Ten Days of Birthı

BRANDEIS SERIES IN AMERICAN JEWISH HISTORY, CULTURE, AND LIFE

Jonathan D. Sarna, Editor   Sylvia Barack Fishman, Associate Editor

Ten Days
of Birthright Israel

A Journey in Young Adult Identity

LEONARD SAXE *&* BARRY CHAZAN

BRANDEIS UNIVERSITY PRESS *Waltham, Massachusetts*

Published by UNIVERSITY PRESS OF NEW ENGLAND

Hanover and London

BRANDEIS UNIVERSITY PRESS
Published by
University Press of New England,
One Court Street, Lebanon, NH 03766
www.upne.com
© 2008 by Brandeis University Press
Printed in the United States of America
5 4 3 2 1

We thank the University of California Press for their permission to publish extracts from
"Tourists" and "An Arab Shepherd is Searching for His Goat on Mount Zion" by Yehuda
Amichai in *The Select Poetry of Yehuda Amichai* (1996).

Library of Congress Cataloging-in-Publication Data
Saxe, Leonard.
Ten days of Birthright Israel : a journey in young adult identity / Leonard Saxe and Barry
Chazan. — [1st ed.]
    p.   cm. — (Brandeis series in American Jewish history, culture, and life)
Includes bibliographical references and index.
ISBN-13: 978-1-58465-541-1 (cloth : alk. paper)
ISBN-10: 1-58465-541-0 (cloth : alk. paper)
1. Taglit—Birthright Israel (Organization)   2. Jews—United States—Attitudes toward Israel.
3. Young adults—United States—Travel—Israel.   4. Jews—United States—Identity.
5. Zionism—United States.   6. Israel and the diaspora.   7. United States—Ethnic relations.
I. Chazan, Barry I.   II. Title.
E184.36.S65S29   2008
305.892'4073—dc22   2008001419

 University Press of New England is a member of the Green Press
Initiative. The paper used in this book meets their minimum
requirement for recycled paper.

For

Marion Gardner-Saxe and Anne Lanski

"How Joyous is the woman, mother of the children"

אם-הבנים שמחה הללויה

Psalm 113

and

Daniel Saxe and Idan, Adi, and Lia Chazan

"Parents are honored through the merits of their children"

הא למדת שבזכות הבנים אבותיהם מתכבדין

Tanhuma Vayikra 5

Contents

Ten Days of Birthright Israel

Next Year in Jerusalem

1

By the rivers of Babylon—
there we sat down and there we wept
when we remembered Zion.
On the willows there
we hung up our harps.
For there our captors
asked us for songs,
and our tormentors asked for mirth, saying,
"Sing us one of the songs of Zion!"

How could we sing the Lord's song
in a foreign land?
If I forget you, O Jerusalem,
let my right hand wither!
Let my tongue cling to the roof of my mouth,
if I do not remember you,
if I do not set Jerusalem
above my highest joy.
—Psalm 137

After nearly ten hours in flight, the distinctive blue and white fuselage of an El Al 747–400 broke through thick clouds over the Mediterranean Sea and descended toward the Israeli coast. It was early morning, January 4, 2000, and the overnight flight from New York was at full capacity. Most of the four hundred passengers were college students, most under twenty-one years old, and almost all arriving in Israel for the first time. Excited by the prospect of being in Israel, and overstimulated by traveling on a plane filled with their young adult peers, very few of the passengers managed to sleep. This particular flight carried students from colleges in the northeastern United States, and most of them had not known one another before they arrived at the airport. They were all Jews, but their common heritage did not, at the time, evoke strong feelings of kinship. Only a few had a deep commitment to their religion, or even to their ethnic identity. Many of them had little in their backgrounds that connected them to Judaism, the Jewish people, and to Israel.

Shortly after daybreak, the 747 made a gentle touchdown at Ben-Gurion Airport. Ben-Gurion is Israel's principal international gateway and is located a few miles southeast of Tel Aviv. After a short taxi from the runway, the plane parked at a stand in the middle of the tarmac. Almost in slow motion, the tired passengers fought their sleep deprivation and made their way down the movable stairs that had been brought to the plane's forward and aft doors. Many noticed for the first time that the words "Birthright Israel" were emblazoned on the side of the plane.[1] As they stepped onto the tarmac, some, like University of Maryland student Randy Portman, kissed the ground.[2] He had never done anything like this before, but he saw other students doing it, and it seemed like the right thing to do.

Another student, Steve Rosenberg from Rutgers University, roused himself and made his way down the stairs. Steve was active in his campus Hillel organization, and visiting Israel had been a lifelong dream. When he first heard about Birthright Israel, it seemed too good to be true. The trip was advertised as a "gift"—the "birthright" of every Jew. There had been a lot of interest among Rutgers students about going on the trip—many more had applied than there were seats available—and he felt especially lucky to have been selected to go. Almost five years later, when recalling the moment, he remembered a "beaming smile" as he began to experience the fulfillment of his dream.

Normally, airport shuttle buses would have taken everyone to the passenger terminal; instead, the Birthright Israel pilgrims were taken to a nearby El Al hangar. There, they joined another six hundred or so college-age peers. Randy recalls stepping into the hangar and hearing a blast of Israeli music and people beginning to dance. "[There was] so much energy and power . . . I remember running around and jumping and dancing and singing . . . [we were] all going around in circles and at that point I [felt], 'This is going to be the most amazing thing that's ever happened to me.'" These new arrivals were the vanguard of a newly established program, and no ordinary ceremony would suffice. With all the celebratory energy that could be generated in the early hours of the morning, the Birthright Israel participants were welcomed by the mayor of Jerusalem Ehud Olmert, and the minister of justice, Yossi Beilin: "*baruchim habai'm l'aretz!*" (welcome to the Land).[3]

The students and other young adults who landed at Ben-Gurion Airport that morning in January 2000, were about to begin an intensive ten-day educational program that would let them experience Israel—its ancient history, its modern development, its people and places. They would learn about a society that has evolved into a state created by the United Nations in the aftermath of the Nazi Holocaust and World War II. Israel is a society and country that seems to undergo perpetual change, provoked by three millennia of Jewish history and its more recent history as the Jewish homeland, as well as the contemporary challenges of relating to the Arab world. For ten days, the program was designed to expose the students to Jewish life in modern Israel, juxtaposing the ancient with the modern, the religious with the secular.

In the several weeks from late 1999 through early 2000, more than six thousand North American young adults and another thousand from nearly a dozen countries came to Israel as birthright participants. By the end of the summer of 2007, more than 150,000 young Jews from North America and around the world had accepted the gift of a Birthright Israel trip and become alumni of the program.[4] Most of the program alumni are from North America, the other major center of contemporary Jewish life.[5]

The goal of this book is to share what we view as the extraordinary story of Birthright Israel and to try to explain how and why it has affected the lives of its participants. Our fundamental perspective is that of educators and social scientists. We have been involved in developing and studying Birthright Israel for nearly six years. We have seen, sometimes with awe and naive surprise, how the program engages participants intellectually, emotionally, and behaviorally—and how its effects seem to last far beyond the time that participants spend together in Israel. We are not dispassionate observers; Israel is central to our own Jewish identities. We have traveled with and studied thousands of participants and, doubtless, our intellectual and emotional sensibilities have converged. But we are writing this book because we believe that Birthright Israel models the best of educational programs. Although its significance has direct relevance to Jewish education, the program's lessons transcend issues of religious and ethnic identity and the concerns of worldwide Jewry.

There also is a second goal. As academics interested in social psychological and educational theory, we are interested in young adults' quest for meaning and the dynamics of their identity formation. Through description and assessment of Birthright Israel, we want to understand the power of immersive group experiences to foster learning and identity formation. And, given the particular context of Birthright Israel, we want to understand the role of travel—both as a way for individuals to appreciate their heritage and to comprehend the contemporary world. We want both to tell a rich story about a specific educational program and to address larger issues about young adults and how they live and learn.

In terms of the contemporary Jewish community, Birthright Israel is the largest educational experiment ever attempted. No other systematic effort to innovate in Jewish education approaches the scope and reach of Birthright Israel. From a social scientific perspective, the program provides a laboratory to study how experiential education can be used to affect knowledge and behavior. The Jewish community outside of Israel has long-standing concerns with how it transmits its culture; increasingly, there is concern about how it creates connections among Diaspora and Israeli Jews. Parochial concerns notwithstanding, the implications go far beyond the Jewish community: as a study of ethnic identity formation in postmodern society, Birthright Israel has the potential to illuminate a central contemporary debate. The program offers important lessons about how young adults struggle with issues of personal identity and meaning-making, and how intensive exposure to one's heritage can be a strong and positive catalyst for identity formation.

A PLANE LANDS

The Birthright Israel flight from New York on January 4, 2000, was overbooked and a few lucky students were given business-class seats. A few rows ahead of the passengers with extra legroom sat a first-class traveler, Michael Steinhardt, traveling with his wife and partner, Judy. When the plane landed, Steinhardt walked down the steps to a waiting VIP van and was escorted to the hangar. In 1960, at age nineteen, Michael Steinhardt had graduated from the Wharton School at the University of Pennsylvania with a degree in finance. He had then spent his professional life as a Wall Street investor and built a reputation as one of the savviest minds in the business.[6] One dollar invested in his hedge-fund company in 1967 was worth hundreds of times more only twenty-five years later.[7] Steinhardt closed his firm in 1996 and turned his attention and his fortune to Jewish philanthropy. Troubled by his assimilationist friends, he wanted to use his marketplace-honed intelligence to benefit the Jewish community. This project—Birthright Israel—was his latest and perhaps most significant venture.

While Steinhardt was in flight, closing in on the Israeli coast, Charles Bronfman—his philanthropic partner—was having breakfast in his home in Jerusalem's Talbieh neighborhood, awaiting the arrival of the first large contingent of participants. Although Steinhardt and Bronfman shared a passion for Jewish philanthropy, the two men could not have been more different from one another. In contrast to Steinhardt, who had grown up poor in New York City (his father had left the family when Steinhardt was very young),[8] Bronfman was a scion of one of the world's wealthiest families. His father, the legendary Samuel Bronfman, had built Seagram's from a small Canadian liquor distributor into one of the world's largest and most successful corporations.[9]

Although denizens of very different worlds, Bronfman and Steinhardt shared a deep concern about the future of the Jewish people. They were troubled by the increasing numbers of Jews who were losing a connection to their heritage. The ambitious goal of the two philanthropists was to alter assimilationist trends. They aimed to shift the orientation of an entire generation of Diaspora Jews from a trajectory of noninvolvement with the Jewish community to one of identity and engagement. They decided that it was the "birthright" of every Jewish young person to be able to learn about his/her heritage and homeland.

Upon arriving in the hangar, Steinhardt, a stout man with a no-nonsense persona, was moved to tears. He was overcome by the sight of a thousand young people dancing at such an improbable hour in such an unlikely setting. The crowd's size, the intense joy being expressed, and the reality of seeing an idea he had nurtured come into being—all contributed to this uncharacteristic reaction. Later, he would say that he was not surprised by the response. He had been confident about how the program would be received. Apart from Charles Bronfman, however, few shared his perspective.

Although Bronfman and Steinhardt backed their vision for Birthright Israel with a substantial investment of their own money, initially, their ambitious blueprint was not endorsed by most leaders in the Jewish community. Some were opposed, some were neutral, and only a few were supportive. Although neither Bronfman nor Steinhardt would be comfortable being compared to Theodore Herzl, the modern progenitor of Zionism, their efforts to gain the support of the organized Jewish community were not all that dissimilar from the struggles Herzl faced a hundred years earlier. In 1896, Herzl, a journalist whose own tendencies toward assimilation were jolted by the Dreyfus trial in France, wrote *The Jewish State,* advocating the Jewish settlement of Palestine. Now, just a little more than one hundred years later, Bronfman and Steinhardt were advocating another project on a grand scale to bring Jews to Israel. Granted, this time there was a State of Israel to visit. Nonetheless, as during Herzl's era, getting the community to share their vision presented a challenge.

BIRTH OF AN IDEA

The story of how Birthright Israel developed has several threads. For a long time, the Jewish community in North America had been studying how to integrate the Israel experience into Jewish education.[10] Many in Israel had been both partners and developers of their own Israel educational projects. The actual Birthright Israel program had its origin in a casual conversation. Charles Bronfman and Michael Steinhardt met over dinner at the Israel Museum in

Jerusalem in 1997. At one point, they went out for some fresh air and a stroll in the museum's Billy Rose Art Garden. Steinhardt pressed Bronfman on how they might do something "big" to alter the Jewish future. Surrounded by ancient antiquities, with the hills of Jerusalem as a stunning backdrop, Steinhardt wanted to build on Bronfman's efforts to bring more youth to Israel and proposed bringing tens of thousands of young adults to Israel as a way to "plug the dam of assimilation."[11] Such a program, he opined, could both make a measurable difference in Jewish Diaspora life and demonstrate how to use philanthropy effectively. A visit to Israel would no longer be something done only by those young Jews who were already committed to being Jewish. It could be something experienced by every young Jewish adult.

The idea was not entirely new. There were, to be sure, a host of predecessor programs that brought young Jews to Israel, and Charles Bronfman was one of the most committed supporters of these efforts. Bronfman had already demonstrated his commitment by launching a philanthropic organization in the late 1980s that made educational travel to Israel for young people one of its priorities.[12] Thousands of young people, mostly high school students, had participated in an "Israel experience" as part of these programs. Even at their height, however, the numbers were still quite small relative to the number of potential participants. Perhaps, more important, most of those who went on these trips were from families that were already highly Jewishly engaged. The programs primarily served those who were least likely to be at risk of assimilation.

Bronfman and Steinhardt were Birthright Israel's progenitors, but Yossi Beilin has been called by some its godfather.[13] Yossi Beilin—who, as previously mentioned, was one of those greeting the students at the El Al hangar— is a well-known political figure in Israel, having served as a member of the Knesset (Israel's parliament) for more than a dozen years and as minister of justice. He is a former political science professor and, perhaps, Israel's leading "dove." He was instrumental in developing the Oslo Accords and was co-signator of the 2003 Geneva accords.[14] Beilin was born in Tel Aviv into a family that had strong ties to the early Zionist leaders. He is, perhaps, the quintessential Tel Avivan—a secular Israeli who believes in Zionism. Beilin manifests his Zionist concern both through his political work and through his writing about the relationship of Israel and the Diaspora. A speech he gave in 1994 planted the seed for Birthright Israel.[15] In his book *His Brother's Keeper: Israel and Diaspora Jewry in the Twenty-first Century*,[16] Beilin argues that the relationship between Israel and Diaspora Jewry needs to change fundamentally. Beilin's central argument is that Israel should no longer be a supplicant, the object of Diaspora alms. On the contrary, Israel is a vibrant society, one of the most productive in the world. In his view, American Jewish philanthropy should be redirected to Jewish education in the Diaspora. And, as part of that redirection, Beilin proposed a voucher that would enable seventeen-year-old Diaspora Jews to come to Israel and learn about their heritage. His initial view was that of a youth "jamboree"—a pilgrimage, a celebration, and rite of passage.

It had become increasingly evident to the Jewish community, particularly in North America, that travel to Israel was an important element of Jewish education.[17] Nevertheless, the idea that all Jewish children and young adults were entitled to a trip to Israel—that it was an actual "birthright"—was novel. Steinhardt and Bronfman, inspired by Beilin, began to develop the idea by consulting with a broad range of educators and social scientists who had been involved with Israel Experience programs.[18] Travel programs for young people and adults emerged after the creation of the State of Israel. For millions of Jews from European and Middle Eastern countries, travel to Israel was about *kibbutz galuyot* and *aliyah*—finding a new home and life in a Jewish State. For the millions of Jews (mostly from North America and Western countries) who did not move to Israel or intend to move there, the Israel trip became part of the challenge of Jewish identity and education; it became linked to the journey toward Jewish self- and collective identity.

Beginning in 1948, and particularly after the 1967 Six-Day War, Israel trips have become a promising resource of world Jewry to educate and affect the Jewishness of young and old alike.[19] In the 1950s, led by the Jewish Agency for Israel (JAFI) and by Jewish youth organizations abroad, short-term youth trips (from four to eight weeks) to Israel began to develop. This development was accompanied by the creation of long-term study programs in Israel for university-age students.[20] Around the same time, Jewish philanthropic agencies began to organize what came to be denoted as "missions" to Israel for philanthropists and Jewish lay leaders.[21] These efforts received their greatest impetus in the late 1960s, after the Six-Day War. The war not only transformed Israel's territory, but changed its image, particularly among world Jewry. Israel was a brave and successful country, a model society that every Jew could be proud of.

No doubt, the broader accessibility and ease of international travel in the 1970s and 1980s, as well as increasing financial resources for travel and leisure-time activities, also contributed to the trips' popularity.[22] In 1987, nearly thirteen thousand young people came to Israel on experience programs sponsored by the Jewish Agency and a host of North American and Israeli organizations.[23] By the end of the 1990s, thousands of youth were traveling to Israel on a plethora of short-term programs.

For the most part, Diaspora participants in these short-term programs were high school students affiliated with synagogues, day schools, camps, and youth movements. Most of the teenage travelers who participated in these programs went to Israel for four to eight weeks during their summer vacations. The most common pattern was a group of some thirty to forty youngsters participating in programs that combined tours of the country with discussions, study, and group activities. For the vast majority of these young people, these trips constituted their first visit to Israel.

In the 1980s, the phrase used to describe visiting Israel went through a metamorphosis: what initially was referred to simply as an "Israel trip" became an "Israel experience." The use of a new term, intentionally or not, was rooted in John Dewey's notion that true education is rooted in experiences.[24] The change in terminology affirmed that going to Israel was a powerful Jewish educational opportunity. Yet it was not simply a matter of being exposed to didactic lessons.[25] It had to do with the entire "experience." The change in name reflected the commitment to Israel travel as an important resource for Jewish education and identity formation.[26]

Another milestone in the history of youth travel to Israel was the emergence of post–high school, pre-university, yearlong study programs in Israel. The target audience for these programs was the graduates of Jewish day schools, mostly those sponsored by the Orthodox community, but also students from the newly emerging non-Orthodox day schools.[27] By the 1990s, the post–high school year in Israel (sometimes called the "gap year") emerged as the norm in the Orthodox educational world. As such, it constituted an indispensable additional educational setting and way station for indepth Jewish education.

The thousands of youngsters going on these programs spawned an Israel experience cottage industry, comprised of scores of sponsors. Some of the sponsors, such as the Jewish Agency, the Reform movement in the United States (UAHC [now URJ, the Union for Reform Judaism]), the Conservative movement (USCJ, the United Synagogue of Conservative Judaism), and Young Judaea brought thousands of youngsters annually. As well, there was a score of smaller programs, sponsored by a mix of Jewish educational organizations such as Livnot U'lehibanot, Muss High School, Nesiya, Pardes, Project Oren, and Shorashim. Each sponsor targeted a different audience and often had special religious, cultural, or academic foci. The majority of participants who took part in these programs were from North America. The programs cost millions of dollars and employed hundreds of executives, Jewish educators, administrative staff, support personnel, and tour guides.

As noted earlier, in the late 1980s, Charles Bronfman (with his late wife, Andrea) established a foundation, one of whose main goals was to foster educational travel to Israel for young people.[28] The foundation, now called the Andrea and Charles Bronfman Philanthropies (ACBP) in the United States (in Israel, Karen Karev), supported research, pilot programs, coalitions of national organizations, and lobbying. The emergence of a foundation led by highly respected lay leaders and accompanied by research, policymaking, and implementation measures provided youth travel to Israel with a new voice and helped Israel travel become more central on the agenda of contemporary Jewish life.

In the mid-1990s, influenced by the Bronfmans' foundation, several national and international organizations came together to create Israel Experience, Inc., an advocacy agency for educational travel to Israel.[29] Israel Experience, Inc. became a voice and lobby for Israel travel. It conducted research on the economics of trips and their impact; as well, it developed alternative models. The organization awarded incentive grants for new educational programs, and provided marketing and recruitment techniques. Although Israel Experience, Inc. had limited resources, it became the prototype for a cooperative venture among Jewish communities, private philanthropists, and Israeli partners. It was a crucial precursor of Birthright Israel.

Israel Experience's programs included ten-day, multiweek, several months, and yearlong study programs. They were sponsored by a broad array of agencies, were aimed at diverse age groups, and had distinctive orientations. For some of the major youth movements associated with religious denominations (for example, NCSY, Orthodox; USY and Ramah, Conservative; NFTY, Reform)[30] as well as nondenominational groups (for example, Young Judea), an Israel trip became a centerpiece of their youth programming. Often, these programs were coordinated with summer camping[31] and youth leadership activities. Some of the best Jewish educators became involved with Israel trips, hundreds of teen leaders spent summers in Israel, and there was growing excitement about this new arena in Jewish education.[32]

This "good feeling" was buttressed by a growing body of empirical research that pointed to the powerful and long-term impact of the Israel experience on Jewish identity.[33] Over several decades, a diverse collection of anecdotal reports, personal memoirs, qualitative and quantitative scientific research studies, and several doctoral theses on Israel trips had accumulated.[34] A 1997 summary of this research concluded:

- Israel experience programs generate high satisfaction and enjoyment by participants and emerge as young Jews' most positive Jewish experience;
- Participation in an Israel experience program makes an important contribution to general adolescent development; for example, enhancing self–esteem;
- There is a strong connection between adult Jewish identity and participation in an Israel trip during adolescence;

- The experiential educational model of Israel experience programs is seen as responsible for the strong impact on attitudes and behavior, as well as toward support for Israel and a sense of Jewish peoplehood.[35]

The overall conclusion of research in the late 1990s was that "youth travel to Israel is one of the most powerful resources that the North American Jewish community has at its disposal to face the challenge of adult Jewish identity and involvement."[36] That said, the research was nonexperimental and did not compare equivalent groups of program participants and nonparticipants. Those who went on the trips were most likely to be the already engaged, and conclusions about impact were often tautological. Of course, those who went on Israel trips would have a strong connection to Judaism; they were already from families where engagement with Jewish life was a high priority.

More powerful was the fact that the majority of young Jews—indeed, the majority of all Jews—had never visited Israel.[37] Although thousands of adolescents and young adults participated in the programs, the ranks of participants were still a small fraction of the total number of Diaspora Jews.[38] The Israel experience trip was, perhaps, a wonderful educational product but it was not an experience most young Jews were taking advantage of in the 1990s. "Longing for Zion" has been part of Jewish tradition for thousands of years, ever since Jews were sent from Jerusalem to Babylon in 586 B.C.E. Virtually all Diaspora Jews can recall the closing words of the Passover seder (ceremony): "l'shana haba'ah b'yerushalayim" (next year in Jerusalem). Nevertheless, after nearly sixty years of Israeli statehood, the majority of world Jewry had never spent time in Jerusalem. Prior to Birthright Israel, those who did go to Israel were a select number of the most highly affiliated. The Israel experience market belonged to the families of the most committed Jews. Most unaffiliated Jews, even most Conservative and Reform Jews, did not send their young to Israel and did not go themselves.[39] The idea of going to Israel for a visit was nowhere on the radar screen for most North American Jews.

FROM IDEA TO REALITY

When Bronfman and Steinhardt first embraced the Birthright Israel concept and offered to provide millions of dollars of their own funding to jump-start the effort, they faced substantial opposition from leaders in the Jewish community. They needed the support of the community if the program was to be successful and, at least at first, such support was not forthcoming. A number of critics scoffed at the plan and called it "Bronfman's blunder and Steinhardt's stupidity."[40] One Jewish communal leader, the prominent Australian businessman Isi Leibler, wrote an op-ed in which he declared: "The reality is that the Birthright Israel concept is bizarre. . . . well-meaning American Jewish philanthropists, desperate for solutions, have mistakenly adopted the quick fix—a 10-day free trip to Israel for every youngster to overcome all the problems of Jewish identity and miraculously generate a Jewish renaissance."[41]

Critics' primary objection was that an investment of more than two thousand dollars per participant would be largely wasted. From the naysayers' vantage point, it was not clear how ten days in Israel would be anything more than a good time at someone else's expense. The Jewish community had a host of competing priorities, ranging from formal Jewish education to local and international Jewish social welfare programs. It was folly, they believed, to invest large sums of money in short-term informal educational programs for college students and young adults.[42] The injury was, perhaps, compounded by the program's target audience: young people, many of whom were from affluent homes, who had not expressed an interest in Israel and who had shown little or no commitment to the Jewish community.

Michael Steinhardt had not become wealthy by listening to others; indeed, he had developed a reputation as a "contrarian." Undissuaded by the criticism, Steinhardt forged a partnership with Charles Bronfman, who had long believed in Israel experience programs. The two philanthropists were convinced that the Birthright Israel experiment was worth trying, and confident that the investment would pay off in the creation of a new generation of engaged Jews. They contributed more than $10 million of their own funds to get the program off the ground. But to implement their vision, Bronfman and Steinhardt needed to expand their partnership. Despite their considerable resources, their vision was far larger than anything that they were willing to support and sustain on their own. Others would need to join in to finance the project.

Within a relatively short period of time, Bronfman and Steinhardt had created a coalition involving nearly a dozen other philanthropists and Hadassah, the Women's Zionist Organization of America.[43] In retrospect, it is not clear that all of those who provided financial backing were enamored of the idea or thought it likely to be successful, but Steinhardt and Bronfman were powerful salesmen. That they also were willing to commit their own resources made them powerful role models. In the end, key to their success in launching the program was that they were able to obtain the backing of Israel's prime minister, Ehud Barak. With the prime minister's support, they gained agreement from the State of Israel to provide $7 million of funding for the first year. Later, they gained the support of Jewish communities from around the world, and the communities, too, pledged a similar amount.

The two philanthropists had, in a time frame that seemed like warp speed compared to the glacial speed of development of most Jewish educational programs, assembled the fiscal resources to conduct a large social experiment in Jewish education and identity development. Their grand vision of bringing one hundred thousand young Jews to Israel in less than five years was now at least a possibility. Although by the time the first planes landed in Israel only part of the funding was in hand, they had assembled a remarkable coalition to fund the program.

Financial issues aside, Bronfman and Steinhardt had also created an organization, with offices in Israel and North America, to develop and manage the initiative. The founders realized that to make Birthright Israel "work" they would need professional guidance from those who knew the mind-set of their target audience and understood education. The program would have to be more than a tour: it would need to have rich emotional and intellectual content, yet be attractive enough to draw tens of thousands of young adult participants who up to this point in their lives had not been all that interested in Israel.

Steinhardt and Bronfman wanted to create major change and overcome the reasoning that had kept Diaspora Jews from acting on their feeling of connection to Israel. Perhaps the key development that made Birthright Israel feasible was a collaboration between the philanthropists and educational trip organizers. Unlike prior efforts, which involved single philanthropists or communal organizations, Birthright Israel was conceived of as a partnership—not only among funders, but also between birthright and organizations that had the ability to recruit and provide educational programming for young adults.

Initially, the most important of the provider/educator organizations was Hillel: The Foundation for Jewish Life. Hillel is the dominant Jewish organization on college campuses and has been a presence among university students since 1920, when it was formed as a unit of B'nai Brith. Currently, there are Hillel houses on more than 120 campuses in North America, as well as a global network of 500 regional centers around the world.[44] Richard Joel was the president of Hillel at the time Birthright Israel was formed. Joel had been a law school professor and became the head of Hillel International in 1988. He had transformed the organization: its structure and fund-raising, how it related to the Jewish community, and its relationship to each of Hillel's campus chapters.[45] When Joel began at Hillel, the campuses were regarded as a "vast wasteland" of Jewish community life. He worked tirelessly to change that situation. A traditional observant Jew, he refocused Hillel's mission with the slogan "maximize the number of Jews doing Jewish with other Jews." Joel had engineered a remarkable transformation of Hillel.[46] Finding the means to engage young American Jews with their peers in Israel, and with Israelis in general, was a natural way to accomplish his goals.

In less than two years from the time that Steinhardt and Bronfman first discussed the idea, the project was given a name, Birthright Israel, and an organization was created to oversee the trips. The central Birthright Israel organization[47] decided not to run the trips themselves. Instead, the educators who were Birthright Israel's professional leadership took the radical step of developing a network of independent trip organizers whom they funded to conduct Birthright Israel trips. To ensure that that the program's objectives would be met, the Birthright Israel organization created an elaborate set of standards and monitoring procedures to assure quality. In addition, a computer-based registration system for North American participants was created.

LAUNCH AND BEYOND

Registration for Birthright Israel in North America began in August 1999, just as the academic year at colleges and universities started. The criteria for participation were designed to be simple and straightforward: One had to self-identify as Jewish, be between the ages of eighteen and twenty-six, and never have visited Israel as part of an educational program. Spurred, in large measure, by campus Hillel organizations, applications to participate in Birthright Israel flooded in. By the time registration closed in October 1999, almost fifteen thousand young Jews from the United States and Canada had signed up to participate in the first trips. Several thousand other young adult Jews signed up for trips from Argentina, France, and Russia.

In North America, demand for slots in the program was so high that lotteries were conducted. There were attempts to balance groups by gender and some favoritism was applied, in particular, to ensure that the program served the least engaged Jewish youth. In the end, however, most of those who got slots were simply lucky. Many of the early participants were recruited by Hillel organizations at universities across the country—from large state universities, to small colleges, and from highly selective private universities and open-admission commuter schools. Hillel recruited and planned programs and provided North American staff; they contracted with educational tour operators in Israel, however, to conduct the actual trip.

Implementation of Birthright Israel was, by design, decentralized and, along with Hillel, more than five dozen organizations initially applied to become trip providers. Some of these provider groups, like Kesher (the college arm of the URJ) were affiliated with Jewish religious denominational groups, while others were national Jewish organizations, such as the Jewish Community Centers Association. Other provider organizations were independent and Israel-based. These groups included private touring companies as well as nonprofit educational and religious organizations.

Many of the groups that initially traveled on Birthright Israel were composed of students, often from the same campus. But Hillel was not the only provider and, even when it arranged trips for its students, it was not always possible to organize groups neatly by campus. Participants were organized in bus groups, each of which had a capacity of thirty to forty. The non-Hillel groups drew strangers together from all across North America, although friends would often travel with one another. As it turned out, the most effective way to advertise was word of mouth—the buzz carried far and wide. Even though program organizers had planned to spend a large budget on advertising, virtually all of the applicants learned about the program from siblings and friends.

The young Jews who danced in the El Al hangar in January 2000 represented the first wave of participants in Birthright Israel. Nearly eight thousand came during that winter break, primarily from North America, with some from the former Soviet Union, Europe, and South America. The participants were a diverse group. A few were themselves relatively recent immigrants to North America, particularly from the former Soviet Union and North Africa. Most, however, were second-, third-, and even fourth-generation American Jews. Culturally and religiously, they represented the full spectrum of Diaspora Jewry. Like the American Jewish community, the participants were mostly religiously liberal or conservative, with many refusing to identify with any denomination—considering themselves "just Jewish."[48] Although some who identified as Orthodox Jews participated, they constituted a relatively small contingent in North America. Many of the Orthodox students who applied were, in fact, ineligible because they had traveled to Israel previously on an educational program.

Over the next seven years, more than 150,000 young Jews from more than two dozen countries participated. The numbers would likely have been larger, but shortly after the program began, Israel experienced a spate of terrorist attacks that killed and wounded hundreds of civilians. Although violence had never been eliminated, even after the 1993 Oslo Accords with the Palestinian Authority, in October 2000, the leader of the then principal opposition party in the Knesset, Ariel Sharon, made a symbolic visit to the Haram al Sharif/Temple Mount. The Temple Mount is a holy site to Muslims in the Old City of Jerusalem and is the site of the Al-Asqa Mosque. The Temple Mount stands on top of Jews' most revered site, the Western Wall.[49]

On the day following Sharon's visit, Palestinians held a demonstration at the Temple Mount that turned violent and resulted in a confrontation with Israel police and military.[50] It marked the beginning of several years of violence that caused more than one thousand deaths among Israeli civilians and more than twenty-five hundred among Palestinians.[51] Public facilities in Israel, buses and restaurants in particular, were targeted by Palestinians willing to give up their lives as suicide bombers.[52] Israelis initially called what occurred *"ha'matsav"* (the situation), while the Palestinians called it the "intifada" (uprising). Although violence had been a fixture of Israeli life over the previous decade,[53] what occurred after the Temple Mount incident was unprecedented. It had repercussions in every segment of Israeli society, most significantly in the political realm. This particular incident also altered Israel's image and relations with the world.[54]

The most direct impact of the situation on Birthright Israel was that it heightened concerns about safety among prospective participants as well as their parents. The program still attracted large numbers of applicants, but by the time it came to confirm participation, there was often drop-off. There was in fact a series of terrorist incidents from 2001 to 2002—public bus bombings in Jerusalem, Haifa, and elsewhere—that occurred just as registration confirmation deadlines approached. The terror situation seemed to peak in 2001; by 2003 waiting lists had again developed. By summer 2006, the waiting list for the trip was more than double the number of available slots (10,000). In 2007, as a result of a large new gift by philanthropists Sheldon and Miriam Adelson,[55] the program brought more than thirty thousand North American participants to Israel and had nearly fifty thousand applicants.[56]

PARTICULARLISM IN AN AGE OF UNIVERSALISM

With hindsight, it is clear that Birthright Israel overcame a host of challenges to create a program that young adult Jews would want to take part in—regardless of their backgrounds and prior engagement with their Jewish identities. One challenge was to overcome what was, particularly for North American participants, Birthright Israel's countercultural stance. In postmodern Western society, why should a program that caters to fostering the ethnic and religious identity of a particular group be of interest and be successful? Should not a program that emphasizes peoplehood, rather than individualism, be anathema? Why would young adults give up opportunities to earn money, get ahead academically, or take a "real vacation" simply to learn about their heritage? In our market-based economic situation, how does "not for credit" education, delivered informally, attract participants and lead them on a path of self discovery?

The story and analysis of Birthright Israel that unfolds in the ten chapters of this book—paralleling the ten days of the trip—provides a set of answers to these questions. The questions are not independent; thus, trying to unpack Birthright Israel requires a description and analysis of the multiple elements of the experience and an assessment of its impact on participants. In trying to understand and assess Birthright Israel, our goal is to draw both particularistic and universal lessons. Our intent is not only to contribute to understanding contemporary ethnic and religious identity, but also to understand educational processes and how to engage young adults in meaningful experiences.

To some extent, Birthright Israel is countercultural. It is a group-oriented experience in a Western cultural context that seems increasingly individualistic. Nevertheless, the program may resonate with the needs of contemporary North American young adults and a growing interest in communal activities. As much as contemporary life emphasizes individualism, there has been a revival of interest in spirituality and communal life. Involvement in ethnic and religious communities by contemporary young adults is not, however, what their parents and grandparents experienced. Young adults are finding their own highly individualistic way in a newly complex world.[57]

To oversimplify, there seems to be a change in how young adults view the individualism that characterized the 1980s and 1990s in America. Consider, for example, the case of Sheila, a young woman described by sociologist Robert Bellah and his colleagues in their 1985 classic on American perspectives, *Habits of the Heart*. Sheila is not Jewish, and thus not a prospect for Birthright Israel, but she is an archetype of a large group of young Americans. As part of the study, Sheila is asked what her religion is. Her narcissistic reply is "Sheilism": she regards herself as a person of faith and she listens to "just my own little voice."[58] Although Sheila is representative of many contemporary young adults, our sense is that this type of individualism is seen by many others as insufficient. In this sense, Birthright Israel is the counterreaction of contemporary young adults to the individualism and the lack of genuine connection with others that characterizes their iPod–instant message lives.

Another contextual answer is suggested by political scientist Robert Putnam in his sociopolitical treatise, *Bowling Alone*.[59] In the language of social capital adapted by Putnam to describe the value of our relationships with others, Birthright Israel is designed to create "bonding" social capital, a sense of connection to others who share a common background. Bonding social capital is potentially essential to creating "bridging" social capital; in effect, it is the glue that allows members of disparate subgroups to come together as a society.

BEGINNING A JOURNEY

When the inaugural participants in Birthright Israel left the Ben-Gurion Airport hangar in early January 2000, they began a journey that was designed to let them see, feel, and experience what it is like to be part of a people and a tradition that spans more than three millennia. Metaphorically, and perhaps in the context of Western individualism, the experience was planned as one of self-discovery. But the journey taken by Birthright Israel participants seems somewhat more than an individual journey to understanding. There is something unique about young Jews from North America traveling to their homeland with others to a place that has been at the center of their forebearers' hopes and dreams. As well, there is something unique about making a journey to Israel at a critical developmental point: as one is making decisions about career and family that will frame one's adult life. But Birthright Israel is also unique in that it incorporates a very different model of education than most had experienced before—one created to arouse their senses, stimulate their minds, and engage their physical being.

For Jews around the world, whatever their level of commitment to prayer and to involvement in the Jewish community, there is a familiar refrain said communally at the end of the Yom Kippur service and the conclusion of the Passover seder. The words "l'shana haba'ah b'Yerushaly'im" express the hope of Jews to return to Eretz Yisrael. It is a hope that has both physical and spiritual dimensions. The name Jerusalem, according to one interpretation, is built on the root for peace (shalom) and, in Hebrew, is a plural word (Yerushaly'im). There are, it suggests, multiple paths to achieving peace and, symbolically, many ways to be part of the Israelite people. Thus, participation in Birthright Israel is not only an opportunity to be in Eretz Yisrael, but also to be connected to the Jewish people. As Jamie, one of the inaugural birthright participants in January 2000 might have said, it's a "cool" concept, and, as several thousand Birthright Israel participants wrote in evaluation surveys, it is pretty "amazing."[60]

Our world is increasingly dominated by negative models of ethnoreligious identity, conflict over competing claims to land, and culture wars that pit individuals and groups against one another. The history of the Jewish people is, likewise, a story mixed with extraordinary accomplishment and equally extraordinary tragedy. Jewish culture has survived longer than any other culture and Birthright Israel was designed to ensure that Jewish life continues and thrives. Birthright Israel calls out for study and understanding, both as an effort by a religious and cultural minority to ensure continuity and as an educational program for young adults. By attempting to alter the trajectory of identity development of young adults, Birthright Israel offers a unique window into ethnicity, emerging adulthood, and education.

In the chapters that follow, we describe, unpack, and try to understand the meaning of the journey taken by those who have accepted the Birthright Israel gift. Just as the ideas, history, and creativity of those who created the program have broad roots, its implications have multiple branches. It is an innovative educational venture, a social experiment and an endeavor that seeks to alter the ethnic and religious identity of an entire generation. The book is designed to guide the reader through the educational and cultural journey undertaken by program participants. Although our view of the program is decidedly positive, our goal is to not to promote the program but to explain and critically assess how and why it operates. In the next chapter, we explore the context within which the program was initially developed.

Dreams Realized and Shattered

ISRAEL IN THE MIND OF AMERICAN JEWS

2

They say there is a country
A land that flows with sunlight
Where is that country?
Where is that sunlight?
—Saul Tchernikovsky
Wherever I am going—I am going to the Land of Israel
—Reb Nachman of Bratzlav

For most of the Jewish immigrants who heeded turn-of-the-twentieth-century calls for Jewish resettlement of Zion, the beaches of Tel Aviv were their first sight of the Holy Land.[1] Jerusalem may have been the focus of aspirations to return to the Jewish homeland, but Tel Aviv was their port of entry. Today, Tel Aviv is Israel's second largest city, and is the hub of a metropolitan area that is home to nearly half the population of the state. Modern-day immigrants and visitors, like those in Birthright Israel groups, arrive in airplanes; invariably, however, they pass over or just to the south of Tel Aviv. From a distance, its glass-lined skyscrapers immediately capture one's attention and provide a striking symbol of Israel's modernity.

In contrast to Jerusalem, the capital city and home for many of the most traditionally religious Jews, Tel Aviv is often juxtaposed as Israel's secular capital city. It is the country's financial, business, and cultural center. Modern Tel Aviv is flanked on its southern end by the reconstructed port of Jaffa, which juts out into the Mediterranean and is home to the many of the city's Arab population. A promenade along the beach connects the southern and northern ends of the city and serves as the front lawn for hotels, restaurants, and discotheques that line the seashore. Israel follows the Jewish calendar; thus, virtually all schools, government offices, and businesses are closed from Friday afternoon through Saturday night. The exceptions to the Sabbath closing norm are restaurants and entertainment venues, particularly in Tel Aviv, Israel's most Westernized city. The city caters to the majority of Israeli Jews who are not traditionally religious and is therefore a focal point for weekend social life.

On Friday evening, June 1, 2001, religious families throughout Israel had begun their Sabbath observance and, even in secular homes, families and friends were gathered for social time together. Late that Friday night, at the southern edge of the promenade near Jaffa, hundreds of teenagers were gathered outside two discotheques. One of the discotheques was called Pasca and the other was known as the Dolphinarium, the latter named for the recently closed aquarium that it replaced.

The young people waiting to enter the dance clubs were predominantly Russian-speaking students, many from Tel Aviv's Shevah Mofet High School. The 1990s had witnessed an extraordinary level of immigration from the former Soviet Union to Israel. Nearly one million Jews from the former Soviet Union, mostly Russians and Ukrainians, had arrived in less than a decade. The students waiting to enter the disco that night were part of the first generation of these immigrants being raised and educated in Israel. Dancing late on Shabbat evening at the Tel Aviv beachfront was a marker of how quickly the young Russians had been socialized as secular Israelis.

Shortly after 11:20 P.M., a twenty-two-year-old Palestinian from Kalkilia, a town fifteen miles to the north of Tel Aviv that straddles the pre-1967 border with the West Bank, arrived at the Dolphinarium. His name was Said Hotri, and he was no ordinary participant in Tel Aviv's weekend nightlife: it was later determined that he was a member of the militant Hamas organization and had been trained by their Qassam Brigade. Hotri had walked across a field and taken a cab for the less than thirty-minute drive to Tel Aviv. Then, according to one news account, he "wormed his way into the crowd" waiting to get into the discotheque. Strapped to his body was a deadly mix of explosives, made even more lethal by ball bearings, nails, screws, and washers. As he mingled with the throng of young people waiting for the discotheque doors to open at midnight, he triggered his bomb. No doubt Hotri died instantly; in doing so, he also murdered twenty teenagers and a security guard. Another 120 were injured in the blast. Most of the victims were young, as young as fourteen years old.

In Hebrew, a terrorist incident such as the attack at the Dolphinarium is called a *pigua* (strike). On June 1, 2001, the sound of the pigua at the Dolphinarium reverberated through a large swath of Tel Aviv, particularly along the hotels that dotted the beachfront to the north. It also sent political shockwaves around the world, with Western leaders concerned that Israel's newly elected prime minister, Ariel Sharon, would retaliate and set off a new round of Middle East violence.[2]

One of those who heard and felt the blast was Germany's very popular foreign minister, Joschka Fischer. Fischer, coincidentally, was in a hotel just a few blocks from the blast site. Aroused by the sound of the blast and the cacophony of police and ambulance sirens, he went to the scene. He was pained by what he saw and concerned that Israel would feel it had no choice but to retaliate against the Palestinian Authority; in doing so, the fragile Middle East would be destabilized. After a furious round of phone calls and consultations, on Saturday morning, Fisher went to meet the chairman of the Palestinian Authority, Yassir Arafat. Arafat was at his compound in Jericho, a few miles outside of Jerusalem and less than an hour's drive from Tel Aviv. In part as a result of these efforts, and a commitment from the United States to help develop a security plan, Israeli Prime Minister Ariel Sharon decided not to retaliate.

A MOMENT OF DECISION

The physical shockwave that accompanied the blast was felt throughout Tel Aviv. The metaphoric impact, however, was far stronger and reached not only world leaders and diplomats, but the Jewish world, from Jerusalem to New York and beyond. It had a direct effect on Birthright Israel. When the blast occurred, more than a thousand Birthright Israel participants were already in the country for the summer program. Several thousand more students and recent graduates were preparing to leave to travel to Israel.

At the time of the blast in 2001, the largest operator of Birthright Israel trips was Hillel and its campus affiliates. The Hillel organization and the Reform movement, both of which had several groups ready to leave North America for Israel, were particularly concerned with the security situation. By Saturday night, word of possible delay or cancellation of the Hillel and Reform trips reached Charles Bronfman, who was at his home in Jerusalem. Generally mild-mannered, Bronfman received news of possible trip cancellations with intense anger. From Karen Karev, the offices of his Israel foundation, Bronfman held a series of meetings and conference calls with staff and trip organizers, both in Israel and the United States. He was not in a listening/negotiating mood and offered an unequivocal message: the incident in Tel Aviv had *not* changed the situation and this was *not* the time for Americans to abandon Israel by canceling trips. In his view, the tragedy was evidence that Birthright Israel was more important than ever.

Bronfman's perspective on the Dolphinarium bombing, like that of most Israelis, was one of shock and sadness. It was if a member of his family had been attacked. He could not but be revolted by thoughts of teenage boys and girls lying dead and wounded on the promenade, their lives and their families shattered by a nail-laced bomb. At the same time, his mood, like that of most

Israelis, was one of resolve. For Israelis, one had no choice but to continue with daily life and pray that the bombing would not lead to a further escalation of violence. Israelis were no different in that respect from many Americans. Like New Yorkers, who at that time in mid-2001, went to visit or work in New York City's World Trade Center—despite the fact that it had already been attacked in 1993 by Bin Laden's terror network—Israelis went on with their lives, no matter how horrific the news. But Bronfman is not a Sabra (Israeli-born). He is a Canadian Jew who mostly lives in the United States. To understand why, in the wake of the Dolphinarium bombing, he believed that Birthright Israel was "more important than ever," one has to reach into Israel's history and the relationship of Diaspora Jews to Israel.

ZIONIST ROOTS AND ASSUMPTIONS

The relationship of Jews to their homeland is complex and has long been the focus of debate and discussion in Jewish communities around the world. The complexity is both externally driven (by historic anti-Semitism, hatred, and violence toward Jews) and internally generated (by debate over Judaism as a religion, as an ethnic and cultural tradition, and the importance of a homeland). It is a debate, at its heart, about how to live a Jewish life in a predominantly non-Jewish world. The emergence of Zionism in modern times, a politically driven movement to allow Jews to gather in their homeland and escape anti-Semitism, has transformed an age-old debate.[3] Understanding the history of this debate is important to understanding Birthright Israel and the unique role that Israel plays in the psyche of Diaspora Jews.

In the century since Herzl first promulgated his vision of a modern Jewish state in the land of Israel, the dream of a return to the Jewish homeland has become reality. The state emerged in the shadow of the Holocaust—the systematic murder of six million Jews during World War II.[4] For many homeless and stateless Jews after the war, the United Nations' decision to create a Jewish state allowed them to rebuild their lives and, from the remnants of European Jewry, re-create family, religious and cultural life.[5] For other Jews, including those who lived in Arab countries throughout Africa and the Middle East, the creation of the state allowed them to leave countries rife with deprivation and anti-Semitism.[6]

At the end of the nineteenth century, when Zionism was being advocated, the area was relatively desolate and travel to "the Land" was a distant thought for most Jews. Only about ten thousand Jews lived in Palestine in the last part of the nineteenth century. (Of course, the overall population of the country was also not very large.)[7] Although it is unlikely that Herzl's fellow European

Jews read American literature, humorist Mark Twain's description of his trip to Palestine in 1867 captures a sense of the situation. As he described in his travelogue *The Innocents Abroad,* Twain summarizes what he saw: "Palestine sits in sackcloth and ashes. . . . [It] is desolate and unlovely. . . . It is a hopeless, dreary, heartbroken land."[8]

The image of the Land of Israel notwithstanding, the importance of visiting Israel in the Jewish imagination had existed since the beginning of Jewish history.[9] Thousands of years ago, as described in the Book of Genesis, the patriarch Abraham (the progenitor of the Jewish people) went on the first "Birthright Israel" trip from Ur to the Land of Canaan: "Go from your land, from your birthplace, and from your father's house, to the land that I will show you."[10] Genesis describes how the Land of Canaan, present-day Israel, became Abraham's home and the birthplace of his son, Isaac. On Mount Moriah—the site that later became the location of the Holy Temple in Jerusalem—Jewish tradition says that Abraham took Isaac to be sacrificed as a test of his commitment to God. According to the biblical narrative, the Jewish nation was still in formation, and it was forever changed, when years of famine forced Isaac's descendants to travel to Egypt. The Book of Exodus describes their arduous return. Jewish holidays, rituals, and customs, all based on these sacred stories, contain and perpetuate a longing for the Land of Israel.

For Jews, Israel has been the "promised land": a physical place to be a people, but also a metaphoric place where material and spiritual needs would be met. As described in a biblical passage, "Then he brought us to this place and gave us a land, a land flowing with milk and honey."[11] Deuteronomy, the fifth book of the Bible, describes preparations for reentering the Land of Israel and God's covenant with the Jewish people. Inhabiting "the land" is conditional: "Keep, therefore, all the instruction that I enjoin upon you today, so that you may have the strength to enter and take possession of the land that you are about to cross into and possess" (11:8). The instructions focus on creating a society that pursues "justice and righteousness," where concern for the welfare of the less fortunate is primary.

Although Jews have lived in the land that is now the State of Israel since biblical times, Jewish life has been shaped by forced dispersions. In 586 B.C.E., the Chaldeans (Babylonians) invaded the land and forced most of the Jewish population into exile in Babylonia. The Babylonian exile proved to be shortlived, but it had a profound impact on Jewish history. Jewish leaders believed that they had been exiled for their lack of fidelity to Mosaic law and for their failure to create the kind of society that God had instructed. It led to a flourishing of Jewish writing and self-examination that became a central part of Jewish tradition.

The second dispersion began nearly five centuries later, after the Romans invaded Palestine. Although some Jews tried to coexist with the Roman rulers, this relationship ended with the efforts by Roman legions to destroy the Second Temple. In 70 C.E., Roman soldiers laid siege to Jerusalem, killing tens of thousands of Jews and eventually capturing and burning the temple. Jews who escaped went into hiding or, as in the case of those who fled south to Masada, created fortresses. When the fortress at Masada fell in 74 C.E. its inhabitants, rather than allowing themselves to be taken captive, ended their lives in an act of martyrdom known as "*al Kiddush Hashem*" (in sanctification of God's name). At the end of the first century, Rome had clear dominance over the land.

Throughout the last two thousand years, Jewish civilization reemerged—with Jews living as part of larger non-Jewish communities, first in Europe and, more recently, in North America. The Jewish story became directly related to the challenge of Jews trying to adapt to their Diaspora communities. But wherever they lived, Jews never forgot Israel and they always dreamed of "returning."[12] Whether at daily prayers, at the annual Passover seder, or at a wedding ceremony, Jews remembered Zion. Indeed, the story of Jewish attachment to Eretz Yisrael from the time of the destruction of the Second Temple until the establishment of the state in 1948 is a major chapter in Jewish history.[13]

ISRAEL IN THE EYES OF CONTEMPORARY JEWS

The dream of returning to Zion was for a very long time impractical; perhaps as a result, Jewish yearnings about Israel have not always been realistic. Such appears to have been particularly true for American Jewry. The distinguished historian of American Jewry, Jonathan Sarna, has argued that American Jews have long held unrealistic views of Israel.[14] Their view of Israel has been distorted by a lens that helped them cope with their own Jewish identity. In the early period of Zionism, Israel was the "holy" land, where pious Jews engaged in "prayer and study." It was the reverse of the American dream, which focused on material life. Later, articulated by American Zionists such as Louis D. Brandeis,[15] the Land became a utopia, reflecting the perfection of American ideals of democracy and freedom. That the vision and reality did not match—early settlers were not simply engaged in Jewish thought and the political system that developed, while democratic, was not utopian—did not much matter, as few American Jews directly experienced Israel.

The creation of the State of Israel out of the ashes of the Holocaust changed the relationship of Jews to their long-sought land. Establishment of the modern State of Israel allowed an ingathering of Jewish exiles from Europe, North Africa, and throughout the Middle East. For many, going to Israel was not a choice; it was the only refuge that would accept them and allow them to live freely. But for others, it *was* a matter of choice. Particularly for North Americans, who enjoyed the freedom of democratic countries, living in Israel represents an ideological statement. Ideology is embedded in language: thus, in Hebrew, to return to Israel to live is to make aliyah (literally, "going up"); if one should leave Israel, one is *yoreda* (literally, "ones who goes down").

The return of Jews to their homeland has not been an easy process. Since Israel's declaration of statehood on May 14, 1948—nearly six months after the United Nations had voted to accept a partition plan that allowed the Jews to create a state in part of Palestine—Israel has had to fight for its right to exist. In doing so, it has garnered a disproportionate share of global attention and, increasingly, disapprobation. Although Israel's founders sought to create the ideal state that Jews have long prayed for, much of the country's focus on has been on self-protection. The very day it was created, Israel was attacked by Arab countries that rejected the United Nations decision ceding a portion of Palestine to a Jewish state. Following this War of Independence, there were full-scale wars in 1956, 1967, and 1973. The 2006 war in Northern Israel and Lebanon was an extension of an ongoing conflict.

The pressure for aliyah has complicated Diaspora Jewry's relationship with Israel. David Ben-Gurion, Israel's first prime minister, maintained that "only in the State of Israel is a full Jewish life possible."[16] According to this view, a Jew could not be a complete person if he or she lived in the Diaspora. Other commentators, however, like the scholar and founder of the first Jewish Studies program in America, Simon Rawidowicz, argued that one could be fully Jewish in the Diaspora (Babylon), as well as in Israel (Jerusalem). Rawidowiz argued with Ben-Gurion and maintained that it was a mistake to name the country "Israel," as if the People of Israel who lived in the Diaspora did not count.[17]

Ben-Gurion's position created a long-standing tension between Israel and the leadership of the American Jewish community. In Israel's formative years, the point person for Diaspora Jewry in this debate was Jacob Blaustein, an American philanthropist and president of the New York–based American Jewish Committee (AJC). The AJC was the social affairs arm of the Jewish community. Blaustein challenged Ben-Gurion's position and maintained that American Jews, living in a free society, should feel no obligation to emigrate. He and the leadership of the AJC were particularly concerned that American Jews would be accused of dual loyalty.[18] Thus, his dispute with Ben-Gurion was both a matter of Diaspora-Israel relations and an issue unique to Jews' standing in the United States.

In 1950, Jacob Blaustein and Ben-Gurion reached a public accord.[19] The

Ben-Gurion–Blaustein agreement acknowledged that American Jews had no rights with respect to Israeli political decisions and, reciprocally, that Israel could not interfere in Jewish communal life in the United States. It was also agreed that, while Israel needed the "skills and know-how" of American Jews, the decision whether or not to come to Israel—"permanently or temporarily—rests with the free discretion of each American Jew."

Although the agreement between Blaustein and Ben-Gurion provided the framework for Israel-Diaspora relations in the early years of the state, the written declaration has not solved the problem. From the time the agreement was signed to this day, the issue has been debated. Ben-Gurion, in 1960, claimed that it was "the responsibility" of every Jew to make aliyah. He later had to retract his statement and reaffirm his commitment to the original agreement with Blaustein. More recently, in 2006, at the AJC's 100th anniversary celebration in Washington, D.C., Israeli novelist A. B. Yehoshua created a storm of controversy by proclaiming that only in Israel could one live fully as a Jew.[20] Although his position was immediately challenged by both American and Israeli politicians and academics, Yehoshua's comments were the equivalent of picking at the scab of a long-standing wound that has refused to heal.

ISRAEL AND THE AMERICAN JEWISH AGENDA

Much has changed since the early days of the founding of the State of Israel. Concerns about its viability, as well as the responsibility of Jews to immigrate to the land, have somewhat subsided. Although the memory of the Holocaust still remains central to Israeli identity and security concerns remain a focus, Israel is a modern Western society and technological powerhouse. At the same time, Diaspora Jews—particularly those in North America—have, perhaps, been *too* successful in adapting to their host cultures. Intermarriage rates have increased dramatically, and there is widespread concern about communal capacity to sustain engagement in the community and its organizations.[21] In this respect, Birthright Israel may play a critical role. Israel experiences help assimilated Jews understand that they are part of a larger, worldwide community, as well as being Americans.

Substantial evidence suggests that while North American Jewry feels pride, as well as a responsibility to help Israeli Jews, the establishment of the State of Israel was not central to their identity as Jews. North American Jews feel attached and supportive, even if they do not see the State of Israel as central to their lives and identity as Jews. Perhaps even more important, Jewish communities outside of Israel developed their own elaborate religious, cultural, and social action organizations, mostly independent of those in Israel.[22]

Aliyah from North America to Israel has never been large. Some Americans did heed the call in the early days of the state and there was a substantial influx after the 1967 war. Aliyah from North America, however, has never been so high as immigration from countries where Jews have been actively discriminated against.[23] At the same time, Israel has been a central concern of the organized North American Jewish community. Until recent years, the federated Jewish communities in North America gave the majority of their philanthropic dollars to support programs in Israel. Billions of dollars have been raised in response to crises, from wars to needs for immigrant support. The 1967 and 1973 wars resulted in a major increase in support for Israel, as did efforts over the last twenty-five years to bring immigrants from the Soviet Union and Ethiopia.[24] Thousands of "American Friends" organizations exist to support social, health, and educational needs in Israel.

Yet American Jewry's concern with Israel fluctuates with the security situation.[25] In recent years, support has peaked when Israel is under attack; in particular, in the aftermath of the 1973 Yom Kippur War and, in 1991, after missiles reached Israel from Iraq. Jewish concern about issues of survival are an extension of concerns that have been at the heart of Jewish history. From the times of the Babylonian exile to the destruction of the Temple and from the fifteenth-century Inquisition to the Holocaust and the struggle to save European Jewry and establish the State of Israel, survival has been a central concern of Jews throughout the world. Security concerns have shaped Jewish life, even in safe Jewish communities such as those in North America.

Nonetheless, a shift occurred, particularly after 1967, and Israel's stunning military victory in the Six-Day War. Not only did Israel obtain what seemed at the time to be secure borders; it demonstrated that it had the military strength to defend itself. It was the beginning of a movement concerned not only with the survival of Jewish life within Israel, but outside Israel as well. Beginning in the 1970s, the American Jewish community became more and more concerned about its continued vibrancy. In the 1990s, committees and commissions on Jewish continuity and identity were established. The central issue was the degree to which Jews were becoming Americanized and losing their distinctive Jewish attachments and identification.[26]

Evidence of a marked rise in the intermarriage rate, highlighted in the 1990 National Jewish Population Study (NJPS),[27] caused considerable anxiety among American Jewish communal leaders. In particular, the leadership came to believe that substantial numbers of their children and grandchildren were at risk of losing their connection to Judaism.[28] Their response took the form of enhancing support for intensive Jewish educational environments such as day schools, Jewish summer camps, campus programs, university-based Jewish Studies programs, and Israel educational experiences. Funding for all of these from Jewish philanthropic agencies and individuals increased. Israel experience programs thus joined the cadre of educational experiences that would, it was hoped, change the tide of assimilation and contribute to the enrichment of Jewish identity.[29]

Although the organized American Jewish community had deeply supported Israel and its needs for decades,[30] the community never made travel and physical presence in Israel a high priority. But this dynamic began to change, at least in modest ways, during the 1980s. One marked change was that non-Orthodox seminaries made a year in Israel a requirement for rabbinic students.[31] Perhaps more important, during this period, Jewish organizations and philanthropies began to give more attention to Israel travel and education programs. Local Jewish community federations began establishing or expanding Israel-trip incentive funding and, as described earlier, Israel Experience, Inc. was established.[32] Despite these efforts, changes on the ground were minimal: only a small minority of North American Jews went to Israel. Those who traveled to Israel tended to be the most committed and religiously involved Jews.

There were a variety of practical reasons that enabled American Jewry, on the one hand, to support Israel emotionally and financially, but on the other hand, not to visit. One issue was security. Despite the image of Israel as an extraordinary military power, security issues loomed large for many from the Diaspora. For most of its existence, Israel's security situation had been the focus of near-constant media attention. The predominant image of Israel, shaped by television, magazines, and electronic media, was of a country torn by violence and terrorist attacks. It did not matter that reality was somewhat different and that Israel's highways were more dangerous than the buses and public sites that were the focus of terrorist attacks.[33] It did not matter, either, that young adults were probably safer in Israel than their compatriots back home.[34] Participation in Israel trips was highly sensitive to incidents that occurred just before trips begin. Thus, the youth trip business was devastated in 1987 when the first intifada took place; in 1991, before and after the Gulf War; and in 2000 when the second intifada began.[35]

Personal finances were also a consideration, particularly for trips to Israel that targeted young people. For example, six-week Israel teen trips in the 1990s cost from $4000 to $5000.[36] Although many North American Jews were accustomed to spending similar sums for family trips or summer camps, these costs inhibited all but the most highly motivated or resource-rich families from sending their children. Jews, like many other Americans spent money on camp, vacations, and travel for their youngsters, but the Israel trip was not seen in those terms by most American Jews. An Israel trip might have been seen by some as "exotic"; for most, however it was not seen as a vacation or even as a parallel to "fun" at a Jewish summer camp.[37]

In the end, it seems that lack of interest was even more important than the perception of safety. Going to Israel was simply not on the radar screen of most North American Jews and their children. The focus of Jewish education for teenagers was a bar or bat mitzvah ceremony and celebration. In fact, data over the last decade suggest that more than 60 percent of North American Jews celebrated a bar or bat mitzvah with a religious ceremony.[38] Hebrew school was also part of their normative experience: 80 percent of young American Jews had at least one year of some type of Jewish schooling. It was also normative for Jews to marry other Jews, at least until the 1980s.[39] But that appeared to change after 1980; although there is substantial controversy about how to measure intermarriage rates, the assumption, at least in the United States, is that more than half of all Jews who marry, wed non-Jews.[40]

Traveling and spending time in Israel was never seen as a central part of Jewish identity for American Jews. Modern Israel did not, necessarily, need the expertise of American Jews, certainly not as Ben-Gurion had called for during the first decade of the state. For most non-Orthodox Diaspora Jews, Israel was not at the center of their religious consciousness. Most Israelis were secular and those who *were* religious practiced Judaism in a way that was foreign to mainstream American sensibilities. Mea Shearim, the ultra-Orthodox section of Jerusalem, was a tourist attraction rather than a spiritual or educational destination for North American Jews. Perhaps most important, Israelis spoke Hebrew, a language that most American Jews did not understand. They might be able to read Hebrew in their prayer books, but understanding and speaking the modern version of their ancestors' language was not central to their Jewishness.[41]

The bottom line was that there was no critical mass of American Jewry who had traveled to Israel. By 2000, among Jewish adults in the United States, perhaps only 35 percent had ever been to Israel.[42] Orthodox Jews, Jewish professionals, and those with family in Israel were frequent visitors, but the majority of American Jews had never visited their homeland. And, despite substantial hand-wringing in the wake of the 1990 NJPS (National Jewish Population Survey) findings about the dramatically increased rates of intermarriage, there were few calls to make travel to Israel a Jewish priority.[43] Although leadership missions to Israel became increasingly normative, there was no popular culture of travel to Israel, particularly educationally focused travel. The Jewish priority toward Israel was to support Israeli organizations financially,[44] and to help it politically, but not to visit.

Although the 1990s did not witness a marked change in North American Jewish travel to Israel, there were beginnings of an attitudinal shift. In some respects, with the need for aliyah and the need for money no longer a central issue, it was easier to focus on the positive—familial, spiritual, cultural, and religious reasons—for Diaspora Jews to want to experience Israel. It was, perhaps, fueled by what some have called a renaissance in Jewish life in America. There was increased interest in Jewish texts and culture and with moving beyond the superficial elements of Jewish community involvement. Jewish ethnicity was "in." Perhaps emblematic of this was the growing presence of Jewish study programs on college campuses and a revival in teaching Hebrew.

BEYOND TERRORISM

As noted earlier, the June 2001 suicide bomb at the Tel Aviv discotheque reverberated throughout Israel and beyond. Indeed, it was a spark that came close to igniting full-scale war between Israel and the Palestinians. Although widespread war did not break out, for more than two years after the young Russian immigrants killed at the Dolphinarium were buried and surgeons had repaired wounds of the injured, piguim were a fixture of life in Israel. The shock waves of each blast reverberated far beyond Tel Aviv, Jerusalem, and the other cities that were attacked. Their impact was felt throughout the Middle East and Western countries; in particular, they helped shape Diaspora Jewry's attitudes to Israel. Just as the attack set back efforts to force peace between Israel and its Arab neighbors, it also slowed down the development of Birthright Israel and other efforts to make a personal connection to Israel central to developing Jewish identity. Israel might have been in the hearts of many American Jews, but Israel became associated with danger.

Abba Eban, one of Israel's most well-known political figures, was ambassador to the United Nations in 1963, when President Kennedy was assassinated. In a condolence message to the American people on the murder of the president, he remarked, "Tragedy is the difference between what is and what might have been." The murder of young teenagers at the Dolphinarium was a genuine tragedy. It was not simply that more than twenty lives had been snuffed out and that the wounded would be forever scarred. As well, the blast was a fracture point in the dreams of Israel and the hopes of those who wanted to make Israel central to the consciousness of Diaspora Jewry.

The impact of the Dolphinarium tragedy was no doubt magnified because of who the victims were. As *olim* (immigrants to Israel) from the former Soviet Union, they symbolized the ongoing need for Israel as a refuge for Jews from around the world. As youngsters, they represented the hopes for Israel. And, perhaps symbolic of how Israeli culture is far more complex than Jewish culture, they were acting out exuberance reserved for teenagers, living the Western dream of freedom.

For American Jews, particularly Jewish communal leaders, the seemingly random bombings of civilian sites created a dilemma. On the one hand, each attack provided added evidence of the need for American Jews to support Israel. Each bombing was proof of the need to help Israel maintain its security and its essential role as a refuge for oppressed Jews. Israel needed American Jewry's financial, political, and emotional support. On the other hand, the bombings suggested that Israel was more of the Middle East than the West— unsafe and foreign to Americans.

The leadership was torn. They had to highlight the precarious security situation, but do so without undermining efforts to engage American Jews directly with Israel. Birthright Israel was potentially important to the effort, at least in the mind of its organizers. If young adult American Jews could be engaged with Israel, the future could be assured. The leadership recognized that, along with their responsibility to help protect Israel, developing a strong bridge between Israeli and American Jews was a necessity for both communities.

The task that Birthright Israel took on was different than that of previous efforts to engage Diaspora Jews. The security situation was only part of the issue. Among the first several thousand participants who came at the beginning of 2000, the oldest members of the group had been born in 1974, just after the Yom Kippur War. None had lived during the pre-state era of Zionism, nor had any lived through the wars that came to define the borders and status of the State of Israel. Like the Israelites led through the desert by Moses for forty years, they came to Eretz Yisrael with a very different frame of mind than had their parents and grandparents. The history of Zionism and the story of Israel's creation was, for them, a historical tale. The emotional commitment—either of those whose families had come to Israel seeking refuge or those who witnessed history and identified with Israelis—was not present for these Birthright Israel participants. In fact, many had been chosen to participate in the program because they were presumed to have weak ties to Israel and their Jewish identity.

The Birthright Israel program was created, in part, to give flesh to the idealized, but often bare-bones and emotionally sterile account of Israel that many of them had been taught. Most important, the program was created to help participants develop and strengthen their Jewish identities by acknowledging their past and giving them a framework to think about being part of the Jewish people. When the program began, many observers were skeptical that one could educate and motivate comfortable Diaspora Jews to view Israel as part of their Jewish identities. Even those who thought it possible were unsure what could be accomplished in ten days, particularly if the program did not ask for a financial commitment or postprogram payback.

The chapters that follow describe how Birthright Israel teaches the history of the Jewish people and the State of Israel and provides an experience that helps to shape the identity of young adult Diaspora Jews. One way to summarize what the program does is that it uses modern Israel as a laboratory to teach history and create personal connections between participants and their heritage. Participants get to touch, hear, and feel a variety of narratives about their heritage and get to experience being part of a Jewish community and Jewish society.

The theory is, perhaps, much easier to describe than it is to implement. What, for example, is the story of Israel that participants should be offered? Is it the dream of Zion—the spiritual, religious message that has been part of Judaism since the destruction of the Temple? Is it the political story of how vicious anti-Semitism gave Jews no choice but to establish a homeland of their own? Is it the story of how to create a utopian society, one that fulfills Isaiah's prophecy of a "shining light" unto the nations? Or is it the story of how brains and brawn enabled a group of people, drawn from different parts of the world but sharing a cultural heritage, to make the desert bloom and science flourish? No doubt, the narrative is complex and each of these themes strikes a resonant chord with Israelis and participants alike.

The ongoing violence and the absence of peace with Palestinian Arabs add a layer of further complexity. Do the piguim represent continued victimization of Jews? Or do they represent the reversal of roles and Jewish chutzpah (arrogance) about their rights to lands that are the property of other peoples? Or, perhaps, are Jews the human canaries of modern society? Is their travail a harbinger of future conflict, with wars that have no defined borders and combat that makes no distinction between soldiers and civilians?

Since 2001, the leaders and funders of Birthright Israel have decided that the program was more important than ever. Perhaps the Al Qaeda attacks on New York and Washington, on September 11, three months after the June bombing in Tel Aviv, made Israel seem no less safe than anywhere else. September 11 is no doubt a factor; more important, however, is that the persuasive logic of the program as a gift and as a builder of Jewish identity trumped other concerns. It was a logic that appealed directly to the young adults. Although security concerns were to remain an issue—and are perhaps even more important today—the program continued because those who participated returned to their home communities telling others that they had had an "amazing" time. Systematic evaluation data (see chapter 8) reinforced anecdotal reports and made clear that the program had the power to alter the trajectories of Jewish engagement of a generation of Diaspora young adults.

How the program was organized to meet its objectives; how it is structured as an educational intervention; and how it operates for participants, educators, and program organizers are the foci of the next several chapters.

Sites and Sights

3

1.

Visits of condolence is all we get from them,
They squat at the Holocaust Museum
They put on grave faces at the Wailing Wall
And they laugh behind heavy curtains
In their hotels.
They have their pictures taken
Together with our famous dead
At Rachel's Tomb and Herzl's Tomb
And on the top of Ammunition Hill.
They weep over our sweet boys
And they lust over our tough girls.
And hang up their underwear
To dry quickly
In cool blue bathrooms

2.

Once I sat on the steps by a gate at David's Tower. I placed my two heavy
baskets at my side. A group of tourists was standing around their guide
and I became their target marker. "You see that man with the baskets?
Just to the right of his head there's an arch from the Roman period. Just
to the right of his head." "But he's moving, he's moving!" I said to myself:
redemption will only come if their guide tells them, "You see that arch
from the Roman period? It's not important; but next to it, left and down
a bit, there sits a man who's bought fruit and vegetables for his family."
—Yehuda Amichai

The Haas Promenade in Jerusalem was built in 1986 and is named
after the San Francisco family that founded the Levi Strauss jeans company.
The promenade (*Tayelet*, in Hebrew) is a two kilometer–long, stone-paved
pedestrian path that extends along a hill in southern Jerusalem. The path is

partly built on arches that from a distance, give it the appearance of an aqueduct. The promenade overlooks a fold in the landscape known as the Kidron Valley, part of which is the site of the Jerusalem Peace Forest, developed by the Jewish National Fund.[1] The promenade faces the Southern Wall of the Old City of Jerusalem; with only a small bit of imagination, one can see the history of Jewish, Christian, and Moslem life unfold before your eyes. One can see Mount Moriah, the biblical site where, according to tradition, Abraham took Isaac to be sacrificed and where the City of David was located. One can also see the Temple Mount, which sits on top of part of the City of David and which is reputed by Islam to be where Mohammed ascended to heaven. One can also see the Garden of Gethsemane where Jesus was betrayed and the Church of the Holy Sepulchre where Jesus was buried and from where, according to Christian history, he ascended to Heaven. The vista also includes the expanse of modern East Jerusalem, mainly inhabited by Arabs.

On one side, the Haas Promenade is bordered by the United Nations Truce Supervision headquarters, a building constructed in the 1930s as the residence for the British high commander. On the other side, the promenade is bordered by upscale Jerusalem apartments inhabited primarily by middle-class and affluent families. At the western end of the path is the site designated to be the embassy of the United States in Jerusalem. Although the U.S. Congress in 1995 set a deadline for moving the embassy to Jerusalem from the existing location in Tel Aviv outside the capital city, Presidents Clinton and Bush have both delayed implementing the legislation.[2] The complex history of the vista notwithstanding, the panoramic view from the Haas Promenade is breathtaking. The visual stimulation, and its relationship to Israel's history and future, is made even more poignant by sounds that punctuate the air for many visitors. Throughout the day, a visitor can hear the call to prayer from Moslem mosques and the ringing of bells from East Jerusalem's Christian churches. Before 1967, the area of the Haas Promenade was under Jordanian control and few Jewish tourists visited the site. In the nearly forty years since the Six-Day War, the situation has dramatically changed; today, the promenade is often one of the first stops tourist groups make when they arrive in Jerusalem.

Just before nine o'clock in the morning, early in the summer of 2003, two Birthright Israel buses, clearly identified by their regulation banners draped across the fronts and backs, pull up to a small parking area near the highest point of the Tayelet. As the sleepy-looking Birthright Israel contingent disembarks and makes its way to the overlook, they pass an ice cream truck with a vendor hawking popsicles, drinks, and souvenirs, and several young Arab boys selling picture postcards of Jerusalem. The group walks down a set of steps and stands together to take part in a carefully planned program that begins with an introduction to the site and to the grand expanse of Jerusalem in front of the group.

Both bus groups had arrived from Canada the previous day, and the Tayelet was not only their introduction to historic Jerusalem, but the prologue to their engagement with Israel. The *madrich* (guide) begins his rap about the site slowly—a wise decision, because most participants are distracted by their adjustment to the strong sun and the power of what they can see when they turn their heads 180 degrees. His tone is emotional as he tells them that this is one of the grand views of the world and that before them is a "panorama of centuries of history." He continues that there is a special treat that morning: Charles Bronfman, co-founder of Birthright Israel, has come to talk with them and to welcome them to Jerusalem.

For many participants, Bronfman is a mythic figure. Most of those standing in the hot sun already know Bronfman was born in Montreal and they know of his role in the Seagram company, his ownership of the Montreal Expos baseball team, and his legendary philanthropy. Charles arrives, with his leashed dog in tow, just as the buses pull into the parking lot. A number of the participants want to shake his hand and thank him. He seems embarrassed to get such attention. When he moves to the front of the group, his "speech" is not very elaborate. He simply wants his fellow Canadians know that he loves Jerusalem. He tells them about his home nearby and that the Tayelet is part of his daily walk. He tells his fellow countrymen that being Jewish is a great experience and that it is their "birthright" to be able to visit Israel and get to know their ancestral homeland and the people of modern Israel.

Not every Birthright Israel group meets Charles Bronfman at the Tayelet, but often a prominent leader is invited to meet with groups. Some groups have met with Bronfman's philanthropic partners, including Michael Steinhardt and a partner who joined after the program was founded, Lynn Schusterman. Hillel groups have heard from Richard Joel, former president of Hillel International and now president of Yeshiva University, or they have gotten to meet and hear Avraham Infeld, who succeeded Joel at Hillel. Although Joel and Infeld are quite different from one another, they are both extraordinarily effective orators. They are more than a generation apart from the Birthright Israel participants but can connect with participants and help them relate their presence in Jerusalem to their Jewish identities.

After the guest speaker, a trip participant frequently says a few words—reacting, asking questions, and usually expressing thanks for the opportunity to be a part of the experience. Then there is a brief ritual, associated with entering Jerusalem, of reciting a blessing over *challah* (bread) and wine. Some groups then remain at the site for a short period of time, socializing or even dancing, while others devote their time to learning about the history of the distant vistas. In some cases, groups are highly interactive and the outdoor discussion becomes more like a seminar.

Of the presenters who meet groups at the Tayelet, some are brief and inspirational, while others are more long-winded and lecturer-like. All, however, invariably provide historical perspective and awe their audience by reciting some of the facts associated with the view before them. They will say, for example:[8]

> "In front of you is the biblical city of Jerusalem and you are looking at what might be regarded as the cradle of Jewish history."
>
> "The layers of Jewish history spread out before you, beginning with the binding of Isaac on Mount Moriah to the First and Second Temples and the kingdoms of David and Solomon to the destruction of the Temple and Exile, to the eternal Jewish longing to return to this place."
>
> "Contemporary Jerusalem is all around you and is built on this most ancient of Jewish roots here in the Land of Yisrael."
>
> "This ancient heart of Jewish existence has been preserved over the ages, we are here today, and you are part of this chain of history."

As a Yehuda Amichai poem says, "All the generations before me contributed me so that I might be erected here in Jerusalem; That obligates me."[3]

Not all of the background given at the promenade focuses on Jewish identity. Guides will often refer to the profound significance of the site to Christians and Moslems. They do so by pointing to the churches in the Garden of Gethsemane, to the Church of the Holy Sepulchre, and to the mosques on the Temple Mount known in Arabic as "Haram el Sharif." Some groups hear about the site in terms of the contemporary political situation. A guide, for example, will say, "See that building in the right corner of the view. It has been suggested as the eventual home of the Parliament of the Palestinian Authority. Over there is Al Quds University, a major Arab university in East Jerusalem. And there is the new security wall being erected to protect Jerusalem from terrorists." Exactly what a group hears depends on the guide, the group, and when in the course of the trip the visit occurs.

What overall meaning does either a short (half-hour) or long (two-hour) visit to the Haas Promenade convey? Observing dozens of groups and talking to many participants, we see that nearly all come away understanding that Jerusalem is central and key to the Jewish experience. They understand that they are supposed to see links in Judaism among place, religion, and spirituality. An experience at the Tayelet, however brief and subdued, "shouts out" to visitors that the Jewish people were born in this place and have been linked to it for more than three millennia. It justifies the ongoing Jewish connection to the land. The Tayelet allows a young adult Birthright Israel participant to feel that he/she is standing in the amphitheater of Jewish existence. By being there, they are active partners in the continuation of their people's history. The visit to the promenade is part of a journey or travel experience that has been part of the human legacy for centuries.

BEING A TRAVELER

In earlier eras, travel to foreign lands was a long and arduous journey, fraught with adventure and danger. Travelers to the land that is now modern Israel came in brown capes or shining armor as sojourners, soldiers, and pilgrims. Today's travelers arrive on sleek jets that allow them to come and go in what is, relatively speaking, a flash of time. They wear shorts, T-shirts, and fanny or backpacks, carry guidebooks and disposable cameras. Modern travelers, if they are helped on their journey, are more likely to be led by a person called "a tour guide" holding an umbrella or colored flag than they are by their family's patriarch or a senior soldier. Modern travel is basically like wandering— going places without much knowledge of the place or genuine contact with the place or people who inhabit it.

Travel is a primordial human experience. Perhaps it began with the expulsion of Adam and Eve from the Garden of Eden. It continued with Ulysses' odyssey over the seas and the conquests of the Roman Empire. In the Middle Ages, travel took on a new form as the Crusaders rode horses across Europe to the Middle East. Later, it took shape in European exploration of the Americas and the way in which Europeans traveled to Venice, Rome, and Florence for inspiration. In modern times, travel for Americans meant driving. Today, it's more likely flying: to Fort Lauderdale or Cancún at spring break and to Europe and other exotic locations around the world.

In the first seven years of Birthright Israel, the more than 150,000 young Jews who boarded El Al and other flights became a twenty-first-century model of tourist-pilgrim-traveler—probably the most concentrated voluntary wave of tourism in Jewish history. These travelers are, of course, of great interest to those who created and support the program. They hope it will promote Jewish continuity. But the program should also be of great interest to academics and scholars for whom tourism has, increasingly, become a subject of intensive study and research.[4]

What kind of travel is Birthright Israel?
"Tourism" scholars describe several types of travel, making a sharp distinction between "the pilgrim" and "the tourist."[5] Pilgrimage refers to travel of believers to holy sites that already have meaning and significance in the

lives and lore of the traveler. The pilgrim is a traveler from *within* a tradition and belief system. Tourists are different kinds of travelers; they are not necessarily visiting holy sites about which they know anything or in which they believe. They might be described as "curious photographers" taking time off and changing venue from their normal routine.

Birthright Israel travelers are not easily described and are, perhaps, a hybrid. They are not traditional pilgrims. It is not that they are "pilgrim believers" seeking out familiar holy sites or those that have inherent primacy in their faith system. The Birthright Israel travelers may know little or nothing of the sites to which they are traveling; they do not come from within a community of believers who are journeying to sites that they consciously regard as holy; and they are motivated to travel not by "an inner light" but by, among other things, the gift of a free ticket and ten days, all expenses paid.

At the same time, the Birthright Israel travelers are not the classical "if it's Tuesday, this must be Belgium" tourist. Granted the Birthright Israel travelers see a great number of historical sites in a short time, but for the most part, they are interconnected places—integrated by the narration provided by guides over ten days. Participating on a Birthright Israel trip does not have much in common with meandering through Europe. Even if the participants were not themselves motivated, their guides try not to allow them to be in Israel just to "be away"; rather, their purpose is to help participants find meaning in the place and one's relationship to it. As thousands of Birthright Israel participants indicate on their applications, they feel drawn to Israel; connecting with their homeland represents a missing link in their identity development. As one participant described the feeling, "I need to visit my homeland. . . . I want to understand better why my religion feels so right for me."[6] Finally, many were "normal" young adults who were seeking fun with peers on a free, no-strings-attached, overseas trip.

Participants are not disappointed and the founders of the program, Bronfman and Steinhardt, have received thousands of unsolicited thank-you letters. A typical letter expresses profound gratitude for having been able to take part in Birthright Israel and links it to the way in which it helped them develop their Jewish identity. Hundreds of letters include comments such as "My trip to Israel was one of the most special in my life, as I finally was able to see what I had learned about for years in Hebrew school. Standing at the Western Wall, and realizing the religious significance of *my* location, was an amazing feeling."

The Birthright Israel traveler is in some kind of "liminal state" between a "normal" life setting and a new and different world and culture that seems to be about something more than text-messaging and going to a rave. Sociologist Shaul Kelner indicates that the trip is about altering the social setting of these young adults, and placing them in new and unfamiliar settings with the goal of "opening the possibility for existing self-definitions to be shed and alternative ones to be adopted."[7] In that sense, Birthright Israel utilizes the garb of contemporary tourism as a vehicle for identity formation and for generating feelings of peoplehood.

What distinguishes the Birthright Israel participant from other categories of contemporary tourists is that the Birthright Israel traveler participates in a carefully crafted educational experience with clearly articulated knowledge and identity goals. The participants may look more like tourists rather than pilgrims, but Birthright Israel is overtly about learning; hence, the visiting young adult is participating in a genre that may be called "educational tourism."

Birthright Israel young adults are brought to sites that have stories, narratives, and meanings that are framed by someone: a tradition, a guidebook, or a tour leader. The book, tradition, or person gives "meaning" and makes sense out of the stones, buildings, and earth. The sites and sights can and do have multiple meanings and interpretations, but they are brought to the site by educator-guides who carefully weave the narratives. Moreover, major "narratives" of the Birthright Israel trip are stated as required standards. For example:[8]

- Israel is a contemporary modern society
- Israel is connected to main themes of Jewish history
- Key sites in Israel explain the origins of Zionism, the struggle for Statehood, and the ongoing Israeli-Palestinian conflict
- There are core Jewish values reflected within the context of places visited
- There is a connection between Israel, the Holocaust, contemporary Jewish life, and your personal Jewish identity
- Visiting and learning about these sites should evoke deep positive individual emotion, and pride in each Birthright Israel participant for being Jewish

The concept of "framing" is central to understanding how a Birthright Israel trip operates. Students of photography, literary criticism, and contemporary philosophy are cognizant that one does not simply see or experience a sight. Rather, "seeing a site" is always related to framing. The photographer decides to hold the camera in a certain way, to focus on certain things and not others, and to include or omit some people in the picture rather than others. The author writes about an event or theme from his or her perspective and the reader reads the description in his or her room. The readers read not the text that the author wrote, but the one the reader reads. Similarly, travelers who participate in a Birthright Israel group can look around and see many things. One unique feature is that their attention is regularly focused by the curriculum and the tour guides. Their attention is drawn, and they focus on specific "sites and sights" that Birthright Israel and the tour guides think are important.

Experiences on a Birthright Israel trip are framed according to a set of required Educational Standards (see chapter 4). The guides (*madrichim*), along with other staff, are charged with interpreting the standards and implementing a coherent program that integrates the required elements with their own educational and group sensibilities. The educational staff shapes the experiences in a multitude of ways: their initial presentation of "tomorrow's itinerary"; their comments on the bus as the group approaches the site; the words they use while at the site; their summing-up. Groups also take part in a series of at least three "tie-in" discussions designed to allow participants to reflect on what they have seen and heard. The Birthright Israel project took a strong stand from the outset against any sort of overt indoctrination or propaganda. At the same time, like any form of education or educational tour program, Birthright Israel engaged in the activity of framing.

Another striking characteristic of Birthright Israel trips is that they create unique kinds of group experiences for those traveling together. A sociologist of tourism, Victor Turner, called this phenomenon "communitas."[9] In Birthright Israel, it is popularly referred to as "the group." The communitas dimension of Israel experience programs in general, and of the Birthright Israel trip in particular, is one of the defining characteristics of the experience.[10] It is not simply traveling to Israel that matters; it is coming with a particular group and sharing intimate moments, sites, and sights with a group of peers with whom one bonds.

Birthright Israel trips are "educational tourism" and the guide is more of a "tour educator" than a "tour guide." He/she represents the site and fosters construction of a shared narrative that each participant can adopt."[11] The tour educator is an interpretative voice. The educator provides a framework for Birthright Israel participants to understand what they see and also serves to shape the communitas experience.

TRAVELING THE BIRTHRIGHT ISRAEL PATH

Each Birthright Israel group has a somewhat different itinerary, but some sites are required to be part of all trips. Below, some of the core Birthright Israel sites are described. Our focus is not only on the sites, but on the diverse ways tour educators frame what is seen. We shall see places that groups "saw" and some of the different ways in which sites were "framed." As well, possible diverse "meanings" that could emerge from the very same site are examined. Below, visits to four sites are described. They represent the range of ancient, modern, and contemporary sites that are part of each Birthright Israel experience. They represent, as well, the different approaches to engaging participants with the land and culture of Israel.

A Hill in the Desert

After the Western Wall, Masada is the second most popular site on Birthright Israel itineraries. In the first century, as noted earlier, it was the site of a key event in Jewish history. Masada is a rocky plateau on the western coast of the Dead Sea, ten miles north of Kibbutz Ein Gedi and sixty miles south of Jerusalem. It is on the border of the Judean Desert across the Dead Sea from Jordan. Masada is a mountain that at its highest point is four hundred meters above the level of the Dead Sea, the lowest spot on the face of the earth.

The main source of information about the site is from the works of Josephus Flavius, a historian writing during the time of the events that took place there. In 1963–1965 the great Israeli archaeologist Yigal Yadin conducted a monumental archaeological dig and study of the site. Historically, the site on which there was a splendid castle served Hasmonean kings and Herod the Great (37–4 B.C.E.) who used it as a retreat in times of political troubles. In 70 C.E. after the Temple in Jerusalem was destroyed, Masada became the last bastion of Jewish independence, where the most radical of the insurgents retreated.[12] In 72 C.E. the legate of Judea, Flavius Sylva, surrounded Masada with his tenth legion and prepared to ascend it and conquer the last insurgents. On April 15, 73 C.E., led by Eleazar Ben Yair, the 960 remaining men, women, and children of Masada decided that rather than surrender, they would instead kill themselves "al Kiddush Hashem." Only a handful of survivors remained. A Roman garrison occupied Masada until 111 C.E. Eventually, a series of earthquakes caused the collapse of most of the buildings. In the fifth and sixth centuries a group of monks established a small church at the site. After their departure, the site remained deserted until contemporary times. The site is physically remarkable because the castle walls jut out over the edge of the mountain in an otherwise flat body of land bordering the Dead Sea and the Negev Desert.

Masada has assumed an important place in contemporary Zionist lore and legend.[13] The once popular Hebrew phrase *"shenit Masada lo tipol"* (Masada will never fall again), came to mean that Jews would never again be forced to sacrifice their lives against approaching enemies; rather, Jews would fight back and defeat the enemy. Jews would finally, as Zionist ideology centrally proclaimed, become masters of their fate and captains of their souls. For many years, the induction ceremony of Israeli paratroopers took place on top of Masada. It was a way to symbolize modern soldiers' link to an ancient Jewish past. It emphasized the soldiers' role in ensuring that the tragic story of Masada would become transformed into an heroic tale.[14]

Most groups begin the Masada visit early in the morning, hiking up the mountain as the sun rises over the Dead Sea. We observed one group shortly after 4:30 A.M. as they began their single-file march up the mountain. For the thin and agile, it is a vigorous morning outing; for others, it is a formidable physical and sometimes psychological challenge. Little guiding is done on the way up, there is lots of small talk and banter, and there is careful staff surveillance to ensure safety. A cable car is available a little later for anyone unable to climb, but there are no takers on this trip. The group arrives at the top of Masada by 5:30 A.M. They have just completed a demanding climb, and they did it together as a group.

When they reach the platueau, the tour educator takes over. What is the story of Masada he tells? And how do different guides explain it? The Masada visit is, perhaps, the supreme example of "framing" and shaping narratives. Consider how four different guides begin the tour:

> Shlomo begins the tour either at the *mikveh* (ritual bath) or at the synagogue and says: "We are now on the top of Masada. It is the site of the martyrdom, of a group of deeply committed Jews who preferred death to being forced into exile or into living non-Jewish lives. It is the ultimate symbol of Jewish commitment. You will see here a *mikveh,* a synagogue, eating rooms, storerooms, and a Jewish community that even as death lay before them persisted in their commitment to living a Jewish life and Jewish values. Jewish continuity and life was their supreme value and they were willing to sacrifice their lives and the lives of their children for it. This mountain symbolizes commitment and belief in Judaism, its God, and the centrality of preserving its existence. Notice it's not just any old community. It has a mikveh and a synagogue. It's a Jewish community. Jews who were committed to preserving Judaism sacrificed their lives here. This is what is called al Kiddush Hashem."

> Batya begins the tour at Herod's palace on the very edge of the mountain and says: "We are now on top of Masada. It is the site of the martyrdom of 960 Jews. It's also a fascinating site in terms of the struggle of what some Hebrew writers called 'Hellenism and Hebraism.' Herod was of Jewish background, but he adapted Roman customs, built luxurious palaces, and liked the sports, women, wine, and song of the Greek world.[15] The Jews who came here were zealots—they deeply feared the perversion of core Jewish values by the pagan cultures. Herod and his

palaces represented the values and culture of the general world and in many ways our visit up here is about a challenge, dilemma, and choice each of you face: how do you balance your Jewish identity and your general identity, your Hebraism and your Hellenism?"

A third guide, Yaki, says: "We're now on top of Masada. It is the site of the martyrdom of 960 Jews in the year 72 c.e. Imagine you were the Jews up here. What options did you face? Do you think what they did was the right choice? Why? Why not? Are these the only two options they had? Think about these questions as our trip continues."

And, finally, Shayne says: "This place has become central in modern Israeli history. It symbolizes the Jewish connection to the Land of Israel and the refusal to let foreign forces defeat us. The defenders of Masada would rather die than to let the enemy send them into exile. Exile for the ancient Jews was inconceivable. For many decades young people your age were sworn into the paratroopers on this mountain to guarantee that never again will Masada fall—never again will Jewish life be destroyed. For our young people today Masada symbolizes the Israeli commitment to guarantee Jewish survival in a free and independent Jewish homeland here in Eretz Yisrael."

None of these descriptions are totally faithful to the historical record, but then the actual guides are not academic historians. The guides have studied history, but they recount it in a way that is consistent with their own world-view. Most tour guides probably present a bit of each of the four narratives presented here, although emphases in one direction or another emerge. The core message that all of the educators preach is that Masada is a symbol of the deep commitment of Jewish continuity and survival. Being Jewish has involved ongoing life-and-death struggles for survival and there have been Jews throughout history that have risen to the occasion and fought that battle. Masada's existence today is testimony to the Jewish will to survive. The Hebrew phrase "shenit Masada lo tipol" is interpreted to mean that the continuation of the Jewish people is assured.

Back at the base of the hill, the Birthright Israel participants get on the buses, sweating, hydrating with cold drinks, feeling exhausted, but also exhilarated. They ride north or south along the Dead Sea, often in silence, physically and emotionally spent. They are consciously or unconsciously pondering the questions that Masada raises. For a place that is so real, it is nevertheless difficult for the participants to put themselves in the position of those who were at Masada when it was under Roman siege.

On the Shores of the Sea of Galilee

More than 150 miles north of Masada, in an area that is as verdant as Masada is desertlike, most Birthright Israel groups stop at a small cemetery on the southern coast of the Sea of Galilee. It is a short distance from the center of Tiberias, the city that lies alongside the Sea of Galilee and that serves as a "front door" to much of northern Israel. Several of the great Zionist leaders of pre-1948 Israel are buried in the cemetery here: most notably, Berl Katznelson, the major ideologue of the Labor Zionist movement and Moses Hess, a nineteenth-century pre-Zionist thinker who wrote the pamphlet "Rome and Jerusalem." More recently, Naomi Shemer, perhaps modern Israel's most famous songwriter (and author of the song "Jerusalem of Gold") was buried at the cemetery. Invariably, Birthright Israel guides take their groups toward one grave. They typically pause and have their group sit down. In one such visit, a tour educator frames the experience: "This is the grave of Rachel Bluwstein, born in 1890, emigrated to Palestine in 1909, and died in 1931. Evan, would you open that metal container next to the grave?" Evan pulls out a ragged book attached to a chain and hands it to the guide, who continues:

> This is a book of Rachel's poems. Israeli high school students take a school trip each year and this is one of the great holy sites of secular Zionism. Rachel writes of her love and longing for Israel and especially this area. Indeed, she lived for a while just across the road in Kibbutz Kinneret. Let's read a poem [in translation from the original Hebrew]:

> SHAM HAREI GOLAN
> Over there are the hills of Golan, stretch out your hands and touch them.
> In their stalwart stillness they give the command to halt.
> In splendid isolation grandfather Hermon slumbers. A cool wind blows from the peak of whiteness.
> Over there, on the seashore, a low-topped palm tree stands, disheveled like a mischievous infant that has slid down and splashes in the waters of Kinneret.
> How abundant are the flowers in the winter, bunches of blood-red anemones, the orange of the crocus. These are the days when the greenery is sevenfold green and seventy-fold is the blue of the sky.
> But even if I become poverty-stricken and walk bent over and my heart becomes the beacon for strangers, how can I betray you, how can I forget, how can I forget the grace of youth.[16]

The guide continues by instructing his group:

Look across the sea toward the Golan Heights. This may even be the spot where she wrote the poem. The poem is about living for today—here on earth. The Zionist movement was not just about anti-Semitism. It was also about young romantics and idealists, people who believed in seizing the day, people who believed that by working together they could make a better world. In this cemetery are buried the dreamers of a new and better society who came here to build and be rebuilt. Over there, at Kvutzat Kineret, lived A. D. Gordon who came to Palestine in his fifties and preached the "religion of labor." By working, by touching the soil, by redeeming the land we redeem ourselves. We are now heading north into the living museum of Zionist ideology: kibbutzim built by Russian and Czech and American Jews who came to create new lives and new societies. Land, simplicity, communal sharing, reshaping material priorities, the holiness of today, living now. Many died, as Rachel did, of tuberculosis which she had contracted in Russia during World War I; conditions were tough, there were Arab raids, but they persevered. They believed in themselves, they loved every tree and hill here. They were home. Welcome to the home of ideological Zionism. This may be a cemetery, but it's been visited for decades by thousands of young people seeking inspiration for life. As you will see, this area is alive and booming. You have entered the Manhattan of living Zionism. Welcome!

After the cemetery visit, the participants return to their bus and sit back and rest. Most Birthright Israel participants had probably never heard of the names of those buried in the cemetery before they arrived. Most of them had never thought about Zionism as an ideology about earth, land, and control of one's own life. Some doze off as they think about the experience, but most have a hard time sleeping. There are too many new ideas fluttering in their heads; perhaps, even words of poetry remain.

A Yuppie Street in an Ancient City

The German Colony is a middle-class neighborhood in the southern part of Jerusalem. The German Colony was so named because it was founded by German Templars in the last part of the nineteenth century. The colony was modeled on a typical German village of one- and two-story houses surrounded by greenery and pastoral tranquillity. The houses were constructed of stone and many have red-tiled roofs. Today, the houses are spacious villas or have been replaced by newer modern apartment buildings of three to four stories. The neighborhood street names include "Lloyd George," "Smuts," and "Masaryk." The neighborhood is inhabited by Jerusalem's middle class mainly of Ashkenazic origin, with many academics, public officials, writers, students, and civil servants. It is an upscale neighborhood and apartments can run from $500,000 to $2,000,000. Small parks dot the neighborhood. It is a popular area for "Anglo-Saxons" and it is home to Jews who are even more diverse than the typical Jerusalem neighborhood. This is the neighborhood for Jerusalem's yuppie, middle-class intelligentsia.

The main thoroughfare and the heart of the neighborhood is Rehov Emek Refai'im (Valley of the Ghosts Street). Clustered along the narrow boulevard are a string of coffeeshops and restaurants with names like Caffit, Masaryk, Hillel, Aroma. Interspersed are wine shops, gift and jewelry stores, flower shops, and newsstands. There are bakeries and you sometimes hear people at coffeehouses talking about which one has the best Shabbat challah. Along with distinctly Israeli local commerce, Emek Rafai'im has not escaped having a Pizza Hut and a McDonalds.

Friday morning is the time to see and be seen on Rehov Emek Refai'im. Knesset members are buying their challah or holding court at Caffit. Winners of the Israel Prize for literature, cinema, and architecture stroll along the street and have coffee in one of its cafés. The German Colony is home to the offices of the leftist Shalom Achshav (Peace Now) movement, and the leftists regard this area as their turf. Perhaps ironically, many of the shopkeepers are staunch "Likudniks" (the rightist party, formerly headed by Ariel Sharon). Given the intensity of Israeli politics and the freeness with which everyone shares his or her views, it is perhaps surprising that heated debates between merchants and customers are not common.

Before the intifada, the German Colony was off the beaten track of Birthright Israel buses. Most likely, the only way one would know about this neighborhood was if a bus was passing from the southern section of Jerusalem back to one of the hotels in the center of town. This changed in late 2000, after the beginning of a wave of suicide bombings. To ensure participants' safety, Birthright Israel instituted strict control over free time. Thousands of independent nightlife junkies and gift-seeking young adults were no longer free to wander in downtown Jerusalem or neighboring areas such as the Russian Compound. To provide controlled participation in nightlife and shopping, a compromise was reached that enabled Birthright Israel groups to wander in a precisely defined locale that could be monitored by Israeli police and security forces.

Rehov Emek Refai'im was regarded as a well-protected, self-contained area. The business district begins near the old Jerusalem train station and ends beyond Café Hillel. Police, stationed at each end of the street, could check both cars and individuals entering the district. It was one ten-block stretch of shops and restaurants where forty or more young adults could walk, talk, drink, buy gifts, and people-watch. For Birthright Israel's purposes, it was an ideal setting for a "framed" experience. Tour guides would tell more or less the historical facts we have just described and then set their charges free. A somewhat similar site was Sheinkin Street in Tel Aviv, overpopulated by boutiques and young Israelis with pierced body parts.

What was the message of Emek Refai'im? Without much framing, other than providing historical context, the setting allowed Birthright Israel guides to show Israel as a contemporary, Western society where Jews lived normal lives. The stores, the people, and the shopwindows did the job better than a hundred lectures. That the site had many elements familiar to the college communities that many participants came from, from coffeehouses to McDonald's and Pizza Hut restaurants, allowed Israel to be presented as not much different than their home community.

One of Emek Refai'im's core messages was that being part of a Jewish community did not mean that you had to dress or act like the shtetl people of Anatevka from *Fiddler on the Roof.* The withered pictures of a great-grandmother and great-grandfather in the family album described their forebearers' lives, but not modern Jewry. Jews in the twenty-first century looked like familiar people: they wore shirts with polo horses on the left breast; they drank cappuccino, they read Grisham and Huntington (in Hebrew and English), and, as Yehuda Amichai described in his poem "Tourists,"[17] they bought "fruits and vegetables for their families." Amichai, perhaps the best-known Israeli poet before his death in 2000 could ofen be seen in Emek Refai'im. You could meet him walking with his buddies Menachem Brinker or Haim Guri, two of Israel's best-known literary figures. An Emek Rafai'im visit meant being in a living laboratory of contemporary Jewish society, but one that resonated for college-age Jews with the secular environments they knew from their home communities.

Another Cemetery

In 1951, Mount Herzl in Jerusalem was established as the national cemetery of Israel where presidents, prime ministers, government, and Jewish agency officials are laid to rest. It is named after Theodore Ze'ev Herzl (1860–1904) whose remains were interred there in 1951. The cemetery connects to the National Military Cemetery of Israel, where those who fell in Israel's wars and soldiers from Jerusalem are buried. Several sections of the parklike cemetery commemorate special events in Israel's military battles: refugees that the British tried to keep out of Palestine after World War II; parachutists who died trying to reach European Holocaust victims; British and Red Army soldiers; sixty-nine sailors who were lost in the disappearance of the Dakar submarine in 1969; and others.

Cemetery visits are a unique part of Israel tourism; tourists, in muffled whispers, often joke that they have never spent so much time in cemeteries. The Mount Herzl and the National Military Cemeteries send a clear message about the struggle for Jewish survival and the price paid for the creation and defense of the Jewish State. The visitor sees the graves of some of Israel's founders and great public figures, including Herzl, as well as Prime Ministers Levi Eshkol and Yitzhak Rabin.[18] They also "meet" hundreds of anonymous young people, many of the same age and even from similar backgrounds, whose lives were cut short by Israel's wars. Because the cemetery is so large and because there are so many stories, Birthright Israel produced a special educational booklet for tour educators.[19] It provides historical context, relates modern themes to ancient texts, and provides suggestions about how to teach the stories of those buried at the cemetery.

In practice, tour educators emphasize diverse themes when they bring a group to Mount Herzl: heroism; the diversity of countries from which people came; the price paid for the state; the particular heroism of young people of the same age as the visitors. In Birthright Israel groups that visit the cemetery with their Israeli counterparts (see chapter 7), the Israelis almost always tell personal stories of their relatives and friends who are buried there. The decibel level of tour guides at the cemetery is often hushed and the messages about the site are whispered, rather than shouted. Nevertheless, the storyline of struggle, heroism, and youth rising to the occasion is presented loud and clear. This visit is emotional, touching, and sometimes aggressively presented. For some Birthright Israel participants, they feel "put on the spot." The questions, asked or unasked as the group silently files out of the cemetery are, "What have you done for your people?" "What kind of sacrifice are you prepared to make?"

WHAT IS LEARNED FROM A PLACE?

These sites—from ancient Masada, to the cemetery alongside the Sea of Galilee, to Emek Refai'im, to Mount Herzl—represent, in microcosm, the kind of places that Birthright Israel trips include as part of the experience. These are but four out of the thousands of events, sites, and sights on a Birthright Israel trip. Some other popular sites include: the Independence Museum in Tel Aviv (site of the signing of the Israeli Declaration of Independence); the Golan Heights; Sde Boker (the kibbutz of David Ben Gurion); the archaeological digs at David's City in Jerusalem; the Knesset; the Supreme Court; kibbutzim; Yaffo, the Negev, and Eilat; Metulla. What are the overseas visitors "shown" on these trips?

Cemeteries and the sites of ancient settlements aside, perhaps most important, Birthright Israel visitors are shown a modern country of Jews. They see young people their age, modern buildings, hi-tech industry, and contemporary writers and musicians. There is an overt effort to let the Birthright Israel participant know that Israel is not simply a museum of Jewish antiquities. It is that, of course, but it is also a thriving country of Jews who in many ways are like those in other Western cultures and societies. Even the historical sites and the cemeteries are framed in terms of contemporary life.

Israel is also presented as a modern democracy ("the only democracy in the Middle East") facing a long-standing battle with volatile neighbors and enemies. There is great emphasis on Israel's similarity to America in its commitment to freedom, rule of law, checks and balances, and vox populi. Israel's strong commitment to being a Western democracy, whose Jewish values are universal and transcendent, is emphasized in the context of an almost century-long war with hostile neighbors. There is no intentional effort to present a single political view of Israel; guides are trained both to offer multiple perspectives and allow different voices to be heard. But the discordant views are presented as part of the vibrancy of Israel's democratic political structure.

Israel is also shown as a primordial experience of Jewish peoplehood. The land and the sites are used as the backdrop to present the Jews as a people with shared customs, culture, holidays, and memories. Birthright Israel participants are invited to see themselves as part of this colorful, diverse collective peoplehood and "communitas." Birthright Israel guides try to show contemporary Israel as linked to classical Jewish values; most important, justice, peace, study, and *tikun olam* (repairing the world).[20] As part of a Birthright Israel trip, participants may visit hospitals, army bases, absorption centers, institutions of higher learning, ministries of social welfare and education. Each is a modern setting, but they are used to illustrate how Israeli daily life is linked to Judaism's core values.

Although the focus of the program is on modern israel, Birthright Israel participants are repeatedly reminded that they are in a country with rich historical roots reaching back to the Bible. Most group leaders emphasize the long chain of Jewish history and, inevitably, the central role of the Land of Israel in that chain. Israel is presented as both the birthplace of the Jewish people and as an authentic *Alt Neuland*—a very new and real place with roots in the core events, ideas, and places that shaped the Jewish people.[21]

The trips, both covertly and overtly, create links between the major threats to Jewish existence in recent decades—the Holocaust, the Arab-Israel conflict, assimilation, and intermarriage—and Israel as a response to these threats. *Mi-Shoah L'Tkuma* (from Holocaust to renewal) is a central Birthright Israel theme. Israel, though a modern democracy, remains the refuge of the

Jewish people and the guarantor of the survival of the Jewish people. Although some might view the program as a form of indoctrination, for most Birthright Israel participants accustomed to the give-and-take of college seminars, they are simply being invited into a dialogue about Israel. Their tour educator may have a perspective, and some may not be able to disguise their political position, but participants *are* exposed to multiple alternative perspectives—from the Israelis they meet on the bus, to those they talk with at each site. This exposure is not intended to represent all possible points of view, but it represents the range of views held by Israeli Jews.

Core to Birthright Israel's vision is a commitment to the creation of an intimate personal connection between the young Jew from abroad and Israel—what one observer, Clare Goldwater, calls "existential authenticity."[22] Its pedagogy is clearly invested in personal meaning-making and not simply in instruction or even in the transmission of facts. Observations of hundreds of groups underscores that the narratives provided by guides and educators are not overtly preached nor imposed. Instead, they are woven into the experience and come to the surface by the nature of the sites visited and the frames presented. When the education is well done, the information is presented in a way that is respectful of the young adult's need to develop his or her own understanding. Educators try not to cross over that "dreaded" boundary called propaganda. Partly because of their skill, but also because of the participants, they could not propagandize even if they wanted to; it would not be very effective.

That said, sites are presented with varying degrees of narrative framing. Places such as Mount Herzl and the Haas Promenade are given substantial framing. These sites call out for contextualized information. As well, the educator wants to use the site to provide an overall frame for the experience. Often, there are multiple messages and different ways to frame depending where in the trip the visit occurs and the sophistication of the group. Masada is an example of a site that invites diverse framings and interpretations, depending on the trip organizer. In contrast, some sites, such as a visit to Emek Refai'im are visited with minimal framing, and it is assumed that the experience speaks for itself.

The Birthright Israel trip is, thus, an amalgam of a set of experiences that are offered both with and without framing. What is common across the experiences, and the messages that are transmitted, is that the presentation is generally open and seeks a dialectic with participants. Because the central Birthright Israel organization does not implement trips itself and focuses on setting standards, the program cannot guarantee that the open culture is always preserved. Evaluative oversight evaluation of trip organizers, along with follow-up research on participants (see chapter 8), however, generally points to realization of this guiding pedagogic vision. What is clear is that sites, and their presentation, are central to the Birthright Israel experience.

Of course, Birthright Israel trips have some elements in common with the classical religious pilgrimage. They are journeys to important religious sites, and the goal is to enhance the pilgrims' connection to their ethnic and religious group. But Birthright Israel journeys are not necessarily religious and, as Kelner has maintained, the experience itself creates meaning.[23] Sites, thus, are not ends in themselves. In the Birthright Israel context, the sites are vehicles for a larger "sight." They provide a vision of young Jews who are guided to feel a link to the Jewish people, to the State of Israel, and to their personal Jewish identity.

The Birthright Israel program is consistent—doggedly so—in shaping an educational tourism experience for a specific target group of curious young adults. It is aimed directly at linking the heart and soul of the young participant to an ongoing Jewish journey. The sites seen, shown, and shaped for these visitors are stops on a larger journey called "being Jewish." As described in the next chapter, they are used by educators to link the land with people and, in so doing, to form a coherent narrative. The role of the educators and their relationships with participants and their surroundings is central to understanding Birthright Israel.

A People Revolution

4

This country made us a people: our people made this country.
—David Ben-Gurion, 1946

The Birthright Israel group, college students from the East Coast, waited expectantly in the hotel meeting room. They were chatting, flirting, wisecracking, but mostly just hanging out. They frequently turned to the door to see if "he" had arrived. Finally, Natan Sharansky, the former refusenik turned Israeli politician and best-selling author of *The Case for Democracy: The Power of Freedom to Overcome Tyranny and Terror,* entered with his entourage. Sharansky appeared with his signature green army cap tipped on his head, and wearing a short-sleeved white shirt. He was strikingly tall in his shortness, perhaps exaggerated by his quick pace, and the way in which his taller aides and a security person quickly melted into the background.

The head of the organization responsible for conducting this particular trip greeted Sharansky and introduced him to the participants. Although she had sent him background information on the group, she repeated the information publicly, just to be sure he knew to whom he was talking. She also wanted to signal to the audience that Sharansky knew that he was interested in them. The leader was emotional as she introduced the guest to the Birthright Israel participants and told them, "It is not often that one gets to be in a room and has a chance to talk to heroes, and we are here with one of the great modern Jewish heroes of our time: Natan Sharansky. It is my great pleasure to introduce Natan Sharansky to Birthright Israel bus 127." Her emotion was genuine. For her, and others who had themselves been college students . during the refusenik era, this little man was a giant.

Sharansky spoke English adeptly, but in a monotone made heavier by his Russian accent. Nevertheless, every phrase was clearly shaped and each sentence articulated an intelligent idea. He spoke without notes and his eyes panned the attentive audience throughout his talk. Although his speech was likely a version of something he had given a hundred times, his college student audience was made to feel that the speech was as fresh as if it were break-ing news and as if it had been prepared especially for them.

Sharansky's comments began with the expected acknowledgments. He thanked the participants for coming to Israel and praised Birthright Israel for making their trip possible. He talked about how proud he was to have been one of Birthright Israel's first, and most ardent, supporters in the government and to have served as chair of the Steering Committee that oversees the pro-gram.[1] Then, as requested by the organizer, he briefly told his story. Even for those who knew the basic outline, to hear him recount his journey to Israel and involvement in Israeli and world politics gave it new meaning.

Sharansky spoke about growing up in Russia, of being a mathematician, of being a Hebrew teacher, and of becoming a refusenik after seeking to emi-grate to Israel.[2] He explained how that experience led him to become a de-fender of human rights and, as a result of his refusal to bend to the Soviet regime, how he served more than a decade in prison. Much of his prison time was spent under harsh conditions. He spoke matter-of-factly about what it was like to be in the gulag, what sustained him during his imprisonment, and what it felt like to be released. His release, in 1986, and walk to freedom through the Brandenburg Gate, sounded celebratory. He told his story in crisp sentences in a straightforward, almost surgical style. He seemed to be giving the unembellished version, but he painted a rich word picture. No metaphoric pins dropping could be heard, and no one in the room seemed to be breathing.

After describing his own journey, he then described a recent tour he had made of U.S. college campuses. The focus, almost imperceptibly, had switched from his own life to the audience's. Sharansky told participants that the visit had opened his eyes to the challenges facing them, as well as others in the world. He did not present the issue in the often-used formulation, "they are all out to get us." Rather, in a now passionate tone, he highlighted the need to protect human dignity and freedom, and linked Israel's struggle to this universal fight. Sharansky urged his audience to argue Israel's case in a ra-tional, informed, and intelligent way. He called upon the participants from bus 127 to become educated in the "truth" about Israel and to become articu-late spokespeople for Israel and fighters against Palestinian propaganda. Again, he framed his arguments in universal terms: an opponent of terror and a supporter of human rights for *all*, not just Jews.[3] He charged Birthright Israel participants with a mission: become educated spokespeople for a great message of democracy and freedom.

Like virtually all Israelis who speak to Birthright Israel groups, Sharansky used the word "aliyah." But, in contrast to how others treat immigration to Is-rael, his message was not the typical Zionist plea for Jews to emigrate to Israel.

Instead, his call was for Birthright Israel participants to be part of the Zionist cause. It was, like Louis Brandeis's call in the early 1900s for American Jews to join the Zionist cause,[4] a call for Jews to join the struggle for human rights. Perhaps most important, in the context of recent debate about Israel's role in the conflict, Sharansky wanted his audience to see human rights' advocacy as a Zionist effort. His audience seemed mesmerized by his speech and fully absorbed in his message.

At what seemed like the peak of his rhetoric, he abruptly concluded his presentation. In place of a grand crescendo and oratorical flourish, he ended, simply by saying, "l'shana habaa b'yerushalyim." He then invited questions from the participants. The questions came quickly from an eager audience that seemed to burst with enthusiasm but also suggested the diversity of the Birthright Israel participants:

"What was it like in prison?"
"What turned you on to being Jewish?"
"Why did you go into politics?"
"Why did you join the right-wing camp in Israel?"
"What if we think that the Palestinians have just claims?"

He listened to each question carefully and seemed to understand what was being asked before the questioner had finished his or her sentence. Then, he quickly but politely answered each question, brushing aside queries that would have taken him off-message. Like the experienced politician that he is, Sharansky spoke at length about issues that mattered to him. He used the question-and-answer period as a time to reinforce his view of the contemporary struggle for democracy. After ten or fifteen minutes, one of his aides signaled that they were late for his next meeting. As briskly as he had entered, he thanked the group and marched out with his entourage.

Bus 127 had just spent forty minutes with a unique modern Jewish hero. They had the opportunity to see and meet a person that virtually all of them had heard about. They then had the chance to engage in dialogue about his and their own views of Israel and the world situation. For students growing up in the virtual reality era, a personal encounter with a well-known figure such as Sharansky is, perhaps, more memorable than one would expect. For most of these emerging adults, this was the first time they had the chance not only to see a famous figure in the flesh, but to ask a question and receive an answer. The Birthright Israel experience had given them the opportunity to meet face-to-face and voice-to-voice with a leading figure in contemporary Israel and the modern Jewish world.

Natan Sharansky is one of a long list of important Israeli and Jewish leaders with whom Birthright Israel participants have met and had an opportunity to engage in dialogue. The speakers range from leading political figures, including former prime ministers and party leaders, to academic and business leaders, and from philanthropists and writers. The Sharansky encounter exemplifies how Birthright Israel trips involve not only journeys to earth-and-stone sites, but also opportunities for Jewish young adults to engage Israeli leaders in settings that allow discussion and dialogue. The smallness of Israel, the closeness of people of power, the proclivity of this age group for discussion, and the clout of Birthright Israel's philanthropic and professional leadership give participants access to the country's opinion leaders and elite that would be unprecedented in other societies. The sessions with leaders are visits to "holy sites" of a different order than the Kotel (the "Western Wall" in the old city of Jerusalem). They are opportunities for emerging adults on the verge of entering the vestibules of power. In the case of Birthright Israel, it enables participants to understand how Israelis view their past and their future.

A VISIT WITH AVRAHAM INFELD

Avraham Infeld fills up a room. He is a large man in his early sixties and immediately one is drawn to his head—covered by a mixture of red hair, beard, and a *kippah* (head covering). His eyes sparkle and, whether someone is his longtime buddy or a new friend, that person is likely to find Avraham's arm around his/her shoulders even before he or she has had a chance to say hello. When you meet Avraham, he engulfs you and fills you up with his overflowing energy.

Aubrey (now Avraham) Infeld was born in South Africa during World War II. His parents, Lithuanian immigrants, were ardent Zionists and Hebrew-language educators. Avraham's parents ignited his interest in Zionism, and as a teenager he joined the South African Zionist youth movement. In 1959, the sixteen-year-old Infeld emigrated to Israel. He came alone, although eventually his entire family joined him. He served in the Israel Defense Forces' Education Corps, went to university, and then set out to change the world as a teacher and an educator. After the military trauma of Israel's 1973 Yom Kippur War, he came to believe that a key to Israel's survival was deepening the Jewish consciousness and identity of young Israelis, as well as young Jews from abroad. He felt that Israel and the Jewish world would be better equipped to face the challenges of the future if Jews were more conscious of their Jewish roots.

Shortly after the 1973 war, Infeld established an organization named Melitz, an independent education organization devoted to deepening the Jewish consciousness of young Israelis and the links between Israelis and Jews abroad. Melitz has had great impact on Israel. At its peak, in the 1990s, Melitz had seminar centers throughout Israel. In addition, it had scores of affiliated scholars who traveled to Jewish communities abroad, a vast publication program, and a training school for the staff of Israel experience trips and other informal Jewish educational activities. Melitz's headquarters was located in a few nondescript apartments of an old building in a suburb of Jerusalem. Infeld's office was one desk and a bookcase. Modest offices can be deceiving; Melitz's reach and Infeld's voice boomed throughout the country.

Infeld was an early participant in the discussions that led to Birthright Israel. He and several educators initially encouraged Michael Steinhardt's interest in Beilin's idea for Birthright Israel. At one stage prior to the launch of the project, Infeld was involved as planning director. At heart, he was an educator; his passion was not in large-program management. From the inception of the program, he worked closely with Hillel in helping it to realize the program's educational vision. In 2003, Infeld temporarily moved his base to Washington, D.C., leaving his family in Israel, in order to become acting international president of Hillel International. From his base in Washington, he oversaw Hillel's worldwide network of Jewish campus organizations.

Avraham Infeld is a unique kind of teacher. He uses texts, jokes, the group, himself, in order to press his message of Jewish consciousness and identity. He knows how to craft his message to speak to the concerns of young adults, his favorite audiences. He talks, he listens, he shouts, and he answers questions. At the end of an Infeld lecture, the audience has been exposed to a unique amalgam of Judaism and Infeld himself. His South African–accented words are clear, emotional, and rooted in a philosophical sense of how one develops and maintains religious-ethnic identity. He seems to be one of those gifted artisan-teachers who can take ideas, be they esoteric or banal, and make them accessible and relevant to an audience. Few speakers in the Jewish world are more in demand than Avraham Infeld.

In terms of his work with Birthright Israel, Infeld was often with Hillel groups, even before he did a tour of duty as their international president. On one trip, in 2003, Infeld joined several Hillel bus groups that were staying at a four-star hotel close to downtown Jerusalem and the Old City. He met with them in the basement ballroom. The groups that Infeld met been in Israel for several days and it was clear, when he joined them just after lunch, that exhaustion had set in. Whether it was the nonstop touring, the late-night discussions, or lingering jet lag, his college student audience looked as if they had just pulled an all-nighter.

When Infeld started to speak, some had not finished their lunch, and it was noisy as the ballroom was cleared of dishes. Quickly, however, almost magically, the room went silent. Avraham's voice reverberated; as he warmed up the audience with personal anecdotes, the audience emerged from quiescence and paid rapt attention to his words. Infeld launched into his "five-legged stool" speech in which he equates the Jewish people to a stool with five legs (the Hebrew language; the Land of Israel; Jewish values; the Jewish religion; the Jewish community).[5] With great dramatic pause, he said, "Take away any leg and the stool can't stand." As he expounded his view of Jewish identity, he alternately joked, turned serious, and exuded passion. He presented a clear, powerful, and thoughtful perspective on the essentials of being Jewish. When he finished, participants asked questions, raised problems with his formulation, and discussed how the framework made sense to them.

Unlike the questions asked by participants at a Sharansky speech, there is no political veneer to the issues raised by Infeld's remarks. His audience seems to be grappling not with whether they want to join his spiritual army (that seems to be a given) but how his framework helps them understand their lives. Most likely he succeeds because he makes Jewish identity personal and makes his conversation with college students feel like a one-on-one interaction. As if to make concrete his personal approach, when Avraham responds, he does so individually—asking questioners their name or some other information about them—and then responds directly to the issue they have raised.

The stature of Birthright Israel is such that it is able to recruit some of Israel's best teachers, educators, and charismatic personalities and give participants direct access to them. These personalities presented a different persona than the "professional Jew" that the young adults may have been familiar with from their local communities. Informality rules. The speakers generally go by their first names, are dressed casually, and there is no *bimah* (pulpit) or pews that separate participant and teacher, as there would likely be in a synagogue where students have encountered their rabbis. Substantively, they present perspectives on being Jewish that are often very different from those of the Jewish teachers and leaders that the participants had known before. The educators that young people meet on Birthright Israel emphasize Jewish values, Hebrew culture, and meaning-making rather than observance, survival, intermarriage, or fund-raising. Not all speakers have the charismatic appeal of Avraham Infeld, but many shared his successful method of engaging participants in their Jewish journey.

A POLITICAL DISCUSSION

The important figures that Birthright Israel participants meet are not all iconic Sharanskys or charismatic Infelds. Dov Weisglass is a leading Israeli lawyer who, among other distinctions, served as an adviser to Israel's former prime minister, Ariel Sharon. Weisglass is a tall, serious-looking man who wears business suits and color-coordinated ties. His work over the last several years has taken him into the innermost corridors of international politics and decision-making. He's a serious "player" in Israeli politics.

When he meets with Birthright Israel groups, Weisglass precisely and with the patience of an academic lecturer, presents the case for Israel. He begins by explaining that Israel wants to live in peace, or at least in a state of nonwar with its neighbors. He presents Israel's desire for peace not as his view, but simply as a fact. Israel wants peace, he explains, for Jewish reasons, for economic reasons, and because a state should be able to guarantee its citizens a quiet and secure life. He is emphatic in telling his audience that Israel has not initiated the conflict with the Palestinians, nor did it set out to conquer Palestinian lands. Its occupation of these lands happened as a result of Arab attacks on Israel and Israel has retained these lands because it is the only way to guarantee Israel's basic security needs and rights. Israel would like to reach a definitive settlement with its neighbors but so far, for almost four decades, the Palestinians have refused to enter serious negotiations. Israel, he intones, has no choice but to ensure its people's security by retaining control over land that has proven to be a base for enemy attack on Israel.

The lawyer continues as if he were making opening arguments in a trial and talks about the recently announced policy to disengage unilaterally from Gaza. He explains that the goal is to avoid Israeli control of Arab areas and to minimize danger to Israeli soldiers and citizens. In addition, Israel has decided to build a security fence to protect Israeli citizens against terrorists and suicide bombers' easy access. The fence, he makes clear, is not being built in order to create an apartheid state, but as a defense system to protect lives. Finally, he says, Israel's situation must be seen in the context of 9/11. Israel's conflict is not simply a local struggle between two groups fighting over a small parcel of land; rather, it is one battlefield in a much larger global struggle between Western democratic societies and fundamentalist religious cultures. This is not just Israel's battle, he makes clear; on the contrary, it is part of the larger challenge faced by the rest of the democratic world.

Weisglass used language that was concise and reflected precision in the use of words that exhibited his legal and political expertise. His comments were obviously thought through carefully and delivered without rhetorical flash. He seemed to have a good sense of his audience and his arguments were just at the level of complexity that bright college students and recent graduates could understand. The presentation was not that of a fiery Zionist patriarch, nor that of a religious authority. What the Birthright Israel participants heard—whatever their political perspective—were the clear and prosaic words of an intelligent, early twenty-first-century lawyer and reflective human being.

As soon as he concluded, the questions came fast and furious. The audience was not of a single mind and their questions included praise, attack, clarification, and argument. The questions used a panoply of well-known buzzwords that are part of contemporary political discourse, but they also reflected the Jewish vocabulary that many of them had heard during their few days in the country: "Human rights," "Jewish survival," "occupation," "liberation," "Jewish values," "Nazi Germany," "Samuel Huntington," "terrorists," "liberation movements," "security fence," "separation wall," "occupied territories," "liberated territories," "Judea and Samaria." The discussion was intense and intelligent, questioning and respectful, sharp and interactive.

DIVERSE PERSPECTIVES

As part of the Birthright Israel program, most groups are brought together, usually in Jerusalem, for an educational fair and night of music and speeches (called the "mega-event"; see chapter 10). The educational fair includes lectures and discussions led by distinguished political and cultural leaders. Over the first years of the program, presenters have included leaders of various political factions: Colette Avital, Yossi Beilin, Tzipi Livni, Michael Melchior, Bibi Netanyahu, Ehud Olmert, and Yossi Sarid. The presenters also included leading Israeli journalists: David Horowitz, David Landau, Akiva Eldar, as well as a broad range of lesser-known figures who gave participants a sense of how Israeli political and opinion leaders view the country. Sessions at the educational fair tended to be large audience sessions, with one hundred to four hundred participants. The speaker would make a short (fifteen-minute), informal presentation followed by thirty minutes or more of questions and answers.

Observing many of these educational fair encounters made clear that they were not simply about being moved by a hero or charmed by a charismatic educator. They were more like college classrooms or *Meet the Press* television panels where articulate spokespeople were confronted with deep, diverse, and often controversial questions by very articulate young adults, many of whom were students of political science, economics, and international relations. What was noteworthy about these sessions was their intellectual level, their reflective tone, and their back-and-forth nature. They were possible, in part, because the target audience was college students and recent graduates. The sessions were designed to give Birthright Israel participants the opportunity to question movers and shapers of Israeli's policies face-to-face. Although part of the dynamic was that the students were getting a chance to see high-level officials—a chance that in their home country would be rare—observation of these encounters makes clear that the sessions were also a way for students to come to grips with their own view of Israel. Often, when the students challenged a speaker, it was because the speaker was too moderate and suggested territorial or other compromises for Israel.

Although the question-and-answer sessions were oftentimes highly charged, it would be misleading to suggest that they had much to do with how participants formed memories of their Birthright Israel trip. Indeed, their place in the ranking of experiences on the trip is modest.[6] What is significant is that the Birthright Israel participants were given access to a broad range of Israeli personalities and leaders. They had a chance to engage Israel's leading figures on pressing issues. The sessions are, perhaps, the least "intimate" of the encounters of birthright participants; nonetheless, they serve an important role in filling in high level cognitive detail to their physical and emotional experience.

IT'S ABOUT PEOPLE

The famous and not-so-famous figures who speak to Birthright Israel groups are only one element of how the program connects Diaspora youth to Israelis, to educators, and to one another. The encounters with speakers likely play a relatively small role in shaping the experience. Key are those with whom the participants spent their ten days living, traveling, talking, and relaxing. Below are some portraits of these individuals and of others who are key to the people-to-people encounter that is central to Birthright Israel.

Madrichim (Guides/Counselors)

The educators who have the most intimate connection with participants are the madrichim, the Israeli guides and counselors who are with groups from the time they land at Ben-Guirion Airport, until they depart. They are a fascinating group of individuals and, invariably, their personal stories merge with the story of Israel and the Jewish people. Their role in shaping a Birthright Israel program is critical. Two very different guides are described below, each of whom shapes the experience of participants through their own lens on Israel and being Israeli.

Udi

Udi is in his early thirties. He is thin, tall, good-looking, and energetic. He is bilingual, but he makes enough English-language mistakes to mark him as an authentic "Israeli." He has been associated with Birthright Israel since the inception of the program. He is also a professional musician and musical producer, a graduate of the Rimon School of Music. He is deeply involved in Israeli contemporary life and culture. He sees his career as twofold: music and working with young Jews.

He got into this "business" when he himself participated as a teenager in an Israeli-American six-week teen program in Israel two decades ago:

> I went to their high school program because a neighbor's son had gone and said it was great and I didn't have anything else to do. I planned to hate it, be cynical about American Jews, and have fun with American girls. I have been part of that organization ever since. Every year I say this is probably my last, but like the poet Uri Zvi Greenberg, who writes about Jews trying to leave God, it just doesn't happen. It has become part of my DNA.

When asked why he works in this field, Udi cites his family's personal and professional connection to the security and love of the land. He adds that he thinks it is one of the most important things there is for overseas Jews and Americans. We discussed what Udi does as a madrich:

> I see myself as a *roeh tzon*—a shepherd. I want to show them a way. I want to them to be awed and amazed and full of as many questions as answers. I work hard to give accurate portrayals of sites and events, but I also raise questions and give alternative interpretations. I am a *moreh derech* (a trip leader), not [simply] a trip guide.

The other role that Udi regards as central in his work is creating the group. "The first thirty-six hours are critical for me." For him, the group's level and needs tell him how he is going to work with the trip. He adjusts his work according to the group atmosphere. Finally, he emphasizes the centrality to him of the staff as an integrated team, and his organization generally uses staff that has worked together for years. Even so, he says the trip can rise or fall for him on the synergy of the staff: "A staff that models oneness transmits the message of 'we are one' to the Israelis and Americans. I don't want American staff that simply counts heads. If the staff doesn't work well, the trip suffers."

Udi is one of Birthright Israel's highly regarded madrichim and we asked him what he thinks he does that works. He talked about his knowledge of the land and sites (he did say that he periodically studies history, but also admitted that he mostly talks about what he already knows). He used a strange phrase to describe what he thinks makes it work well with him: "I always look at the end." When pressed, he tells the interviewer that he does not come in with a clear point he wants to hammer home or indoctrinate, but he does plan out his days like scenarios or musical pieces. Music is his metaphor, and he compares his educational work to music: "Guiding for me is like my music. It has a form, framework, beginning, and end like any good piece of music—which at the same time has spontaneity and melody and innovation."

Udi, like all Birthright Israel tour guides, is officially accredited by a government ministry; but his "larger" accreditation and achievement is from a vision of guiding, being Jewish ("dear to me"); Israel ("my home") and working with Jews from abroad ("it really matters"). You will hear Udi on the microphone of the bus summarizing the daily news, or looking out over Kuneitra (a Syrian town on the Golan Heights) explaining the most precise details of the Syrian-Israeli border. At night, one can find him in the lobby of the hotel with a group of Birthright Israel participants or on the lawn of the kibbutz, discussing rock and roll, love, and Israeli hip-hop.

One place you will not ordinarily find Udi is in a synagogue. He is a fully secular Israeli and is not Shabbat observant. Nevertheless, each of his groups begins Shabbat with *zmirot* (songs) and a series of traditional rituals, *Kiddush* (blessing over wine), and the *Motzei* (blessing over bread). The meal ends with *Birkat HaMazon* (blessing over a meal). He arranges for participants in all of his groups to be able to go to diverse synagogues of their choice. Although he is not observant, he makes observance available to his entire group and utilizes his co-staff to create a Shabbat atmosphere. He does not hide his way of being Jewish, but he does not flaunt it in order to denigrate religious adherence.

Udi is a talented tour guide, an interactive educator, and, for most of his group members, a very cool contemporary Israeli. He is also an unmovable Israeli on certain issues. Udi is someone that you schmooze with, hang out with, argue with, like, and sometimes (albeit rarely) do not like. He exudes charisma, can reflect on what he does, and he knows the land intimately. He also, like all educators, can "screw up." He can lose track of time, he can be too emotional, and he's fatigable—his guiding lacks crispness after a fourteen-hour day. From the best to the worst of Birthright Israel tour guides, there are great moments, and there are what in Hebrew are called *fashlot* (screwups). He is not superman, but an example of a very good tour educator who does his job well. Ultimately, he is what the American education theorist Joseph Schwab called an "accessible model,"[7] an educator who teaches through both his words and his actual behaviors. The accessible model exemplifies teachings and is able to be approached in a very real and personal manner.

In the summer of 2006, shortly after Hezbollah launched an attack on northern Israel that led to six weeks of intense warfare, the connection Udi has with his groups is made evident. He claims that he is amazed, but he has received hundreds of e-mails from participants dating back to the first round in the year 2000. They ask how he is doing, they express concern, and they send love. He reflects on the outpouring of concern: "Maybe I changed them, but I have been changed forever by them." Udi was asked, "What are you going to do this coming winter?" He replied: "*Habibi*, you gone loco? I have my dates already for my thirteenth round of Birthright Israel groups."

Francis

At least in her biography and outward appearance Francis is the non-Udi. She made aliyah to Israel in 1968 from New Zealand. In contrast to Udi's distinctively Hebrew name, Francis's appellation is the name of a Catholic saint. While Udi is a young bachelor, Francis is female, married, and the middle-aged mother of three grown children. Those who know her well say that she has never used the word "awesome"—differentiating her sharply from the young adults from North America. Francis is attractive, but no part of her body is pierced, tattooed or, indeed, uncovered. Unmistakably, she is an adult, even though her profession is to lead young people on tours of Israel.

One might think Udi is the prototype of Birthright Israel's ideal guide, while Francis the compromise resulting from too few Udis. That is not the case, however; going on a hike with Francis alters any stereotypes you might have about her and her facility to connect with college-age adults from abroad. She is witty, quick, and soft-spoken; yet, she can be forceful and even use off-color words in a way that seems natural. To listen to her presentations recalls Udi's musical metaphor. Her talks are built like Ravel's *Bolero* or Lizst's *Les Préludes.* She starts softly and gently, but builds to an emotional crescendo that can leave one speechless. This is not someone trying to earn some extra shekels or working to keep herself busy. Rather, Francis is a passionate educator whose life is ignited by Judaism and Israel. Her work is to ignite others with the same vision. When asked about her work as a tour guide she says:

> I'm fanatical about Jews being Jews. I want to "convert" Jews to being Jewish because I think being Jewish is great. I don't guide places. I guide people. I know all the facts about places but they don't particularly interest me. I'm interested in shaping stories—about places, people, and lives. I live in Israel, love Israel, and it's my home, but I'm a Jewish tour guide not a tour guide of Israel.

When asked about what techniques and tools she uses to guide Birthright Israel groups, Francis quickly responds:

> I have a point of view and I present it. It doesn't attempt to indoctrinate, but I want them to know being Jewish is a way of looking at life and the world. I am serious when I explain sites but I also laugh about life and use my wit as if I were at home. I use biblical texts a lot because I want them to see the connection between Israel and Judaism. I also tell my stories— about my life, my children, my feelings. I'm not afraid to make myself part of the landscape.

Francis has worked for various tour operators over the years and with both young people and adults. She says that she likes doing Birthright Israel trips because it is "God's work." She does not love doing what she considers "baby-sitting"—say, when participants shop on Ben Yehuda Street (a pedestrian way in Jerusalem)[8]—and while she appreciates Birthright Israel's plethora of rules, she says she is a bit too old to have to worry about all that stuff. "In the end, we talk, we explain, we walk, we cry, we have fun, and this little project cooked up by a few 'guys' changes lives and has moved the Jewish world." She is secure enough in who she is, and what she does, not to worry about projecting any particular image.

Israeli Staff

Udi and Francis are characteristic of Birthright Israel madrichim employed by trip organizers; even so, they can only suggest the diversity of guides' personalities and backgrounds. Some trip organizers have staff who are visibly religiously observant, wearing kippot (head coverings) and, in some cases, *tzitzit* (fringes). Some of the staff are immigrants themselves from the country of the participants. Thus, for groups from the United States and Canada, the staff will sometimes be former Americans. Perhaps, because of having lived in two cultures, they have a unique ability to relate to participants. Some groups have, as guides, sabras (native-born Israelis) who broadcast deep national fervor and passion. The staffing of Birthright Israel trips is as diverse as the twenty-plus trip organizers and the bazaar of Jewish life across Israel's population.

Another of Birthright Israel's goals is to ensure that tour educators of some sophistication lead groups. A particular focus has been on ensuring that staff avoid propagandizing or trying to indoctrinate participants. The challenge has been to find staff who meet strict legal criteria and are both excellent educators and extraordinary group facilitators. This is not an easy task. Although systematic monitoring and evaluation of Birthright Israel trips (see chapter 8), indicates consistent and high levels of satisfaction with staff, there is always the staff person who on a certain day goes overboard in framing an encounter or is painfully boring. It would be surprising, given the 24/7 engagement of participants and staff, if such were *not* the case.

In its early history, the tragic circumstances of Israel's security situation made it easier for Birthright Israel trips to be staffed by Israel's best tour guides and educators. After the Al Aqsa Intifada during 2001, tourists all but abandoned Israel. Israel's best tour guides and educators suddenly found themselves jobless. Consequently, Birthright Israel participants had the good fortune to be guided by Israel's best (in those years, Birthright Israel groups also stayed at some of Israel's most luxurious hotels). For most of Birthright Israel's first five years, trips were led not just by tour guides who knew facts and figures about holy sites, but by tour guide educators who also knew the hearts and souls of young adults from abroad.

At the same time, Birthright Israel itself complicated the tour educator role by requiring that the tour guides leading trips be certified. Certification courses may focus on working with adult tourists from abroad or Israeli high school students. Many Birthright Israel tour educators had such training, but some of the best did not (as they had done their training over many years in work with teen summer groups). Periodically, this legitimate standard backfired on Birthright Israel, by requiring groups to engage tour guides who had the right certification, but the wrong temperament or experience. Over time, most trip organizers enabled their best educators to acquire the certification to go along with the expertise.

In her master's thesis on the role of the tour educator, Clare Goldwater delineates the critical role the staff—particularly the tour educator—plays on this trip.[9] Drawing on both a rich classical sociological literature on tourism, as well as on literary and psychological narrative theory, Goldwater makes the case that in a sense travelers do not see a "country" or even a "site." Instead, they see the country or site *constructed* by the tour guide who frames the objects in front of them. As we saw in the example of different approaches to guiding on Masada (see chapter 3), tour educators guiding the apparently same site may nuance their framing with a different perspective and, sometimes, with totally different stories. In that sense, a Birthright Israel trip to Israel is not a journey to places; rather, it is a journey of narratives.

Overseas Staff

Each Birthright Israel trip is staffed, at a minimum, by an Israeli tour guide/educator, a medic, a security guard, and two overseas staff (individual trip organizers sometimes supplement the required number of staff). Overseas staff play an important role on trips, although there is often ambivalence on the part of the organizers about their ability to represent Israel. The original thinking was that an integrated educational team of Israeli and North American staff was needed. They would work collaboratively to frame, teach, guide, lead discussions, and be individual mentors. Several of the trip organizers have a history of integrated Israeli-overseas staff that enables this desired synergy. Hillel made a core commitment from the outset to send its senior campus directors to be co-leaders of the trip along with the Israeli guides. These directors were skilled at leading the six structured conversations that Hillel built into the program; in addition, many were versed in Israeli sites and sources and could share guiding with the Israelis.

The role of overseas staff is threefold: First, they are expected to serve as co-staff with Israelis and posess the ability to present interesting enrichment comments or perspectives on sites, sources, and experiences. Second, they serve as personal guides, mentors, counselors, and aides to the individuals in the group on both intellectual and emotional issues. Finally, they are expected to become the link that connects the trip to life back home. In the case of Hillel trips or community-based trips, all this would seem to be a natural flow: a counselor meets the group on campus or in the local city, spends the trip in Israel with the group, and helps them connect to the Jewish community when they return home. And, in the best cases, it works just as theorized. The overseas staff member is an exciting indigenous young Jew who has a common language and culture with participants and helps communicate the experience. But in other cases, overseas staff are head-counters, waker-uppers, and an extra body on the bus. Often, trip organizers engaged younger overseas staff whose role became more supervisory and organizational than educational. In some instances, some trip organizers rewarded graduates of former trips who succeeded in recruiting new participants with a return trip as "staff"—light-years away from Birthright Israel's original intentions. Over the years, Hillel found it increasingly difficult to recruit its senior Hillel directors and had to rely on younger, less well-trained, staff. After the first several years of the program, the oversight process began to note some cracks in this heretofore strong foundation.

In response to the overseas staff problem, Birthright Israel strengthened requirements for overseas staff and oversight processes to guarantee that they were fulfilled. Most important, they closed the loophole that allowed tour organizers to use overseas staff positions as a reward for former participants who recruited new participants. In the 2005 revision of its educational standards, Birthright Israel emphasized the central role of overseas staff.[10] The revised standards make clear that having participated in a Birthright Israel trip does not necessarily fulfill the prior Israel experience requirement for staff. The overseas staff person had to be an educator, knowledgeable about Israel and Judaism and had to be an accessible model of diverse ways to live and be committed to Judaism. The standard was designed to encourage both experiential and people-centered educators. The standards set a high bar. They were not always attained, but Birthright Israel made clear the ideal qualities.

THE GROUP

Much of the literature about the Israel experience focuses on the effects of the group. Both Harvey Goldberg of the Hebrew University and Samuel Heilman of Queens College have produced ethnographic studies of high school trips conducted in the mid-1990s. The ethnographies provide thick description of how group effects operate on youth tours,[11] and emphasize the central role of a cohesive group in Israel experience programs. In fact, the group becomes so much unified that a "bubble effect" emerges, to some extent isolating participants from their surroundings. A number of factors influence this dynamic: traveling together for a sustained time with the same group, the bond of the local youth culture that the overseas visitors bring, and experiences that tighten in-group cohesiveness and out-group distancing.[12]

The group is also central to the Birthright Israel experience, even though the targeted age group is several years older than the teenage trips. Typically, Birthright Israel travelers are organized in bus groups of up to forty overseas participants and five to ten Israelis. The unit of travel, organization, and of the ten-day experience is the core forty people. There is essentially only one experience—the mega-event—that encompasses more than a few buses.

Second, as with the high school groups (and all groups that travel together) the intense shared immersion creates a community spirit (communitas)[13] and "total institution"[14] even if only for the ten days. Third, the group discovers norms, mores, and cultural artifacts that bind them. Finally, Birthright Israel's education standards mandate group-building techniques as part of its program, which was aimed at further enhancing the educative effect of the group experience.

At first glance, the Birthright Israel group experience seems to offer the same pattern as the prior Israel trip experiences: close bonding, rituals, and unconditional love. This led some observers to conclude that the bus unit was and would remain the primary unit of loyalty of Birthright Israel participants in the years to come: "Bus 127 will survive forever!" In fact, such does not seem to be the case. The bus group is very important for ten days as a conduit to exchange ideas, share experiences, and strengthen identity. In many cases, friendships develop that continue for months and years to come. But the more common pattern is a sense of group loyalty to Birthright Israel as a whole. The shared visit to the Supreme Court becomes a hazy memory; over time, the group becomes the more than one hundred thousand young adults who shared an experience. This larger "group" was clearly reinforced by participation in mega-events and by a carefully tailored campaign by Birthright Israel aimed at creating the Birthright Israel "brand." The overall result is the creation of a sizable culture of young adult Jews who have together discovered something new, exciting, and positive about being Jewish. That bond lasts longer than the proverbial T-shirt now in the back of the participant's closet.

PHILANTHROPISTS

Although none of the philanthropists actually travels with a group, the two founding co-chairs of Birthright Israel, Bronfman and Steinhardt, along with Lynn Schusterman, see many of the groups and are known by all of the participants. Their role deserves mention, along with that of the other individuals who shape Birthright Israel trips.

Bronfman and Steinhardt have already been described. Lynn Schusterman, head of the Charles and Lynn Schusterman Family Foundation, is one of the most powerful and influential philanthropists to emerge recently on the Jewish scene. She is a figure of strong passions and demanding standards. At the same time, she is a diminutive woman who, at first glance, seems reserved. But any note of reticence disappears when she is among Birthright Israel groups. At mega-events, as soon as the music begins, she transforms herself from a major power broker to a human dynamo. She is in the middle, singing, dancing, and, most of all, smiling from ear to ear. Her trademark phrase at mega-events is "Shalom, y'all" and her closing phrase is always "I love you." From anyone else, it would sound kitschy; from Lynn Schusterman, it is genuine. Her emotiveness reflects her midwestern way of expressing her joy in being part of the Jewish people.

Lynn and her late husband, Charlie, saw their first Birthright Israel group on a Friday evening in the winter of 2001, when they came to the Mount Zion Hotel in Jerusalem. Charlie immediately sat down at a table of Russian participants, and Lynn found a group of students from a college Hillel. They joined in the meal, singing, and dancing. The couple even stayed as a seasoned teacher engaged a room full of one hundred Birthright Israel participants. At 10:00 P.M. on that Friday night, they were treated to a reading of Yehuda Amichai's poetry. It was the teacher's way to involve participants in understanding contemporary Israel—"Jerusalem doesn't need a mayor; it needs a ringmaster"—and it deeply affected the Schustermans. They were both exhausted after a long flight but were swept off their feet by the energy and passion they experienced in those few hours. From that moment on, Lynn Schusterman became one of the major figures in Birthright Israel. After Charlie died in 2000, the program became her passion and Birthright Israel became a living memorial to her life partner.

Schusterman was one of a larger group of philanthropists who contributed millions of dollars to Birthright Israel.[15] She also belongs to that small group of philanthropists who help compose the unofficial "permanent adjunct staff" of Birthright Israel trips. Lynn Schusterman, along with the founding philanthropist partners Bronfman and Steinhardt, has participated in every round of Birthright Israel trips, visiting and speaking to dozens of groups. At the mega-event that brings participants together for a concert and rally, she will often make a brief speech. She is treated like a rock star, with people reaching out to touch, kiss, embrace, and, of course, to have pictures taken with her.

Among Schusterman's special interests are Hillel groups and Russian students. She generally visits these groups while they are hiking or seeing a historic site and she acts as a participant. Her preferred approach is to talk to participants as they are walking or having a meal. If she gives a speech-like presentation to a group, she shares brief words of excitement and appreciation. Her presence for Birthright Israel participants was that of a major philanthropist who became even more involved because of her excitement about these young people and her unadulterated joy in being Jewish. As the program has matured, she has become very involved in post-program activities and has developed a number of programs to bring Birthright Israel alumni back to Israel.[16]

Michael Steinhardt, at least physically, stands in sharp contrast to Lynn Schusterman. Although he shares Lynn's passion for spreading "Jewish joy," he comes across as a serious businessman. He too has assumed mythical proportions as one of the often mercurial movers and shakers of contemporary Jewish life. But when he visits groups, he typically sits quietly and responds, almost matter-of-factly, to questions. The participants get a glimpse of his passion when he begins an effort, often raucous, to engage in Jewish matchmaking. He will begin with a straightforward question: "How many of you are romantically involved" or "How many of you want to be fixed up?" He will then pick out participants that he thinks might be good couples and tries, in public, to make a *shidduch* (the Yiddish term for a match). So legendary are his efforts at matchmaking, that a myth emerged—it turns out that it is partially true—that he would pay for the honeymoon of any couple that meets as a result of a Birthright Israel trip.[17]

Among the key philanthropists, Charles Bronfman spends the most time in Israel and sees the most groups. Perhaps if he hadn't been a Bronfman he could well have been an interactive and approachable educator. He regularly visits groups, not only to observe, but to engage in discussions with participants. When Birthright Israel trips are taking place, you might find him on the lawn at Ramat Rachel (a kibbutz on the outskirts of Jerusalem), at the Jerusalem Museum, or in any one of a number of hotel meeting rooms.

Invariably, Charles Bronfman's encounters with a Birthright Israel group begin with a brief statement that allows him to "connect" with participants. Depending on the occasion, he might salt his comments with down-to-earth and even off-color language. He often remarks that he doesn't "give a damn" what kind of Jew they are, as long as they choose to be Jewish. Then he will say, "Enough of my jibber-jabber. Talk to me, ask me anything. Tell me why you're here." There's a pause; you can almost hear his audience saying to themselves, Is this multimillionaire serious? Then the questions flow: "Why did you give your money for this?" "Why do you like Israel so much?" "Can one make money in Israel?" "What is your Jewishness about?" He usually ends talks to Birthright Israel groups by telling them that they are a generation that has a chance to choose anything, including whether to be Jewish: "It's your choice. We wanted to give you a chance to experience one of the great moments in Jewish life as you face your choices. Now go home, choose as you will, and God bless." Charles Bronfman does not meet the legal requirements for a Birthright Israel tour educator, but this philanthropist-educational entrepreneur may be one of the best educators in the Birthright Israel system.

Meetings with each of the philanthropists generally end with photographs. Participants are invariably left with a "wow" feeling about the group and the Jewish future. To Birthright Israel participants, these wealthy individuals are not simply icons, power brokers, or hard-nosed philanthropists, but real human beings. They demonstrate their genuineness by meeting with the participants to talk, dance, and listen. These meetings between philanthropists and participants have become an important part of Birthright Israel trips. They enable young Jewish adults to meet face-to-face in an intimate setting with Jewish leaders they would not otherwise meet.

Perhaps one reason the encounters with philanthropists are so important is that they provide a contrast for participants' prior experience with Jewish leaders. For many, their experiences have been with rabbis in gowns on pulpits, famous speakers in large halls, and middle-aged men in suits haranguing them about intermarriage, anti-Semitism, and assimilation. Suddenly, young Jewish adults sit on a lawn or in a room with three individuals who, instead of seeming like icons, are genuine people who speak a language they understand, and have feelings that they can connect with. The removal of the metaphoric pedestal is mind-boggling, and many a young person goes away thinking, "Maybe I could be where they are some day."

LOOKING GLASS SELF

Classic sociological theory, associated with symbolic interactionsim, posits that we learn about who we are and modify our self-perception by paying attention to how others see us. To use the term coined by Cooley a century ago, we use others as a "looking glass self."[18] The encounters that Birthright Israel participants have with Israelis—regardless of how formal or informal—are central in shaping the experience and determining much of what a participant learns. What is, perhaps, extraordinary is how many such personal encounters a participant can have in a relatively short time.

We have, however, not yet mentioned the most important group of people whom Birthright Israel participants encounter: their Israeli peers. They will be the focus of the next chapter and reflect how the "people factor" is critical to understanding Birthright Israel. When the program was developed,

Birthright Israel educators shifted the Israel experience from an exclusive pre-occupation with buildings and sites to a balance between this approach and that of Israel as a contemporary society. Birthright Israel's educational standards reflect an attempt to present a kaleidoscope of people, to illustrate the diversity of Israel's populace, while breaking down simplistic stereotypes.

In a sense, Birthright Israel wanted to recast the question "What is an Israeli?" to "Who are the Israelis?" Birthright Israel educators clearly sought to break the stereotype of the Israeli as a needy refugee or as a close but ne'er-do-well relative.[19] They wanted to change the perception of Israelis that, good intentions notwithstanding, Israel and Diaspora Jewry over the decades had created. Educators also wanted to created new interfaces with Israelis. For too many tourists to Israel, their encounters, other than with a tour guide, were mainly through people in the service industries (waiters, room clerks, store clerks, taxi drivers), and stores or sites that catered to tourists (souvenir shops, museums). Ironically, the waiter or hotel clerk was often Arab, rather than Jewish. A key element of Birthright Israel's program was to change this pattern and develop significant encounters with a broad range of Israelis. This aspiration has been only partially succeessful because the trips are in the hands of trip organizers. They have responsibility for choosing the "people," and necessarily followed their own views in choosing who was engaged. Moreover, ten days is a short time to meet the diverse mixture of Israelis who make up the country.

To achieve these goals, the program wanted to capitalize on the group itself for both educational and for public relations reasons. The program's educational architects believed that Jewish young adults needed an intense injection of powerful positive social networking—something that Jewish life abroad had not been providing. Its public relations and marketing gurus quickly learned that word-of-mouth was the best public relations tool to recruit more participants and convince philanthropists, the government of Israel, and the communities of the value of this investment.

It is unlikely that the Israel experience field will be able to go back to former models after the "people-centered" experience that Birthright Israel introduced. No doubt, programs will have to be adapted for different age groups and needs, but it seems unlikely that the Israel experience program can ever again be a people-less Israeli experience. And it is doubtful that future incarnations of the Israel experience can take place without what has become known as "the jewel in the crown" of the Birthright Israel trip—the *mifgash* (shared encounter) with Israeli soldiers and peers. In the next chapter, we shall meet some of the Israeli soldiers and students who have populated the Birthright Israel buses over the past five years. Israeli peers of the Birthright Israel participants play a critical role in helping to shape the educational content of the experience.

Shared Encounters

5

Behold how good it is for brothers and sisters to sit together.
—Psalm 133
Looking at the Jews as such, I can't say I enjoy it much. Looking at the rest,
I'd say I'll be Jewish any day.
—Albert Einstein

The members of bus group 242 passed through the jetway connecting El Al Flight 008 to the recently opened, ultramodern, Terminal 3 at Ben-Gurion Airport. They are wisked by a moving walkway along the top level of the terminal and taken by a long pair of escalators into passport control. After having their passports inspected by the border control officer, they arrive, a few minutes later, in the main baggage hall. There they collect their knapsacks, duffle bags, guitars, and assorted suitcases, load them on luggage carts, and walk out the group exit. Thirty North Americans, age 22 to 26, of various sizes and shapes, wearing long pants or shorts, baring their midriffs or wearing shirts down to their knees, and exhibiting pierced ears, noses, and other body parts, step out onto the cement of the Land of Israel and behold buses, blue sky, and hordes of people.

In older times, pilgrims arriving in Eretz Yisrael were reputed to bend down and kiss the earth. Today, new arrivals to Israel go directly from their plane to an upper floor of the terminal and do not actually touch the ground until they have claimed their luggage. The participants of group 242 are greeted with a new ritual. Waiting for them are ten young people of their age, dressed in jeans, shorts, and T-shirts emblazoned with "Birthright Israel" and the trip organizer's name. The ten Israelis distribute Birthright Israel T-shirts to the dazed Americans, pull them into a circle, and with guitar accompaniment, begin a slow, then increasingly faster, circle dance, while singing a chant with two Hebrew words that repeated over and over:

ACHIM ACHIM ACHIM ACHIM ACHIM (Brothers)[1]
SIMCHAH SIMCHAH SIMCAH SIMCHAH SIMCHAH (Joyous)

The participants in group 242 begin their Israel journey by putting on their new T-shirts, dancing in the middle of an airport, and then getting on a bus with their new Israeli peers, with whom they will spend the next ten days. On the bus, Israeli sitting next to American, the ten-day journey into the heart of Israel begins.

A NEW WAY TO "SEE" ISRAEL

From the outset of Birthright Israel, the program's educational leaders believed that young Jews from abroad must be able to spend quality time together with Israeli peers. They felt that young Jews had to experience Israel in a new way. This vision of a shared encounter was not, however, a Birthright Israel innovation. The concept was inherited from pioneering work that was begun in the mid-1980s by a young educator from Chicago, Anne Lanski. She created an organization devoted to changing Israel trips from "visits to Israel" to mutual experiencing of Israel by Israelis and North Americans. Lanski created high school trips, young adult trips, and even a summer camp that involved equal numbers of Israelis and North Americans. Later, she extended the model to Birthright Israel.

Another young Chicago educator, Charles Herman, began to include Israelis in his Nesiya program (focused on arts and culture education). As noted earlier, in the early 1990s Charles and Andrea Bronfman made the mifgash one of the centerpieces of their foundation's agenda. In the mid-1990s, the Bronfmans partnered with JAFI's Department of Jewish Zionist Education to create the Mifgashim Center. The center was headed by an Israeli educator, Elan Ezrachi and focused on developing programs that would advance encounters between young Jewish peers.[2]

Why did Lanski, the Bronfmans, JAFI, and Birthright Israel believe that a "new way" was called for? The traditional—and believed to be quite successful—Israel trips reflected experiences heavily rooted in visiting the numerous and diverse historical, religious, and contemporary sites of Israel: Yad Vashem, Ammunition Hill, the Museum on the Seam, the Western Wall, Beit Hat'fuzot (Museum of the Diaspora), the Golan Heights, the City of David, Tel Aviv, Independence Hall, Rabin Square, Eilat, Sde Boker, Masada, the Dead Sea, Mea Shearim, the Galilee. These visits were generally moving and powerful, yet there often was a sense of looking within from without; that is, of seeing Israel through a bus window.

The new focus on mifgash emphasized experiencing real people along with seeing historical sites. It stressed viewing Israel from within the heads and hearts of Israeli peers, rather than solely through a bus window or a guide's narrative. The mifgash approach focused on contemporary, as much as historical issues. Advocates of this new direction understood the term mifgash in an educational (and social psychological) sense: enabling authentic encounters between young Israelis with young Jews from abroad as part of organized educational trips. They wanted to take advantage of the educational potential in such encounters to create a better understanding of contemporary Israel and to the respective cultures of the participants.[3] As part of the Andrea and Charles Bronfman Philanthropies' flagship project to advance Jewish life by bringing young people to Israel on educational experiences, mifgashim were incorporated in the program.[4] By the end of the 1990s, almost 80 percent of all Israel trips for teenagers included a mifgash component.

It took Birthright Israel some time to determine how to implement the mifgash effectively. The original educational standards provided guidelines for a mifgash, indicating that it could last from a few hours to ten days.[5] After one year of trips, the Birthright Israel educational staff and the team conducting evaluation and oversight reported inadequacies and wide discrepancies with this standard. Many of the groups had met with Israelis (often high school students) for only a few hours. Such visits did not seem very successful and failed to create meaningful relationships between Diaspora and Israeli participants. It quickly became clear that the mifgash could only be effective if it were implemented differently.

A TURNING POINT

In the second year of the project, the Birthright Israel leadership decided to take definitive steps to turn the mifgash experience into a meaningful element of the program. First, it returned to the vision of the Chicago-based trip organizer and pioneer of mifgashim, Anne Lanski. Lanski, who still heads the organization she founded, Shorashim (roots), had long argued that "the mifgash is not another program or activity." Rather, in her unassuming but decisive way, she saw mifgashim as an overall framework for how educational tourists should experience Israel. To anyone who would listen, she would explain: "Israelis are not dancing bears in a circus or pictures at an exhibition. They are real human beings who, together with Jews from abroad, are the Jewish people. The Israel trip should be a journey in Jewish peoplehood and, to do this, you need Israelis and Jews from abroad for the entire trip. They have to live and talk and play and experience and laugh and cry and do everything together. Their experiencing of Israel together is the Israel experience." Lanski was insistent that a two-hour, or even two-day, mifgash is entertainment and not a true meeting of souls. Thus, all of her Shorashim Birthright

Israel trips have included Israeli participants, from the time the plane lands until the group leaves.

The Birthright Israel leadership was eventually persuaded by these arguments and decided to adapt Lanski's vision to all of its trips. Having decided to take this approach seriously, Birthright Israel obtained a seed grant to hire a mifgash coordinator. They engaged a talented Israeli educator, Ofira Bino, to supervise and coordinate these efforts. Birthright Israel also attracted financial resources to provide partial subsidies for Israeli participation. Perhaps most important, Birthright Israel successfully gained the agreement of the Israeli Defense Forces (IDF) Education Corps to release soldiers for five days to participate in mifgashim.

Bino understood the core vision in much the same way as did Lanski. To realize it in the context of Birthright Israel, she created workshops to train staff in implementing the mifgash (utilizing the experience of a small number of trip organizers for whom this was their specialty). Bino conducted orientations for all Israelis before the trip and debriefings afterward. She personally recruited the soldiers and students for the groups. In 2001, some 80 percent of mifgashim were two days or less. By 2006, fully 80 percent of the mifgashim were five days or more.[6]

Within two years, Birthright Israel transformed its approach to the mifgash experience. Birthright Israel even decided to break with one of its founding principles: rather than outsource the effort, it decided to manage mifgashim in-house. In part, this change was necessary because the Army (IDF) became a partner and Birthright Israel needed someone to coordinate soldiers' participation. Only one staff person was added to Birthright Israel's central organization, but she became directly involved in the educational program, far more so than in other spheres of Birthright Israel. The mifgash component became central to the program, with training, recruitment, and quality of mifgash experiences steadily improving. It was a costly change to the program, as the expense of placing additional participants on a bus was significant. In retrospect, as the stories of some of the groups below suggest, the investment paid off handsomely (see also chapter 8).

HIKING IN THE NORTH

Group 242 wakes up at 6:00 A.M. They begin their ascent of Jilaboon (in the Golan Heights) less than an hour later. It is hot, the terrain is difficult, and for many of the North Americans, it is a physical challenge. Itzik climbs in front of Hilary and gives her a helping hand. He tells her about *masa kumta*—the twenty-mile army hike wearing full gear, the final requirement for the officers' training corps. Shmulik points to a house in the distance and says "Beth, that's where I live." They climb, drink water, laugh, sweat, help each other, cry, touch the soil of Eretz Yisrael together, and for a few hours their bodies are, it feels, connected to the Land of Israel. That afternoon, the bus takes them along the winding roads of the Golan Heights.

As they travel through the Golan, the guide points out where Syrian encampments were located prior to the Six-Day War and describes the nearly abandoned Syrian town of Kuneitra, which had been the Syria's regional military headquarters. From the eastern side of the Golan, he looks down with the group on the Sea of Galilee, Kibbutz Ein Gev, and the city of Tiberias. Then, he asks Carmi to tell about his eight-month army stint on the Golan in the winter of 2003. There is an eerie hush as Carmi speaks about his experience, both the physical difficulties of being a soldier and the joy of comradeship he felt with his unit. It is so quiet that one could almost hear the hot breeze of a Galilee afternoon.

The group then travels to Katzrin, a modern Israeli town established in 1977 on the site of a Jewish village that was destroyed by an earthquake more than a millennia ago. Remains of the village and a synagogue that was built in the fourth and fifth centuries are still visible. The aunt of one of the Israelis in the group invites everyone into her living room and feeds them homemade strudel. With the strudel comes her own highly charged political speech on why Israel should never give back the Golan. With passion, she tells the group: "We built this house, our children were born here, and this is flesh of our flesh, bone of our bones."

The day ends at a youth hostel, located on the shore of the Sea of Galilee. On the wide lawn that overlooks the lake, the lights of Ein Gev and the Golan settlements can be seen flickering in the distance. Beer flows that night, to quench thirst, not to create drunkenness, and the participants quickly become wrapped up in their words, emotion, and, eventually, exhaustion. Some of the Americans seem awestruck by their exchanges with the Israelis. They are overwhelmed and do not seem prepared for such an emotional experience. Even without the strudel-maker's speech, they feel the link of the land to the people. "These aren't territories," says Stacey from Denver, "they are parts of the body and soul of the people here. Now I understand what the Zionists meant when they talked about 'returning to the Land.'"

Not all members of the group share Stacey's perspective. Other passionate voices argue the opposite position. "With all due respect to Kobi's aunt," says Alicia, ". . . and the strudel was great. She and her kids are living on some else's land. You can't build a house illegally, have kids, and then cry that it's wrong to uproot us. The land belongs to Syria just as the West Bank and Gaza belongs to the Palestinians. I understand the inner soul of these settlers better now, but you can't just take someone else's land. And there will never be peace until the land is returned."

Yaniv sits quietly, partly because his views are not far from Stacey's. He feels uncomfortable, however, agreeing with her here. After all, symbolically and otherwise, he is representing the Israel Defense Forces. Shai, another soldier, is not quite so diplomatic. He turns to Alicia and tells her, "*Hamuda* [my sweet one], you know I love you, and after these few days and we're going to be friends forever, but you're full of shit. You just can't understand. You don't live here. You don't serve in the army. You don't put your life on the line. You live in a comfortable house in New Jersey. That strudel and that house in Katzrin are our homes like your house in New Jersey and we have the right and the duty to be here forever."

The evening continues with a few more beers and a lot more voices. Eventually, the group members split up and went back to their rooms to catch a few hours' sleep. Some are unable to get the discussion out of their heads, and a few are seething with anger. Others are enchanted with the magic of the Galilee night. Most, in their vernacular, are just "wiped out," physically and emotionally. Shai and Alicia—adversaries in words—are last seen headed off to a darkened area of the youth hostel. Day five of bus 242's trip has ended.

What happened during those few days? The superficial answer is that two subcultures of young adult Jews—from Israel and the Diaspora—shared an experience. They rode on the same bus, ate the same food, and heard the same words of a tour guide trying to explain what they were seeing as they traveled through the countryside. They sat together on the same lawn on the shores of the Sea of Galilee on a beautiful summer evening. They developed relationships with one another, some intense, others less so, not unlike those they had with peers in other parts of their lives.

One key to the creation of a sense of a groupness and peoplehood is shared experiences. Shared experiences bind you in the present and become shared memories of the past in the future. Two years later, Larry from the North American group, e-mailed Arye from the Israeli contingent. He wrote, "Remember that night that we sat on the shore of the *Kinneret* (Sea of Galilee) and wondered if we'd ever find our true love?" This group of North Americans and Israelis underwent a common set of experiences; in doing so, very different peers quickly found many common agendas: dreams, worries, love, jobs, and parents. To be sure, the North Americans and Israelis experienced the same events differently. The North American Birthright Israel participants could not really forget that their Israeli counterparts were soldiers, and the soldiers, no doubt, could not forget the job that would shortly summon them back. Differences notwithstanding, a peer-to-peer culture of young Jewish adults began to be created in the hills of the Galilee.

The tour educator does a start-and-stop narration as the bus inches slowly southward on the Coastal Highway. Israel's road system has become increasingly traffic-congested and it gives tour guides lots of time to provide commentary about Israel. As the bus plods toward Tel Aviv and passes through Herzliya, a northern suburb, some participants listen avidly while the educator talks about the hi-tech companies that are housed in the glass and concrete buildings that face the highway. Others in the group sleep. Shai and Alicia are in the back of the bus focused on each other.

Kikar Rabin

Eventually, the bus arrives at Kikar Rabin (Rabin Square) in Tel Aviv and stops close to the very spot where Prime Minister Yitzhak Rabin was assassinated in November 1995. Today, the site includes a monument, the original words of lamentation written on the walls by the young in the days immediately following the murder, and a designation of the exact place where the assassin walked into the small parking lot and unloaded his pistol. The tour educator explains the sequence of events and then offers commentary on the challenge to Israeli democracy that evening represented.

The group listens attentively. Each of them—American and Israeli—knew something about the event, but being at the site makes discussion of the assassination far more real than if the group had simply read about it. The power of experience is magnified when Israelis in the group talk about where they were when it happened. Some were teenagers and they recall crying through the night and traveling to Tel Aviv the next day to light candles, bring flowers, and sing (they became known as *n'arei Rabin* [Rabin's young people]). Others were youngsters and watched their parents cry. They did not realize exactly what had happened, but they somehow sensed that Israel would never be the same. One of the Israeli group members cannot restrain himself: "That son of a bitch [Rabin's assassin] was a so-called religious Jew who studied at Bar Ilan University. He did it because his rabbis gave an 'OK' in their Torah classes.[7] The religious world killed Yitzhak Rabin."

The tour educator steps in and tries to deflect the anger at the religious community. He provides more details, including the overwhelming condemnation of the act by much of Israel's religious leadership. "How could a Jew kill a Jew?" asked Kevin. "Sometimes we're our own worst enemies," says Dina, a soldier on leave from Haifa. She continues: "In the time of the Second Temple, Pharisees and Sadducees and Sikarim spent their days fighting each other.[8] Look at the religious and secular and right and left here today. Sometimes, I think if the Arabs just left us alone, we'd destroy ourselves by ourselves." The North Americans are shocked by her words, shaken that this kind of dissent existed throughout Jewish history. They are amazed to hear Dina, "the silent one" in their group, speak up so passionately and knowledgeably.

The visit at Kikar Rabin ends and the group continues with dinner in Kerem Hateyemin, the Yemenite quarter of south Tel Aviv. At dinner, they talk about Rabin, religion, and Yemenite food. Dina is actively involved in the discussion. An anthropologist who stopped by the restaurant would not have been able to tell, at least from the content of what people said, which were the Israelis and which were the Americans. Like a group of college-age students anywhere, their conversation is a mix of profound and mundane commentary. The difference, of course, is that the group includes students and soldiers, and the discussion is framed by their having spent the day confronting critical social issues and questions of their own identity.

Jerusalem Hills

The Tefer (seam) trip is a three-hour Jerusalem route around the city, traveling along roads that separate Jewish and Arab neighborhoods. For one bus group the trip begins in the suburb of Gilo, a Jewish neighborhood built after the Six-Day War in the southernmost part of the city. The tour ends on Mount Scopus in the north, the site of Hebrew University's main campus. The vistas are breathtaking—as are the contrasts among neighborhoods. Equally stunning is the way in which, in the course of a three-hour trip, it is possible to see the entire story of the Israeli-Palestinian conflict compactly arranged like a Monopoly game right before your eyes.

The trip begins at the school in Gilo where the group sees sandbags barricading the playground and pockmarks on the school wall. These marks are the result of shooting that took place during the Second Intifada.[9] The bus parks near a street with a fence decorated with murals painted by local residents. "Over there is the village of Bet Sahur. For months, Gilo was shelled on a nightly basis. Just beyond Gilo is Bethlehem. To the right is the bypass tunnel to Gush Etzion and Jewish settlements in Judea and Samaria," says the tour guide. "That's the road I take to go home" says Esther, whose family lives in the West Bank town of Efrat. "You can see how the conflict is literally in our backyard. Jewish settlements are next to Arab settlements which are next to Jewish settlements. It's a keg of dynamite waiting to explode." "Who was here first?" asks Hilary. The answers to her question fly fast and furious as the group sets out for its next stop.

The bus stops near a monastery in a deserted area. "See that isolated group of huge apartment buildings with the newly paved roads? That is Har Homa, a new Jewish suburb of Jerusalem financed by a wealthy Jew named Moskowitz from Florida. People willing to buy apartments there receive special mortgages to make them more attractive. It has given young couples the opportunity to have decent housing at a reasonable price. "*Mi zeh ha moskovitz hazeh?* [Who is this Moskowitz?]" mutters Avi to Shmulik. "*Lama haYehudim haeylu machnisim et harosh ba inyanim shelanu?* [Why do these Jews stick their noses into our business?]" "*Halas achi, heym po* [Enough, buddy, they're here,]" says Shmulik, pointing to the Americans in the group.

The next stop is the Tayelet, the site from which the group had previously viewed the grand vista of all of Jerusalem (see chapter 3). This time they are going to see only one object: "the wall" or "the fence" or "the security barrier"—the controversial dividing construct that Israel has been building from north to south to prevent terrorism. One of the Israelis speaks up: "Down there is the house of Benjy Segal who used to be director of Camp Ramah in Israel. Stones were often thrown in his living room. Now, there's the security fence that runs right down the middle of the Arab town Abu Dis, dividing the town into two. I was told that it can take Arab kids from one side of the fence an hour to get to their school, which is on the other side."

The bus now drives along a four-lane highway, Route 4, which skirts the western (Jewish-populated) part of Jerusalem on the left and the Old City on the right. On the left is downtown Jerusalem, the King David Hotel, the YMCA; on the right, the Arab old city, Arab East Jerusalem, the Arab marketplace and the Temple Mount. The driver stops the bus for a moment at an empty lot. "This used to be the entry point between Jordan and Israel from 1948 until 1967" says the tour guide. "The place was called the Mandelbaum Gate, named after Mandelbaum who had a house here. This was the only official passageway between the two sides."

On the left side of the highway there is a collection of ultra-Orthodox men and women, distinguished by the men's black garb and the women's covered heads. They are headed toward the alleyways of Mea Shearim, the ultrareligious section of Jerusalem. Someone takes out his camera, but Kobi grabs it and says, "Don't, they will start stoning us for taking their pictures." On the right side of the highway, groups of East Jerusalem Arabs are milling around. Shai quips, "The Jews will stone you on the left, the Arabs on the right, everybody must get stoned!" The group, both Israelis and Americans catch the Bob Dylan reference, and laugh. The madrichim, who were not part of the conversation, wonder what they have missed.

Today's trip ends at a lookout at the Hebrew University campus on Har Ha'tzofim (Mount Scopus). Mount Scopus was the original site of the university, which opened in 1925 and was, by the time the State of Israel was established in 1947, a well-respected research and teaching institution. During Israel's War of Independence, Mount Scopus became isolated from western

Jerusalem. As part of the agreement that led to the end of fighting after the War of Independence, a small garrison was kept there, under the protection of the United Nations.[10] In 1967, when Israel took control of a unified city, it again became linked to Jewish Jerusalem and once more became the main campus of the university. Mount Scopus is today surrounded by both Jewish and Arab neighborhoods. The tour guide concludes: "In this short trip you have seen it all—the story of the conflict that is our daily life." Once again he quotes from his favorite poet, Yehuda Amichai:[11]

An Arab shepherd is searching for his goat on Mount Zion
And on the opposite mountain I am searching
For my little boy.
An Arab shepherd and a Jewish father
Both in their temporary failure . . .
Searching for a goat or a son
Has always been the beginning
Of a new religion in these mountains[11]

CONTRASTING EXPERIENCES

These two experiences, at Kikar Rabin and the Tefer trip, reflected several motifs of the mifgash element of the Birthright Israel trip. Both experiences placed the subject of the Israeli-Palestinian conflict front and center. They sharply presented the issues "on the ground." They enabled participants to observe borders, villages, geography, and issues that have been the source of specific disagreements. No less important, however, experiencing these places along with Israelis added a new dimension to examining the conflict. It enabled overseas visitors to see the experience from the personal perspective of young people who live in Israel but are also soldiers in the IDF. It was a very different perspective than that provided by watching the news on CNN or reading a newspaper such as the *Los Angeles Times*. And it was not quite like taking a college course on Israel or contemporary politics. It was not even equivalent to having a tour guide show you the country. The experience— with a group of peers—provided a multifaceted lens for viewing what Israelis refer to as *ha'matzav* (the situation). As part of a mifgash, Birthright Israel participants used one another and their Israeli peers as sources and filters for insight and understanding.

There are several striking dimensions to viewing the conflict in this way. First, the overseas visitors saw that there was a diversity of opinion in Israel about the conflict with the Palestinians. There were very left, very right, centrist, and very confused viewpoints in Israel, just as there were abroad. There were intense discussions and conflicts over these issues, but the Birthright Israel visitors understood that the disagreement was not a Diaspora-Israel argument. Indeed, there was genuine diversity of opinion among Israeli Jews, in particular about the best strategies for dealing with the conflict.

Second, the overseas visitors experienced the often demonized Israel soldier as a human being. Proximity to real people in this instance, removed the stereotypic horns and guns of the "soldier." Never again would the members of the group see Israeli soldiers as anonymous fighters. Forever they would see them as young adults much like themselves—with fears, hopes, and dreams, just as they had. For some overseas participants, they realized that were it not for an accident of family history, they could be the one in uniform and responsible for defending the State of Israel.

Despite the diversity of views found among the Israelis, the overseas participants experienced an unequivocal unanimity among the Israelis that what they were doing as soldiers was necessary, justified, and a significant affirmation of their Jewish-Israeli identity. The Americans met a unified group of young adults who were deeply patriotic and deeply loyal to their country, their home, and its future. This was clearly a new way to see the conflict, and it had a profound impact on them.

These two visits—Kikar Rabin and the Seam trip—also opened up a Pandora's box of issues regarding the religious-secular divide in Israeli society. Granted the religious-secular debate is generally presented on Birthright Israel trips by lecturers and journalists. But riding the bus and hearing comments and commentary from religious and secular Israelis on the bus made the topic come alive. Moreover, the intensity of the matter burned through the faces and words of the Israelis at Kikar Rabin when the subject of Yigal Amir and Bar Ilan University surfaced; they, again, surfaced when the group goes to Har Homa and Mea Shearim. The centrality of this subject to the psyche and soul of Israeli life was revealed within the walls of the bus, around the dinner table, and at late-night discussions.

What the mifgash accomplished on these two specific programs was to explore simplistic pictures of Israel as the pastoral Promised Land of prophets, a country of holy men and women. The experience forced visitors to face the reality that Israel is a modern country, faced not only with a set of international issues, but with mundane problems like traffic jams and never-ending construction, as well as a host of social problems, from domestic violence to road rage. Regardless, they also learned that Israel is a country full of people with great passion, very deep human dilemmas, and some who earn the appellation, "holy people."[12]

The madrichim of another bus group give several options for *erev Shabbat* (Friday night). The bus group divides into two subgroups, half of whom go to the Kotel, and half of whom visit a liberal Jerusalem synagogue. The synagogue is Kol Haneshama, affiliated with the Reform movement (URJ in the United States; in Israel, the Union for Progressive Judaism).

Later, a visit to the Western Wall is described in detail (see chapter 6); for the moment, our focus is not on the site itself, but with the reaction of the Israeli participants to the experience, and the impact of their participation on the visit. As they approach the Wall, male Israelis don the paper head coverings that they pick from a box nearby, while the women are shuffled to the smaller women's section. Some of the Israelis recalled being at the Kotel for a ceremony on Holocaust Memorial Day or being there for a bar mitzvah celebration. All of the Israelis remember Naomi Shemer's famous song written on the eve of the Six-Day War, "Yerushalayim shel Zahav" (Jerusalem of Gold). For most of the Israelis in the group, this place is a central national site, affirming the existence (and for some, eternal existence) of the Jewish State.

On this visit, however, the Israelis spend more time looking at their American friends than they do at the Wall. They are alternatively bewildered, confused, puzzled, and deeply moved by the reactions of their American peers who approach the Wall with notes, tears, and intense emotion. An observer recalls the comment of an Israeli tour guide: "You can only have your first experience at the Wall once and I regret that I can't share the same 'first' experience again." Many of the Americans stand before the Kotel as in a trance; clearly, it is a deep personal, spiritual moment.

On the leisurely walk back to the hotel under a starlit Jerusalem sky, the Americans say such things as "If only my grandfather would have been alive to know I was here" or "I felt at one with the entire history of our people" or "I felt holiness for the first time." The experience for the Americans is clearly moving and spiritual. The Israelis, however, are inspired by the Americans' reactions to a place that, for many of them, has more symbolic than actual import.

A different kind of religious experience is had by the other group that goes to the liberal synagogue, Kol Haneshama. Although it may not seem so, the visit is particularly odd for the Israeli participants. For most Israelis, including those who do not pray regularly at a synagogue, a synagogue usually means an Orthodox religious service, often at a small shul (synagogue in Yiddish) and always with separate seating for men and women. The group at Kol Haneshama enters a modern synagogue with families, men, women, and guests from abroad all sitting together. The rabbi speaks a blend of Hebrew and English, and the congregation joins him in well-known and moving tunes, humming and singing. Many women wear kippot (head coverings) and the American visitors obviously feel at home. At one point, the congregation sings the well-known song *"Od yavo shalom aleynu v'al kulam—salaam, shalom, aleynu v'al kol ha'olam"* (Peace will yet come to us and to all people—Salaam [said in Arabic], Shalom [said in Hebrew]).

The service ends with the rabbi asking everyone to close their eyes, take a deep breath, and cleanse themselves from the week's travails. Then, after a long silence, the entire congregation sings a melodic verse from Psalm 150: "Kol haneshama t'halel ya" (Let all that breathes bless the Lord). The Americans are clearly moved and several say this is the most spiritual experience they have had since coming to Israel. Some Israelis also seem highly emotional, although Israelis in the group are somewhat bewildered by the sight of men and women sitting together and women wearing kippot. Even many secular Israelis feel that, if they were to go to a synagogue, it would be an Orthodox "shul." Some of the Israelis are quietly muttering about "this strange tribe who are our brothers and sisters."

These two visits clearly are a striking example of how the mifgash provided a new insight for Israelis into the nature of American Jewry. It put them face-to-face with a diverse group of young Jews, from the very knowledgeable, affiliated, and committed, to those with little religious involvement or Jewish literacy. They met many Jews who were products of intermarriage and some who observed non-Jewish rituals in their homes. They experienced the contemporary American version of denominations face-to-face and saw that Jews were not necessarily exclusively *datiim* (religious) or *hiloniim* (secular). The Israelis finally appreciated what teachers in school and lecturers in the army had been trying to teach them with limited success: that Judaism was for their overseas friends a religion and peoplehood. Erev Shabbat—and the entire trip—was an intense course in contemporary Jewry and Jewish civics for Israeli participants in the mifgash.

THE LAST DAY

On the last day of the trip, one of the mifgash groups visits Mount Herzl, the national cemetery of Israel's founders and the national military cemetery (see chapter 3). The visit to Mount Herzl is, in many ways, the climax of the mifgash experience. It brings together all the themes of the trip and all the pathos, emotion, and complexity of the ten days. The group enters the military cemetery led by the tour educator: "You are entering a holy place—a place that memorializes young people whose lives were cut short. This cemetery is about all of us, it's about people, and it's about people our age. It's about our fathers, uncles, cousins, brothers, and sisters. It's about people who should have been here with you on the bus today but aren't." With seeming purposefulness, the guide continually uses the word "ours"; he means everyone in the group.

The group walks between rows of graves of names unknown to them, but each grave signifies a story and the account is often told by an Israeli member of the group who knows the person buried there. Yossi, one of the Israelis in the group, speaks: "There is the grave of Haim Buzaglo. We were in the same army unit. His family emigrated from Morocco in the 1950s. We were in the artillery unit together. He was killed in Lebanon. He was full of life, loved sports, and Elvis Presley music. His dream was to go to Graceland after finishing the army. He was 'achi' [my brother]." Yossi cannot say any more.

Not all of the graves are of specific people known by the Israelis. They point out graves of new immigrants from Russia, England, and Tunisia who were killed only a short time after their ships had brought them to Israel in the late 1940s or early 1950s: "They never even got to live here." The sounds of this visit are, to borrow from Simon and Garfunkel, "the sounds of silence." There is little of the usual banter; clearly, it is a difficult visit for all of the group members. Many Americans are overwhelmed by the sadness of it all. For others, the memories of soldiers their age is simply too much. For most of the Israelis, it is the most personal of all the sites on the ten-day trip. It is an experience undergone together, yet paradoxically, also a great dividing point between the two groups.

The guide ends the visit with a short statement: "This is a military cemetery. These are people who have given their lives for their people. Each of us needs to ask what we have done for our people." The comment is not very subtle, but it creates the kind of introspective moment that is clearly intended. The group heads back to the bus. It is a lot to absorb, and for most of the young adult participants, it will take time. It will be one of those mifgash moments that seems to characterize what unites and divides Jews in Israel and around the world.

DESTROYING AND AFFIRMING STEREOTYPES

One of the most powerful effects of young Israelis and North Americans traveling together for five to ten days was the shattering of some of the stereotypes that characterize Diaspora Jewry's perspective on Israel. The Americans quickly saw that all Israelis were not like Ari Ben Canaan, the hero of Leon

Uris's novel *Exodus* (Paul Newman in Otto Preminger's film). The North Americans also learn that being an Israeli soldier did not mean that one was a flak-jacketed, helmeted warrior perched atop a huge tank aimed at a Palestinian child.

Some Birthright Israel participants came to Israel expecting to meet pious, black-coated, bearded scholars with wives who wear long dresses and scarves, surrounded by hordes of children. They had an image of Israel that was a composite of *Fiddler on the Roof*, faded family photographs of their parents' "bubbies" and "zaidies," and Crown Heights in Brooklyn, New York. Others expected to see the streets full of pistol-packing, American-born "Rambos," accompanied by attractive, intense, head-covered young wives with several children in their arms. In fact, Birthright Israel participants *did* meet some young "Rambos." They found them, however, not to be Hollywood movie heroes, but passionately ideological Jews who carried a pistol for self-defense on their way home in the territories.

Other visitors, with a smattering of knowledge about Israel, expected to meet sabras on Tel Aviv beaches, pork-eating kibbutzniks, and hip young nightclub swingers who read Grisham novels rather than Gemara (part of the Talmud, the core texts of interpretation in Jewish tradition). Indeed, they did meet many fascinating women and chiseled men, who confirmed that Grisham was popular in Hebrew, as were Tel Aviv's beaches on Shabbat. But at the same time, they learned that the Israelis reading Grisham nonetheless returned home on Friday nights to have Shabbat dinner with their families, quoted biblical passages, and were passionate when it came to the right of the Jewish people to have their own land.

Finally, some visitors had been prepared by their parents and by their prior Jewish education to meet destitute Holocaust survivors and refugees. They expected these immigrants to look different and impoverished, but at the same time constitute "brothers" and "sisters" who needed our help. The overseas students did meet new immigrants from Ethiopia and Russia, along with second- and third-generation Moroccans and Iraqis, but they did not all look so needy, deprived, or even so dissimilar as one might have expected. Some were similarly pierced and wore the same Calvin Klein and Tommy Hilfiger jeans as their American peers. It was clear that they were not asking for charity or philanthropy from their American friends.

The Israelis had their exaggerated stereotypes as well. Some Israelis expected to see younger versions of the wealthy, philanthropic Jews who "dropped into" Israel for a few days to see the needy and the "natives," seek out a bit of Jewish nostalgia, and have their name attached to a building. Almost none of the Americans smoked cigars or wore suits, and it was hard to imagine any of them donating money that would put their name on a building plaque. Furthermore, the North Americans did not fit the religious stereotypes often ascribed to Americans who have moved to Israel and have become key among those who settle in the territories. Most of the American participants came from the unaffiliated sector of American Jewish life and were secular—just like many of the Israelis.

Even in ten days, it seemed that several stereotypes were changed, sometimes mildly, sometimes dramatically. The mifgash showed the Americans that Israelis were a diverse people: some went to the beach on Shabbat, while others wore kippot and went to synagogue; and some, even those who wore kippot, went to the beach at other times. It became apparent to the Americans that all religious people were not "fanatics" and that "secular Israelis" were not devoid of a Jewish soul. All young soldiers were not killer-warriors, nor were they all universalistic and leftist. Probably the most important de-stereotyping was the humanization of Israelis. In Amichai's words, Israel is "a man who has just bought fruits and vegetables." It's not "arches from the Roman Period."[13]

The mifgash demonstrated to the Israelis that not all Americans were overweight, wealthy, or spoiled. It revealed that American Jews were much more diverse than previously realized, from the very involved and committed to Israel, to those who cared little and knew nothing. The mifgash uncovered Americans who had come to Israel for fun, but were also eager to listen and learn. To be sure, there were significant differences between the Americans and Israelis, but not so many as expected beforehand.

Sometimes it did happen that stereotypes were reinforced rather than changed. Overseas women sometimes found the Israeli men macho and chauvinist. Some Israelis were surprised at the ignorance of their overseas friends about Israel. Israelis were seen as strongly nationalistic, and Americans were often seen as ambivalent and insecure in their Jewishness and connection to Israel. Ten days often moderated and even changed preconceptions— and other times reinforced them. Both dynamics were evident on Birthright Israel trips that featured a substantial mifgash.

LEVELERS AND DIVIDERS

The Birthright Israel mifgash revealed what may be regarded as some of the great "levelers" and some of the great "dividers" in contemporary Jewish life between Jews from abroad and Israelis. Being a young person in the twenty-first century was clearly one of the great levelers. These two populations shared many elements of the global village in which we now live: they wore the same jeans, ate the same foods, listened to the same music, worried about many of the same issues, and harbored many of the same desires. Being young and alive in the twenty-first century means sharing elements of a common world culture.

These two groups also shared the word "Jewish." Granted, they may have understood and interpreted the word in many different ways, even fought over it, and been frequently surprised at what the other Jew is like. Yet it was ultimately that word (along with a generous monetary gift) that brought the North Americans to Israel. "Jewishness" was what placed the Israelis on the buses. There also may have been, surprisingly, some vestigial sense of what both Freud and Jung called a shared collective memory that linked these two groups.[14] The trip was full of powerful symbols of Jewish "collective memory." The core sites had multiple meanings and interpretations, but they ignited something in both groups. The dim light of collective memory of many Diaspora Jews was illuminated when seeing these sites, and the powerful spotlights on those two sites took on new meanings for the Israelis when they experienced them with their American counterparts.

The Hebrew and English languages were great barriers between these two groups. The Jewish people today clearly do not have a shared language, and the indispensable role of language for group solidarity is lost in our day and age. The Birthright Israel trip was clearly affected by the fact that it has to take place in "loazit," the word used in Hebrew to describe a foreign language (loazit is actually a Hebrew acronym meaning "the language of idol worship"). No matter how fluent the Israelis were in understanding and speaking English, it was clear that something regularly got lost in the translations—for both groups.

Attitudes to religion also posed significant obstacles in the groups. Israelis, as noted, tended to divide their fellow Israelis into *datiim* (religious) and *hiloniim* (secular). They had little or no understanding of (or interest in) Conservative and Reform Judaism and even less sympathy for them. The stereotypical Israeli quip is "the synagogue I don't go to is Orthodox." Although they might have been respectful of women wearing kippot or *talitot* (prayer shawls), behind closed doors they spoke otherwise. The Americans could not understand how so many Israelis were so ignorant and negative about religion. The Israelis understood the meaning of every word of the Kiddush and Birkat HaMazon, but they were more likely to talk throughout it. Many of the Americans did not understand many of the words of the "birkat" (as it often is denoted in American Jewish slang), but they sang the prayer with conviction and gusto. Very often these two groups seemed like members of different religions.

There are core cultural connections that reveal inherent differences between being a Jew in a society like Israel, where the majority culture is Jewish, and being a Jew in a culture like North America, where the majority culture is not Jewish. Primary public events of Israel culture are Yom Ha'Shoah (Holocaust Memorial Day), Yom Ha'Zicharon (Memorial Day for Fallen Soldiers), Yom Yerushalayim (Jerusalem Day), closed movie theatres and restaurants on Tisha B'Av, class trips to historical and biblical sites and contemporary Zionist monuments. In America, the primary public event artifacts include Fourth of July picnics and double-header baseball games, Memorial Day shopping sales, Thanksgiving, Super Bowl Sunday, and March Madness basketball rivalries. Israeli and American Jews grow up in different incubators.

Finally, perhaps the greatest divider—and the most obvious—is that at age eighteen, Israeli men and women put on uniforms and serve in the IDF for two or more years. Afterward, men serve in the reserves for another twenty years or more. At the same time, North Americans put on Dockers and Gap shirts and inhabit college and university campuses for four to eight years. Whatever the accident of their parents and grandparents' decisions about where to settle—at age eighteen, the paths of these two groups of young Jews diverge.

MIFGASH AND ISRAELIS

Discussion of the mifgash would not be complete without noting its impact on Israeli society. More than fifteen thousand young Israelis have taken part in these mifgashin. The majority have been soldiers from the Israel Defense Forces, while others are university students who have completed compulsory army service but still serve in the reserves. In 2002, the chief education officer of the IDF was approached by Birthright Israel's professionals to discuss the possibility of releasing soldiers for a period of time to participate in the trips. He saw this as a unique opportunity to teach about the Diaspora and to strengthen the tie between Israel and world Jewry. He seized the opportunity and made this a central part of the IDF's educational program on contemporary Jewry.

Although the impact of the Birthright Israel trip on Israelis has not been studied systematically as it has vis-à-vis North Americans (see chapter 8), both internal IDF studies and rich anecdotal evidence indicate the profound importance of this experience. Mifgash has broadened vistas about Diaspora Jewry, created lasting personal ties, resulted in many romances (and even a few marriages) between Israelis and Americans, and gradually begun to filter into the common language of Israeli life. The Birthright Israel program was built to affect the unaffiliated Jewish North American young adult. The experience of the past five years points to rich possibilities for significant impact on Israeli life.

In the summer of 2006 the IDF's research unit conducted a study of the impact of the Birthright Israel trip on army participants. Its main findings were that the experience of participating in Birthright Israel trips had several important effects on the IDF. First, it enabled young Israelis to come to understand Diaspora life surprisingly quickly. The IDF had long invested in lecturers who would explain about Jewish life abroad. The Birthright Israel experience seemed to do the job more immediately, dynamically, and powerfully than the standard lecture. Second, it deepened the Israeli soldiers' motivation and commitment to their army service and the difficult tasks they had to undertake. It was an intense and successful course in deepening identification with the task of being an IDF soldier. Finally, it opened up new understandings for soldiers about the nature and importance of Israel to world Jewry. The mifgash was a powerful and intense short-term course in why Israel matters.

The army's research, combined with Birthright Israel's evaluation procedures (which included thousands of debriefings and letters), points to three areas of profound impact. First, it enriches the young Israeli's understanding of Diaspora youth and life. Second, it deepens (and in some cases creates) the participants' emotional links to the Jewish people as a whole. Third, it changes—sometimes dramatically—the Israeli and Jewish identity of young Israelis. Birthright Israel was established to have an impact on the Jewish identity of unaffiliated young people from abroad. During the six years of its existence, Birthright Israel also became an innovative vehicle for confronting issues related to the Jewish identity of young Israelis.

AN EVENING DISCUSSION

The evening discussion takes place at an undisclosed army base. In the room are fourteen soldiers who have just participated in five-day mifgashim with several different groups. They are a group of young and attractive men who, if it were not for where they are and what they are wearing, might be mistaken for graduating high school seniors from an elite high school or freshmen in their first week of college. Together they compose a very select unit undergoing a long-term training program. These fourteen are part of a small group of individuals who are expected to be the leaders of Israel in the military and in other realms within a decade or two. They are the next shapers of critical areas of Israel's security and civilian life.

After every trip, debriefing sessions facilitated by a Birthright Israel staffer are conducted with soldiers. The debriefing begins with a discussion of the places participants thought were particularly meaningful to the overseas participants—or those not successful. Typically, the Kotel and the Yad Vashem Holocaust memorial are seen as the most powerful. But sometimes the sites do not work. For example, one solider thought that the visit to the Holocaust museum was so difficult to comprehend that it became trivialized. Other parts of the program typically mentioned as powerful experiences included the Golan Heights, Jerusalem, and the shared Shabbat.

Members of the group begin to open up when asked, "Okay, now tell us what happened to you on these five days?" Kobi remarks, "I thought it was going to be five days of *kef* [good times] with nice hotels, good food and sharp American women." "So was it kef?" "Yes, but it was much more than that. I was simply so moved to be part of the group. It opened my eyes to questions and issues I had never thought about before." Eyal chimes in, "I learned about their lives but I also learned about mine, I learned we are different in lots of ways but we're the same in so many ways." Mark adds, "I had a stereotype about North Americans as spoiled and childish—was I wrong! This trip completely changed my world." This latter view is echoed by Eytan: "I changed. I grew in these five days. I'm not the same person. I rediscovered Israel. My feeling for why I am here, why I am in the army, why this is our home became reborn. This trip was for me a journey into being Eytan and being Jewish."

The mifgash experience led to a plethora of written testimonies, poems, diary entries and e-mails about what it meant for Israelis and overseas participants.[15] Consider this email to Birthright Israel from a soldier: "As a soldier I came to believe that the Israel Defense Forces is not just for the citizens of Israel but for all Jews—and among them the people who were in my group, I feel that Israel is not just a home for Israelis but for all the Jewish people. Therefore, this project is of supreme importance so as to be able to come to know the young of the Diaspora and to strengthen our ties with them." Another soldier wrote: "What made the experience so strong was that it enabled us to see the day-to-day experience of our life here through the eyes of the Americans and it made us appreciate so much more what we are doing here."

In the final tie-in session, an American participant sums it up as follows: "I was skeptical about what I might have in common with Israeli soldiers but their inclusion in the trip has been key to its potency. They are wonderful people; provide the best lens through which to explore the cultural differences and their constant presence reminds us that there is a danger and a struggle in the State of Israel. I will never again be able to hear about the Middle East without thinking of my new friends."

The mifgash as much as any other factor helps to shape the culture of the Birthright Israel trips. The structured encounter creates a new way of experiencing Israel. It expands the perspective beyond a bus window, beyond quality tour educators and beyond learned lectures. It opens people's hearts and souls as if they were cameras taking pictures of a society. Sometimes the captured images are one-sided, sometimes painful, but necessarily human and, for the young adult participants, genuine. Symbolically, the arches are torn down and real people at eye level were erected in their place.

The mifgash is the most striking way possible to exemplify Israel's diversity. It quickly debunks the notion that there was such a thing as an "Israeli"; in its place, the mifgash presents snapshots of leftists, rightist, centrists, religious, traditionalists, Ashkenazim, Sefardim, Arabs, radical Orthodox, Zionist Religious, Haredim, and any combination thereof. It shows also that abroad there are Orthodox, ultra-Orthodox, Hasidic, Conservative, Reconstructionist, Reform, unaffiliated, feminist, intermarried, Jewish-Buddhists (Jew-BU), and "just Jewish." It is a quick way to uncover what Amichai has called "a complicated mess in this little country."[16]

During the difficult intifada period (2000–2004), the mifgash became, perhaps, the best advocacy workshop possible to explain and justify Israel's position. Although all trip organizers presented advocacy sessions that made the case for Israel's military actions, the opportunity for soldier participants and overseas Birthright Israel participants to talk—formally and informally—was a wholly different way to deal with the same content. Questions from American participants to their Israeli peers were challenging and forthright, such as "Did you ever kill anyone?" "Why are you in the army?" "Why is Israel in Palestinian territories?" "What about Jewish values?" The answers were equally intense and their genuineness and passion was obvious to all. The encounters were not courses in how to advocate for Israel on campus; instead, they were immersion in the modern meaning of Jewish peoplehood and the issues attendant to Jewish survival. Everyone—American and Israeli alike—came away believing that they better understood themselves and the situation faced by Israel.

It is not yet possible to know what the mifgash will mean ten years from now. Perhaps it will lead to a world Jewry in which Jews from abroad and Israeli have frequent personal contact, a world in which their families are intertwined. It might, however, simply become a pleasant memory that has little day-to-day significance. The experience might be like many photographs from trips that fade and wither with time. This subject is virgin territory; no doubt, later researchers will want to study these participants and try to understand better what their experience meant to them. It is clear, however, that the description of Birthright Israel would have been incomplete without this chapter. The mifgash is a leitmotif that increasingly reflects Birthright Israel's central goal.

DEPARTURE

The bus, full of forty tired, teary-eyed, exuberant people, pulls up to the doors of Ben-Gurion Airport. The duffle bags and backpacks are unloaded; participants line up at the long El Al check-in, receive their boarding passes, and slowly make their way over to the stairs leading up to the departure lounge. The madrichim prod those flying out on El Al Flight 001 (the 1:00 A.M. departure to New York) to move quickly. Twenty North Americans depart, while another ten decide to extend their tickets anywhere from three days to two weeks. Most of the Americans who are staying in Israel are heading to the homes of their new Israeli friends. It is difficult to separate those departing from their Israeli comrades. Tears are streaming down male and female faces. Finally, the circle reconvenes for one last time. The guitar and drum reappear:

ACHIM ACHIM ACHIM ACHIM ACHIM
SIMCHAH SIMCHAH SIMCHAH SIMCHAH,

There are hugs, tears, and smiling. The young Americans slowly vanish up the escalator that will lead them back to their lives in cities and suburbs across North America. Will they ever be the same? The Israelis walk slowly back to the bus taking them home, to the university, to their job, or to their army base. Will they ever be the same? Ten days together that might last a lifetime have ended.

The mifgash, however central, is only one element of the ten-day experience. In the next chapter, the educational theory underlying the program is described.

6 Pedagogy for People

A new "learning" is about to be born—rather it has been born. It is learning in reverse order. A learning that no longer starts from the Torah and leads into life, but the other way around: from life, a world that knows nothing of the Law, or pretends to know nothing, back to the Torah. That is the sign of the time.

. . . There is no one today who is not alienated or who does not contain within himself some small fraction of alientation. All of us to whom Judaism, to whom being a Jew, has again become the pivot of our lives. . . . we all know that in being Jews we must not give up anything, not renounce anything, but lead everything back to Judaism. From the periphery back to the center, from the outside in.

—Franz Rosenzweig

It is 3:30 on a Friday afternoon in early January 2002. The Jerusalem weather is crisp, but not really cold, and one can feel that the city is in its final preparations for Shabbat. There are only a few cars on the road and the ever-present parade of buses that use the city's bus-only lanes has tapered into a mere trickle of diesel exhaust. Soon, sirens will wail, signaling to Jerusalem's Jewish residents that it is time to light Shabbat candles. Two tour buses arrive at the Sheraton Plaza Hotel to pick up a group of nearly eighty Birthright Israel participants and take them to Kabbalat Shabbat services.[1] The Birthright Israel participants, mostly college students, are not yet ready to leave. Several hotel elevators have already been switched to Shabbat mode and automatically stop at each floor, so everything takes longer. The bus drivers, eager to get home to their families, begin a loud but essentially good-natured tirade. Their fulminations do little to get things moving more quickly.

Most of the students are dressed nicely: T-shirts, sweatshirts, and torn jeans have been replaced with clean slacks and skirts. No one is noticeably dressed formally, but it is clear that they are dressed differently than usual and that they realize that Shabbat is about to begin. One of the students shows up in the lobby in a T-shirt, decides he is underdressed, and goes back to his room, further delaying the group. Finally, the buses fill up and leave. From the hotel's location on King George Street, just across from Jerusalem's Great Synagogue, the trip to the Old City on traffic-free streets takes only a few minutes.

The bus parks just outside the Zion Gate of Jerusalem's Old City. The stop gives the students fairly direct access to the Jewish Quarter. They could have entered the Old City through the Jaffa Gate, but that would require walking through a small portion of the Arab quarter. Given the atmosphere in Jerusalem at that point in 2002, and Birthright Israel's emphasis on safety, the normal route is avoided. There is a subtle irony, as there are bullet pockmarks all over Zion Gate, reminders of the fierce battle in the Old City that took place during the 1967 Six-Day War.[2]

The students walk through the Jewish Quarter past a number of stores and restaurants, now closed for Shabbat. The arch of the destroyed Hurva Synagogue frames the passing clouds. The group is headed for its third visit to the Kotel, site of the remains of the Western Wall of the Second Temple, destroyed in 70 C.E. by the Romans. The first time they saw the Kotel was just after their arrival. They had gone in the evening, when the Old City had an ethereal quality, its walls bathed in light. On a subsequent visit, they toured the Western Wall tunnel and met with Jerusalem's mayor, Ehud Olmert. Olmert that week had, in a move drenched with symbolism and politics, temporarily moved Jerusalem's City Hall into the Old City.[3]

The streets on the way to the Kotel as Shabbat approaches are somnolent. As the students get closer to the plaza entrance that leads to the Wall itself, the quiet has the effect of intensifying the dramatic view. The stairs that provide access seem to hang in the air above the Kotel plaza. At the end of the stairs is a security area where young soldiers stand guard, most of them no older than the Birthright Israel participants. The security personnel, along with police supervisors, perfunctorily check each participant as he or she goes through the entrance. The madrich has pointed out who is part of the group and it is like having a VIP pass. One participant later remarks that Israeli security is very different than anything she has seen in the United States.

The students walk across the plaza and approach the Kotel. They walk slowly, partly because others are doing so, but also because the site is overwhelming. The wall is physically imposing, but its size is magnified by what they know of its history as a holy site. Most of the males in the group are not wearing kippot and generally do not carry them in their pocket, so they each take one from a public table. Soon, only kippot made from stapled pieces of cardboard remain. The cardboard head coverings do not fit very well, and the evening breeze makes it difficult for the Birthright Israel males to keep them on their heads. One student, not wanting to be seen in a cardboard kippah, pulls a jacket over his head. Another student hands him a wool cap to serve as a head covering, and he smiles broadly.

No one is quite sure when things will start or what will happen—there are no chairs and this does not look like any synagogue they have seen before—so the students mill around and talk among themselves. Hasidim, charismatically religious Jews who follow religious practices their families brought with them from Europe, arrive for their own services. Even in their clean Shabbat clothes, the American students are clearly distinguishable from the fur-hatted, black-coated Hasidim. One student comments that the way the Hasidim pray is sort of like the way he plays sports—hard. He remarks that he wishes he could pray like that.

Another Birthright Israel group, a group of students from South America, shows up. Eventually, someone begins to set up folding chairs in a corner of the plaza, and soon the rabbi leading the services arrives. The rabbi is a former American who made aliyah some years earlier. His youthful face, bushy but neatly trimmed beard, and twinkling eyes provide a hint that this evening's service will not be like a service they might go to at their parents' synagogue.

The rabbi begins with the traditional opening Kabbalat Shabbat psalm, Psalm 95. The melody is from a Shlomo Carlebach tune, *"l'chu n'rannenah"* (Come, let us sing to the Lord). The rabbi's soulful voice and heartfelt expression clearly has an impact on the students—it seems a sublime moment for many. Almost instantly, a group of regulars at the service jump up and begin to dance in a circle. They are tremendously fervent and energetic. A student in the Birthright Israel group, Jonathan, later says, "I've had Shabbos experiences in the past but nothing [like this]. . . . I don't know, I can't even describe it in words. Hopefully, I'll continue to have this again and again."

Jonathan's feelings are clearly shared and many in the group seem emotionally swept-up by the experience. As another participant, Perry, put it, "I had a little bit of hesitation in going to the Wailing Wall [another name for the Kotel] because I really didn't know what to expect. I thought that it would just be a bunch of very formal prayer, which I was not very much interested in, but to my surprise, when there was a lot of that celebration and dance, it was something that was very enjoyable, and it gave me a new perspective on the celebration of Sabbath."

Almost all the members of the group join in the dancing. As the circle turns, their faces are revealed one by one, expressing surprise and delight. They seem to be having a great time. It is like a party, but there is no mistaking it for a distinctly Jewish religious event. Later, Greg comments, "It was incredible. The energy, we were dancing, and singing and praying, was amazing.

I mean there was a crowd of probably a couple of hundred people standing there watching us because we were so loud and energetic and everything. And for me, I haven't felt energy like that in a long time. It was cool."

What is surprising, even to the seasoned researchers who were accompanying the group and had been with other groups to the Kotel, is the uniformity of the reactions. More than a dozen members of the group are interviewed and each gives a similar account. They talk about the beauty of the experience and how much energy they felt from their engagement in Shabbat. Words like "amazing" and "powerful" pervade their comments. What seems clear is that these American young adults have never really experienced a traditional Shabbat; they did not have what social psychologists call "schemata" to appreciate it. Traditional observance of Shabbat was, at least in their prior experience, a time when you were not allowed to do things you like to do and that make life "easy": drive a car, turn on a light, or watch a movie. They were surprised by the Kotel experience of joyfulness. They were, in their own language, "amazed" at how putting aside the secular concerns of the week could be incredibly liberating and, even, fun.

OLD WINE, NEW BOTTLES

One way to summarize the central goal of Birthright Israel is that it aims to alter the trajectory of Jewish engagement of young Jews and point them toward involvement with their community and their Jewish identities. The initial hope was that by providing an educational trip to Israel, young Jewish adults from Diaspora communities would come to appreciate their Jewish identity more fully. That appreciation, in turn, would make Judaism a more important part of their social identities and lives. Identity development is not something that lends itself to traditional educational modalities. If, for example, Birthright Israel took a traditional, cognitive learning approach—if it chose to focus on providing information through lectures and readings that would help participants gain a better understanding of their heritage—the program would likely be a failure. Or, if Birthright Israel were just a tour of Israel—if it chose to focus only on exposing young adults to a variety of tourist sites—it would also likely fail.

What Birthright Israel elected to do, instead, was more complex and included cognitive, emotional, and behavioral elements. It is, perhaps, a model of how any educational endeavor, regardless of its goals, should function. Even though touring historical sites was not the primary method for engaging participants, the tourist element—visits to specific sites in Israel linked to ancient and modern history—became central to the program. Since the

Pedagogy for People 97

founding of the State of Israel, visits by Diaspora Jews have become ritualized experiences. As noted earlier, prior youth education trips had mostly targeted adolescents (see chapter 1). Much was learned from these Israel experience programs,[4] and some of the lessons were incorporated into Birthright Israel, even though the program focused on an older group: college students and recent graduates, ages eighteen to twenty-six.

Perhaps, the most important change from earlier trips was that prior programs were designed and marketed primarily to those who were part of Jewish educational programs and already engaged with Judaism and Israel. In contrast, many of those who participated in Birthright Israel (and, indeed, were part of their primary target group) were Jewishly unaffiliated or, at least, had little current or ongoing contact with the Jewish community. Thus, for example, among participants in 2007, more than 60 percent had no contact with formal Jewish education after the age of thirteen.[5] They did not necessarily seek to join Birthright Israel to learn about Judaism; rather, they chose to participate because they heard that it was fun and, in some cases, because it was cost-free.

There were a host of challenges to creating an effective curriculum for Birthright Israel. It had to be one that could be implemented by different providers and for diverse groups of participants. Although there were available program models, what had worked in the past had to be adapted for an older, less Jewishly knowledgeable and engaged group. For the program to be transformative—and able to accomplish its goals of engaging participants with their Jewish identity in only ten days—it had to be powerful. To be effective, the program would have to "work" for those who had been exposed in childhood to mediocre, as well as good Jewish education. It had to function for those who had already decided they were part of the Jewish people, as well as for those who were ambivalent.

Although Birthright Israel's educational process was not driven by social psychological theory, the program's impact can be described in terms of Kurt Lewin's change model of "unfreezing, change and refreezing."[6] By creating an emotionally overwhelming experience, Birthright Israel, first, helps participants open themselves to learning. Then, by engaging them in a host of activities, it helps them *un*learn some of what they already knew or thought they knew. Finally, by providing content and exposure to different role models, the process helps participants develop new ways of thinking about their Jewish identity and heritage.

Despite the program's aspirations to renew Jewish identity, proselytizing was not considered appropriate. It would likely be counterproductive; more important, such an approach was contrary to the Jewish tradition.[7] Nor could the program explicitly promote aliyah, a central mission of one of the program's sponsors, JAFI.[8] And, aside from the difficulty of attracting North American youth to live in Israel, the integrity of the program's educational focus had to be maintained. It was not a program goal to encourage immigration, and no one wanted participants to return home and warn their friends that the program had a hidden agenda.

At the same time, if the program was just another tour to an exotic destination, it might be enjoyable, but it would not necessarily influence Jewish identity. The approach needed to be fun, meaningful, educational, and innovative. The task was to develop an educational approach that would ignite Jewish souls, engage Jewish minds, and provide models of Jewish behavior. In the following section, the theory and philosophy underlying these aspirations are described. Molded into an educational strategy, it has implications beyond the admittedly parochial interests of Birthright Israel. The strategy had to be sufficiently well-structured but flexible. It had to enable the Birthright Israel organization to set standards and develop feedback mechanisms for trip organizers and providers.

THE CHALLENGE: INSPIRING YOUNG ADULTS

Finding ways to inspire college-age and twenty-something Jews is no easy task. It is not that contemporary young adults are not as motivated, nor even as smart as previous generations; they are probably more so. Rather, it is that any effort to engage them competes against other attractive ideas and possible identities.[9] Perhaps best symbolized by the Internet, which gives one 24/7 access to almost limitless information and connections with others across the world, the contemporary dilemma is information and experience overload. Part of the developmental struggle of emerging adulthood is how to handle being particularistic—about friends, family, ethnic/religious roots—in a world that values universalism.

Inspiration and experience

One lesson from past Israel experience programs is that the critical educational component of travel to Israel is the experiential nature of the journey. Experiential education, while it was underutilized in Jewish education more generally, is not new to secular or Jewish educators. In the early twentieth century, America's great educational philosopher, John Dewey, developed a theory that placed experience at the center of human life and education.[10] Dewey believed that thinking, at its core, is a practical rather than a theoretical activity. Therefore, he reasoned, education is very much about the link between experiences and thinking. In two of his central works on education,

Democracy and Education and *Experience and Education,* Dewey proposed that particular kinds of learning are most effective when rooted in experience. According to his analysis, the act of education is about creating opportunities for learners to undergo experiences that are regarded as worthwhile or educative. Dewey's educational theory shifts the locus of learning from education as "filling up empty heads with content" to a dynamic interaction among the individual, experiences, and thinking.

More than sixty years after Dewey's experiential principle was first expounded, Birthright Israel applied it to developing standards for their curriculum. Israel is, in several respects, a veritable laboratory for experiential education programs. For most participants, it is a distant place that offers an incredibly rich array of Jewish sites and experiences that cannot be duplicated anywhere else. From past experience, one can be confident that a carefully structured program in Israel has the potential to evoke lasting change in participants.[11]

As Dewey would have recognized, however, it is not readily apparent which experiences might touch which individuals. One person might be inspired by contact with Israel's ancient past, while another might be inspired by its hi-tech future. Regardless, the experiential framework suggests a different approach to education than is the norm in higher education. The individual inspired by biblical history might best be reached by visiting biblical sites, where his/her own relationship to the story can be made palpable. Others, with a political bent, might gain a better appreciation of the geopolitical complications of Israel's defense issues with Syria by visiting the Golan Heights and seeing the topology of the land and the sites of the battles during 1967 and 1973.

In either case, the essence of the experiential approach is to avoid the simple sharing of information—as would be the case in listening to a lecture or plowing through the reading list of a college course. Perhaps, as the story we have just read of one group's Shabbat experience illustrates, key elements of Judaism may not be teachable; they need to be experienced. One does not have to conduct the experiment to know that participating in a Carlebach minyan at the Kotel is far more effective in generating appreciation for Shabbat than hearing a lecture that describes and analyzes the beauty of Shabbat. The experiential approach does not preclude lectures, readings, or timelines; rather, the formal material provides background to the experience that is foreground. The staples of formal education are designated to supplement and enhance what each participant experiences.

Although the way in which ideas and meaning were woven together was an outgrowth of each staff's pedagogic experience, echoes of the strategy are reflected in the work of modern educational theorists. For example, Howard Gardner's theory of multiple intelligences and routes to knowing suggests a very similar strategy.[12] Gardner maintains that the modernist tradition reduces "knowing" to a monodimensional structure defined by discursive or cognitive knowledge, whereas in fact, there are diverse ways of knowing. There are, to use his term, multiple intelligences. Jewish education had been dominated by a modernist perspective, sometimes without even incorporating its cognitive veneer.

A Birthright Israel trip attempts to disabuse participants of the notion that Judaism is accessible only if one has mastered traditional Jewish texts. Instead, Judaism becomes accessible experientially, and participants are given the opportunity to participate in Judaism not just cognitively, but also through aesthetic, kinesthetic, and other modalities. Participants get to experience Judaism through art, music, architecture, and dance, as well as through intellectual discourse. It was not deliberate strategy, but Birthright Israel might be regarded as a test of Gardner's ideas as a theory of Jewish epistemology.

The educational approach adopted in the standards for Birthright Israel experiences encompasses all five senses. Participants *see* exhibits at museums (Yad Vashem, the Holocaust Memorial), *hear* the unique sounds of Israel (the siren that goes off just prior to Shabbat), *smell* the "aromas" of the country (the sea, the mountains, and the desert), *taste* Israeli delicacies (from Middle Eastern to East European foods), and get to *touch* the land (the smooth stones of the Kotel). For young adults accustomed to experiencing the world through the Internet and instant-messaging, the sensation-driven trip has an almost radical quality.

Ideas and identity

The college students and recent graduates who participate in Birthright Israel are accustomed to a kind of formal education that emphasizes didactic presentations; they are expert at listening to lecturers and repeating what they have heard on tests. Some, no doubt, have had experience attending interactive seminars and others have conducted independent research, but most have not done these things in the context of Jewish education. With only a few exceptions, Birthright Israel participants are not deeply versed in theories and narratives of Judaism and Zionism. At best, they might be familiar with history and sociology and have some knowledge of the current situation in Israel— more likely from CNN and their local newspaper than from in-depth study.[13]

The educational challenge is complicated by the Internet mind-set of this group[14] and their attention span, which has been simultaneously dulled and overstimulated by multimedia. To maintain interest, the program needed to include intelligent and reflective presentations of core ideas at a level that would be sophisticated enough to engage them without boring them. It would be misleading to imply that the ten days of a Birthright Israel experience were designed to be the equivalent of a college course. But it would also be incorrect to conclude that the program is not an intellectual experience. It was designed to stimulate participants' understanding of history and contemporary life. Likely, it has different effects for those who come to the program with substantial intellectual currency; in particular, those who have had prior exposure to Israel studies.

THEORY IN ACTION

The program was designed to engage those with little prior knowledge and to offer, for all participants, new perspectives. The underlying principles shaped the educational standards that were to become the backbone and organizing framework of Birthright Israel activities. The political, cultural, and philosophical ideas that participants were asked to grapple with ultimately led to a personal set of existential questions, summarized by, "What does it mean for me to be Jewish?" The Birthright Israel educational standards were designed to produce curricula aimed at helping participants answer these questions, both by facilitating their understanding of what they were seeing, and by structuring means that would allow them to internalize the information. Thus, there are two synergistically related central themes of Birthright Israel: ideas and meaning-making.

Operationally, the first objective of the program was to present participants with rich intellectual content that would enable them to understand what they were seeing. Without such information, it would be hard to help them develop the schemata they need to understand a host of other issues. It was also recognized, given the age cohort, that participants would ask themselves what each experience meant to them personally. This inner process of making personal meaning, however, is not just about identity exploration in the abstract, it is also about participants' personal Jewish identities. It is their Jewishness that enables them to be part of the program, and they are visiting Israel, a Jewish state.

In practical terms, an emphasis on ideas and meaning-making required that the experiential educators who led the program be analytic when presenting and discussing ideas, and existential when linking ideas to meaning. They try to find a balance that allows experiences, ideas, and discussions of personal meaning to coalesce. To accomplish this goal, the Birthright Israel curriculum requires trip organizers to conduct discussion sessions at regular intervals. The sessions were not intended to inculcate specific ideologies; rather, they are designed to provide opportunities for analysis and examination of issues that had surfaced during the trip. Topics parallel the main themes of the overall program and include:

- What is Zionism?
- Who are the Jews?
- The Middle East conflict
- Jewish values
- Jewish pluralism
- Civil rights

Many trip organizers incorporated additional discussions sessions. Hillel, for example, incorporates into each of their trips a series of "Six Conversations." The goal of the conversations is to help participants process what they are seeing; in particular, to help them make connections between their experience of Israel and their Jewish identity. The discussions reflect Hillel's mission as a religious and cultural organization for Jewish college students. They see their task as helping students integrate elements of their ethnic and religious identities.

Another trip organizer, Maayanot—which is connected to Chabad, a religiously traditional movement committed to effecting all Jews—conducts discussions of religion and science.[15] Yet another organizer, Kesher (an arm of the Reform movement), is concerned with presenting perspectives on religious pluralism. Some of its conversations are designed to help participants understand the position of liberal Judaism in Israeli society and the complexity of religious discourse.

Participants on many trips also had opportunities to meet with leading Israeli figures to discuss "big picture issues." Some groups, for example, visited with Muki Tzur, a leading thinker from the kibbutz movement. Others were taught by Professor Gadi Wolfsfeld of the Communications Department of the Hebrew University, who showed them news clips from CNN, BBC, ABC, NBC, and CBS and then engaged them in an analysis of techniques and misconstructions used in contemporary communications. Still others met with David Horowitz, editor of the *Jerusalem Post,* Israel's English-language daily newspaper, who shared his perspective on current events. And others got to meet with a broad cross-section of members of the Knesset who shared their view of the political situation and often did so in the context of their own life story. Still other groups met with Holocaust survivors who, no matter how many times they tell their story, never fail to tell it with passion—as if the events of World War II were last month.

Many organizers brought their groups to the Knesset, the Supreme Court, or the Foreign Ministry to meet with leading Israeli political and government leaders. As described earlier (see chapter 3), some groups have held question-and-answer sessions with political insiders, as well as some of Israel's most knowledgeable pundits. Other groups had the chance to meet with the then-president of Israel's Supreme Court, Justice Aharon Barak, a world-renowned jurist. And some met with the finance minister (and former prime minister), Benjamin (Bibi) Netanyahu. In each case, the goal of the encounter was to help participants understand how Israeli leaders thought about and analyzed their society.

Lofty visions and concrete goals

As an educational program, Birthright Israel has sharply defined goals, delineating specific types of experiences. This practice is rooted in the theory of general education that an educational program requires both a well-defined grand vision (distal goals) and precisely defined operational targets (proximate goals). If Birthright Israel were to be successful, it would need a clearly enunciated and precisely stated educational mission that could then be translated into specific education practices.[16]

The "grand vision" of Birthright Israel consisted of three long-term goals. Success with respect to these goals would only be apparent after the passage of time. These goals were:

- To reach a sector of young American Jewry (popularly known as the "unaffiliated") that had been regarded as detached or alienated from Jewish life by providing them with an Israel experience
- To launch young unaffiliated Jews on a "Jewish journey" that would lead them to a lifelong involvement with Jewish life
- To create links among these young Jews, the State of Israel, and the Jewish community in the years to come

To translate the vision into standards for curricula, several proximate goals specified the content of the ten days. Trip organizers were trained in how to meet these goals and a monitoring and evaluation system was developed. If trip organizers failed to achieve the goals, they were sanctioned or even dropped from the program. The operational goals included:

- The presentation of a concise, "bird's-eye" overview of Jewish history, denoted as "the narrative of Jewish history"
- The portrayal of Israel as a modern contemporary Jewish state
- The demonstration of the connection of Judaism to Jewish values by encountering specific examples of these values (with special emphasis on the value of Shabbat)
- The perspective of Israel as a country of diverse views and as an exemplar of the centrality of pluralism to Jewish life

For each of these proximate goals, trip organizers had several options:

- At least one Holocaust-related site: Yad Vashem in Jerusalem or Masua near Tel Aviv[17]
- At least one site related to Israel's political institutions: the Knesset or the Supreme Court
- At least one site related to Zionist history: Independence Hall, Metulla (Israel's northernmost town), or Rabin Square
- At least one site related to Jewish values, in particular Tzedek and Hesed: Yad Sarah, Malben, or Alyn Hospital[18]
- At least one site related to contemporary Israel: a high-technology company, a scientific research facility, or a university
- At least one Jewish historical site: David's City, Masada, Caesarea, or Bet Shean[19]
- At least one experience of contemporary Israeli arts/culture: museums, films, artists, musicians

By laying out the vision in this way, the planners did not intend to inculcate a specific ideology of Judaism; rather, they wished to expose participants to a set of Jewish educational concepts. The goals did not specify what a participant—or any Jew—must do or believe. Instead, the prescribed educational experiences and methodologies were provided in order to facilitate the Jewish journey of a young adult. The goals were initially presented in a publication called *The Birthright Israel Handbook*.[20] The handbook is a detailed manual that explicates the overall vision, describes an educational methodology, and presents examples and options of program possibilities. In addition, the Handbook delineates staff, legal, and logistic requirements.

To ensure the educational goals were met, an independent education research company based in Jerusalem (Moach Eser) was contracted to develop an assessment plan and to conduct ongoing observation of a sample of trips by each organizer.[21] The focus of the assessment was on quality assurance, and it had several objectives: (1) to determine whether the standards of the program were being upheld; (2) to provide trip organizers with feedback that could help to improve programs; and (3) to provide Birthright Israel with overall feedback on trends, areas of strength, and issues that needed to be changed/improved. Two months after the completion of the trip, each trip organizer received a detailed observation report on their groups.

In the last several years of the program, the Birthright Israel organization has organized a week of intensive meetings among trip organizers, their staff, and Moach Eser to review specifics of the assessment reports and to discuss how to improve each program. The oversight and evaluation process has assumed a significant role in Birthright Israel both as a means to ensure educational quality and to maintain a high level of adherence to logistical, safety, and security standards. Reviews of individual trips have sometimes been accompanied by fines and sanctions. At the outset, the process created some difficulties. The Israel experience field had heretofore operated independently and with little oversight.

In practice, the educational monitoring process was supportive and provided objective feedback to providers about their staff and trips. Those trip organizers with a disproportionate number of logistical or educational irregularities were, however, summoned to meetings with the Birthright Israel's educational and logistical staff. They were provided feedback and given an opportunity to make changes in staffing, their program structure, or whatever was diagnosed as the underlying difficulty. Over several years, a handful of groups were suspended from conducting further trips for failure to follow the guidelines. Several groups had financial fines levied. But the system has functioned to ensure a degree of program uniformity across providers and to assure quality.

Exploring identity

Evaluation surveys administered to Birthright Israel participants before their trips indicate that the desire to have fun is a central motivator for young adults to apply for a trip (see chapter 8). This response is not surprising as the program was designed to attract unengaged Jews. Engaged Jews, who might have a more Jewishly focused motivation for applying, were often ineligible because they had already been to Israel on a peer educational trip.

In seeking fun, participants were reflecting their desire to engage in exploration appropriate to their developmental stage. The age group eligible for Birthright Israel, eighteen to twenty-six, coincides almost exactly with a developmental period termed "emerging adulthood" by psychologist Peter Arnett.[22] Building on earlier work by psychoanalyst Erik Erikson[23] and others, Arnett argues that emerging adulthood is distinct both from adolescence and young adulthood, the corresponding stages of Erikson's model.[24] Arnett argues that societal changes in the age of marriage and parenthood have created a distinct period of emerging adulthood in modern society.

Emerging adulthood is characterized by two primary transitional qualities: accepting responsibility for one's self, and making independent decisions. A key feature of emerging adulthood is identity exploration. Young adults, however, do not just explore in order to prepare for becoming an adult, they enage in exploration for its own sake and to explore different worldviews. Values acquired from family during childhood and adolescence are reexamined and questioned. To the extent that the emphasis during this time is on being self-sufficient, it is reasonable for young adults to want to develop their own worldviews rather than to unquestioningly adopt the one their parents gave them. Arnett and Jensen, in a study of emerging adults' religious beliefs, found that there is a strong need to formulate a belief system that arises from their own independent reflections.[25]

Thus, from a developmental psychological perspective, the tendency for young adult Jews to leave Judaism behind is not necessarily about Judaism; rather, it is a naturally occurring process endemic to this age group.[26] But this model does not explain fully the process that individuals go through, in part because many Birthright Israel participants have had little knowledge or experience of Judaism to leave behind. If one takes the Arnett and Jensen model to its logical conclusion, it is conceivable that Birthright Israel would have the strongest effects on those who came on the trip with little or no Jewish identity. They have no preexisting worldview to question and reject. For them, Judaism itself is a novel worldview—and, from the hopeful perspective of those who conceived of Birthright Israel, a more attractive one to embrace.

Arnett's model suggests that Birthright Israel's creators had a strong theoretical foundation for assuming that the trip would have an important impact on participants' Jewish identities. Application of Arnett's model suggests several reasons for the program's success. First, because identity develops over time, Jewish identity could indeed be influenced by the trip. This conception in some ways challenged an assumption among leadership in the Jewish community that adult Jewish identity could only be shaped by rich Jewish family life and Jewish education. Second, it suggests that carefully sequenced experiences in Israel could challenge and perhaps alter the worldviews of participants. Third, while the ten days might affect identity and increase Jewish knowledge and sense of Jewish peoplehood, they could not be expected to increase directly participants' engagement in Jewish organizational life or their observance of Jewish ritual. Such changes would require a different educational model and a longer period of time.

Social interactionism

To be sure, Erikson and Arnett's ideas provide useful clues about the identity journey of Birthright Israel participants. A number of other theoretical models, however, suggest that the social environment is also important in shaping meaning and identity. Participants on Birthright Israel trips might give personal meaning to their new experiences in Israel, but these meanings would in all likelihood be strongly influenced by peers and group leaders. For example, the Kotel is just a large stone wall, albeit an impressive one, unless one knows its history and significance in Jewish tradition. Yad Vashem might evoke strong feelings in participants, but when participants see others similarly moved, the emotional power is reinforced. A camel ride is, perhaps, exotic, but riding in a large group at sunset through the Negev, and discussing biblical descriptions of the desert, makes the experience memorable. Being with a group of Jewish peers, especially when one normally lives in a world relatively devoid of other Jews, strengthens one's identification with Judaism.

Sociological and sociopsychological theorizing supports these suppositions. One theoretical view, referred to as the Chicago School of Symbolic Interactionism,[27] posits the way in which meaning is socially influenced. College students can be influenced because they are part of a new set of social groups with very different norms than their parents. Tajfel's social identity theory and Turner's self-categorization theory, key to contemporary social psychological views of identity,[28] both emphasize the role of social grouping and social relations in shaping identity. These theories argue that a powerful and attractive social environment significantly influences identity.

Multiple approaches were employed by Birthright Israel to influence the social environment and, through it, Jewish identity. First, and perhaps most important, participants travel together for the entire ten days on the same bus with up to forty fellow participants. This requirement influenced identity each moment: as participants shared experiences, they bonded and reinforced the meaning of the experience. Second, mifgashim were organized to allow participants to get to know—and contrast their lives to—Israeli peers. Finally, most groups had the chance to attend what the organizers came to call a "mega-event" (see chapter 10). As the name implies, it was a mass gathering of current Birthright Israel participants (at Jerusalem's International Convention Center or a large outdoor venue). Participants listen to philanthropists, Jewish community leaders, members of the government—sometimes even the prime minister—and are able to see spectacular performances by some of Israel's most prominent singers and dancers. The experience is capped by discotheque dancing into the early hours of the morning.

The important role of the group had already been highlighted in the Israel experience literature. As noted earlier, Heilman[29] and others have described the key phenomenon as the "bubble effect." He observed that the group creates its own culture and animus. The group sometimes played as much a role in the total experience as did Israel itself. Birthright Israel wanted to preserve the positive aspects of this group phenomenon for several reasons. Based on a long tradition of social psychological theorizing,[30] it was assumed that proximity to a group of like-minded and potentially attractive peers would strengthen the power of the experience. If young Jewish adults were to see others like themselves searching for Jewish meaning and caring about their Judaism, it would be a powerful educative force. In addition, the group proved to be an important pedagogic device for stimulating creative, provocative discussions of key issues that arose. Heterogeneity within groups often helped this process; it enabled participants to see their uniqueness, as well as their commonalities.

Person-centered education

Perhaps no principle was as important to Birthright Israel's implementation as its focus on participant needs. As noted earlier, part of the curriculum across providers includes discussions with participants regarding what they are experiencing. In its second year, Birthright Israel published a teaching guide for trip organizers and madrichim entitled *Talking About Tie-Ins*. The guide was designed to help lay out the educational goals and strategy of the program: "BRI [Birthright Israel] trips are committed to an educational approach which actively engages and involves participants. In addition to a rich travel and learning program, BRI trips are individual-focused and aimed at enabling participants to reflect and think about what the trip means for them personally and as Jews."[31] The content of the pamphlet focused on how to conduct prescribed tie-in sessions and allow members of each group to share comments, reflections, feelings, and personal implications of specific visits and activities. Beyond specific content, the guide was a way for Birthright Israel to teach its "learner" or "client-centered" educational approach (rooted in the writings of John Dewey, Martin Buber, Carl Rogers, and Abraham Maslow).[32] This "person-centered" approach regards the individual as the focus and subject of the learning act. It argues that learning takes place mainly (and, in its radical formulation, *only*) through the active engagement and involvement of the learner. Such engagement is the key to unlocking the teaching-learning moment.

From the perspective of educational theorists who argue for this learner-centered approach, the main preoccupation is the centrality of the learner: everything revolves around his or her needs. Birthright Israel adopted this strategy and each of the standards it developed for its tour operations made the participants' learning—or, more precisely, their experience of the program—the centerpiece. Although Birthright Israel was not intended to be a form of therapy, it shares with therapeutic modalities a central commitment to the well-being and welfare of the "client."

To accomplish the goals of learner-centered education required a suitable culture, and key was the development of staff that was committed to each individual participant and his or her personal growth. For this reason, the program created "bus units" of no more than forty participants, in some cases as few as thirty. Each bus had three or four staff, including, by requirement, both Israelis and madrichim from the participant's home country. Tour organizers selected both male and female staff members, who were deliberately chosen to represent a diversity of Jewish perspectives—religious and cultural. Most important, organizers were required to train staff in this all-pervasive person-centered approach.

MULTITASKING STAFF

Understanding the role of the staff is essential to explicate the Birthright Israel experience. Among staff, there is a central tour educator–guide who usually led the group. This person is either a native-born Israeli or a longtime immigrant now living in Israel (recall Udi and Frances, chapter 4). There are also, typically, two staff members from the home country of the participants. They are also required to have appropriate educational background and experience. The staff plays three key roles in a Birthright Israel trip.

First, the staff frames the experience. Staffers accompany their students to diverse venues and explain the site and the sight being seen. The Birthright Israel staffer is, in Dewey's terms, the shaper of the experiences that the participant will have and as such plays a primary role in affecting the way the trip is seen and understood. Given the educational approach of Birthright Israel, this task is as seminal as any teaching or lecturing role one might assume. To be the shaper of experiences on an Israel trip is to influence dramatically the entire personality of the trip. For this reason, some analysts regard the tour educator as the most important educative force in Birthright Israel.[33]

Second, tour educators serve as "accessible models." They are not supposed to function simply as expert information sources; they are also supposed to role-model Jewish involvement, commitment, and lifestyle. Ideally, those who staff Birthright Israel trips are chosen for their knowledge of Judaism and Israel, aong with their understanding and ability to reflect the sensibilities of the Jewish and Israeli souls. Some are young adults who are only slightly older than the Birthright Israel participants and want to share what they have discovered about being Jewish. Sometimes, they are older individuals (including educators, doctors, lawyers) who become involved because they want to inspire commitment and engagement with Jewish and Israeli life. The staff are expected to be exemplars of diverse ways of being Jewish. The most successful are those who make themselves accessible to Birthright Israel participants as both professionals and people.

Finally, in a prosaic sense, the staff are ten-day "24/7" caretakers of participants. They are responsible for wake-ups, health, food, moods, adhering to laws related to drinking and drugs, creature and comfort care. None of these tasks are educational per se, but they are the essence of informal education; without them no education can take place.[34] Taken together with their responsibility as "framers" and "role models," the staffers shape the dynamics and impact of the ten-day trip.

Measuring outcomes

Another element of the educational strategy was the development of measurable outcomes for each trip. The aspiration to influence Jewish identity—a highly abstract goal—could only be realized in the context of a series of concrete experiences. If Judaism, at least metaphorically, is a long-term journey, there need to be specific stops along the way, and a methodology is required to make sure the stops are made. The Birthright Israel program was aimed, fundamentally, at identity development; as noted earlier, however, the program theory required that it engage multiple senses. The program would only work if participants had specific experiences: visiting the Kotel, reading Jewish texts, meeting Israeli peers, studying the Holocaust at a site that recalls the events of World War II, visiting a key site in Zionist history, and experiencing Shabbat. But it was not simply about having a set of experiences. It was about the way in which these experiences were processed to form a gestalt.

Observers and evaluators are charged with ensuring that each trip incorporates the experiences mandated by the standards. Birthright Israel's educational architects concluded that while many forms of Jewish education shared much of the educational philosophy of this program, Jewish education as a whole had been "soft" on translating vision into practice and on requiring "hard" evaluation. The actual "doing" and measuring of Jewish education had been the Achilles' heel of well-intentioned efforts to foster Jewish identity. Under the assumption that identity development is a long-term process that cannot be easily specified, Jewish education had too often become ethereal.[35] It avoided mandating specific experiences, events, and activities, and seemed to function effectively only for those who already were engaged and had a base of knowledge. In contrast, Birthright Israel was committed to specific venues, sites, and sources that in themselves were not the goal but were seen as essential stops on a journey. From a theoretical vantage point, this was an example of what the French postmodernists call *oeuvres:* real acts or works that are manifestations of larger visions and that make the larger visions real and concrete.[36]

A quilted theory

The educational theories and practices employed by Birthright Israel's planners can be thought of as a quilt of synthesized approaches matched to the needs of the age group and the program goals. Sometimes these diverse educational ideals fit together smoothly; at other times, the overt commitment to initiative and creativity conflict with a bureaucratic and stylized commitment to rigid details and measurable outcomes. These clashes were often a source of frustration and confusion for trip organizers and staff. Just as colorful quilts are often made up of preworn fabric from a number of different sources, the components that made up the Birthright Israel program were not themselves new. The innovation was the way in which they were combined and applied to an untested large-scale educational venture. The educational experiment at the heart of Birthright Israel was a synthesis of principles targeted for an age group that had not, until this point, been given sufficient attention by those concerned with Jewish education. The principles were

- focused on learner-person–centered education
- highly experiential
- idea-focused and analytic
- interactive, Socratic, and dialectic in approach
- group-oriented
- focused on core Jewish values and principles
- sharply defined and with measurable outcome parameters

In its juxtaposition of educational principles with traditional Jewish content and themes, the Birthright Israel approach was strikingly innovative. It served as an antidote to many of the standard forms of Jewish education endured by participants over the years. Its design was aligned with principles found in some of the more exciting Jewish educational formats—camping, travel, and youth groups—based on the belief that such formats do make a difference. Ultimately, this theory could best be described as an effort to present a new version of Jewish education that, at its core, is tailored to each participant. The idea is that each person on the program will see Judaism not just as something to learn about, but as something relevant to their individual lives and linked to their personal identity. If the theory is successfully implemented, participants would see Judaism as being active and alive, a positive culture and worldview. It was a break with many of the existing normative patterns of Jewish education.

For Birthright Israel, the whole country is a campus. Teachers are people in shorts and T-shirts who present as straight-talking role models, not remote authoritarian figures. Places and people can be analyzed like texts, rather than having participants engage in traditional text study (for which many were unprepared or uninterested). Judaism is not just something that other people do. Judaism is alive, exciting, diverse, and relevant for many lifestyles and values.

IDEAS AND ACCOUNTABILITY

The other striking dimension of Birthright Israel's education approach is its focus (perhaps, obsession) with programmatic practice. The program was influenced by a philosophy of tightly planned and observed programmatic units. Each of the overarching content areas had to be translated into specific program elements, defined by hours, place, and content. As part of the oversight process, a provider needs to document what it is to teach about contemporary Israeli government structure. Is it going to the Supreme Court or the Knesset? With whom would participants be meeting? What is the expected nature of the discussion? The approach was monitored by the oversight system (see above), an approach commonplace in Israeli education (as well as formal education settings, in general), but foreign to the Israel experience field. As noted earlier, it was initially a source of tension between Birthright Israel and providers.

The monitoring system reflected a preoccupation with details that, for some, was an example of Israeli bureaucracy. It *was,* in part, a bureaucratic requirement, but it was also a reflection of Birthright Israel's business orientation and the fact that the program founders were businessmen, not educators. Accountability was critical and it was necessary to ensure that trip organizers did what they said they were going to do, and what they were getting paid to do. Program funders, in particular the philanthropists, were accustomed to an accountability model and wanted to ensure that their investment was being well used. Such a model was particularly important because there were numerous trip providers and a system was needed to guarantee that they were fulfilling minimal standards.

FUN AND SERIOUS EDUCATION

This chapter makes clear that Birthright Israel was rooted in and shaped by a well-thought-out theoretical framework of the kind one would hope is behind all serious educational systems. No doubt, some will see a discontinuity between a ten-day recreational experience and our characterization of it as based in an elaborate educational theory. There is, perhaps, some irony in the way in which the program and its formulation are different. Nevertheless, Birthright Israel is successful because serious people took the social, emotional, and cognitive needs of those from age eighteen to twenty-six very seriously. They attempted to develop a program that reflects our best understanding of educational, developmental, and social psychological theory.

This overall educational model for Birthright Israel, which combined lofty value statements with implementation plans, forms, observers, and sanctions, although rooted in existing theory, was nevertheless innovative. A system such as this had not been used for Israel experience programs and, perhaps, not in Jewish education anywhere. The extent to which it "worked" will be documented later (see chapter 8). Its impact notwithstanding, the model of education tried to be "state of the art" with respect to both educational philosophy and implementation theory.

Birthright Israel is an educational experiment, with ambitious goals. It was mounted on a scale intended to reach tens of thousands of disparate young adults. The program has a number of unique features, not the least of which is its focus on religious/ethnic identity and the connection of Diaspora Jews to Israel. If these features were not enough, the program was launched during a period of political turmoil: as Israel was embroiled in a new round of violent conflict and, later, as the United States experienced the horrific events of 9/11. The uniqueness of Birthright Israel and the era in which it was launched notwithstanding, it provides a number of potentially valuable generic lessons concerning the education and lives of emerging adults.

The fundamental dilemma that gave birth to Birthright Israel—facilitating adaptive individual identities for emerging adults that include connections to religious and ethnic traditions—is not unique to Jews. The challenge of educating college students about the world, and inspiring them to think about issues that go beyond their own lives, is a broad problem. What Birthright Israel tried to create was an educational framework that acknowledges the interrelationship of cognitive, affective, and behavioral learning. The framework treats education not simply as an exchange of information, but as a way to integrate places and people through shared experience. How this framework serves to engage youth is described in the following chapters. The next chapter deals with the organization that was created to develop and manage Birthright Israel.

An Organizational Culture

7

*Ability hits the mark where presumption overshoots
and diffidence falls short.*
—Golda Meir
If an expert says it can't be done, get another expert.
—David Ben-Gurion

When you sit in Shimshon Shoshani's Birthright Israel office, located in a modern building in a Jerusalem industrial district bordering the main highway to Tel Aviv, you might be surprised to learn that the man in front of you is, at his core, a man of the sea. Shoshani (originally Rozenkranz, but Hebraicized when his family made aliyah) is a distinguished figure who, counter to any stereotype one may have about Israeli informality, is wearing a black suit, blue shirt, and color-coordinated tie. Shoshani is widely regarded as Israel's senior educational professional, having served as director of education of the Tel Aviv Municipality, two separate terms as director-general of Israel's Ministry of Education, director-general of ORT's international educational system, and director-general of JAFI, Israel's immigration, absorbtion, and Jewish education authority. He is widely known and deeply respected in Israeli educational and political circles.

Shimshon Shoshani grew up in the port city of Acco, a mostly Arab enclave just north of Haifa, and spent periods of his youth and young adulthood as a fisherman. Today, he delights in taking guests to "Uri Buri," his favorite fish restaurant in Acco, or to one of his favorite restaurants on the beach near his home in Herzliya. In August 1998, Shoshani was approached informally by representatives of the founding philanthropists to test his interest in heading the fledgling program that was to become Birthright Israel. Shoshani was intrigued.

Most of Shoshani's professional career had been spent working in Israeli educational settings; at the same time, Shoshani had a deep commitment to

Jewish education and identity worldwide. He understood the urgency for boldness in improving the education of Diaspora Jews. Although an Israeli through-and-through, he received his doctorate in education from the State University of New York at Buffalo. He had intimate contact with Jewish communities in North America and around the world and an educator's understanding of the needs of young adults. Shoshani was steeped in educational theory and was expert in theories of educational organization, system building, and innovation. His work as director-general of Israel's Ministry of Education and, later, at JAFI, had brought him in close contact with leading national and international educational figures.[1] Indeed, one of his unspoken dreams was to build a worldwide network of Jewish schools based on the best principles of educational innovation.[2]

When Charles Bronfman and Michael Steinhardt began in earnest to implement their vision for Birthright Israel, they relied on their own staff for advice on the educational vision. In Bronfman's case, several close advisers, including Jeffrey Solomon, president of the Andrea and Charles Bronfman Philanthropies, helped him hone his vision. Solomon is one of the American Jewish community's most respected senior professionals. He has a doctorate in social work and a long record of leadership of Jewish social service and communal organizations. Bronfman depended as well on Janet Aviad, the head of his Israel-based foundation (Karen Karev) and a former political science professor, and several Jerusalem-based educators.[3]

Michael Steinhardt had a similarly distinguished brain trust to call upon. The founding head of his New York–based foundation (Jewish Life Network) is Rabbi Irving (Yitz) Greenberg, one of the visionary leaders of American Judaism.[4] Greenberg has long worked on ways to educate Jews about their tradition and heritage; involvement in the creation of Birthright Israel was a natural extension of his earlier work. Steinhardt also had an Israel-based staffer, the late Shula Navon, who played a critical role as his "eyes and ears" in Israel.

Along with seeking the counsel of distinguished educators, scholars, and Jewish communal professionals, the founders also sought advice on organization and management. From the well-known American management consulting firm, McKinsey and Company, they solicited an analysis of program options. The resulting report offered only general recommendations; it did not provide concrete steps regarding how to actualize Birthright Israel. What was clear from the report, however, was that a leader was needed who could create a new organizational entity. This person would have to be someone who had experience working with Jewish organizations around the world *and* someone who could effectively maneuver his or her way through the intricacies of Israeli bureaucracy. Given these requirements, the list of suitable candidates was quite limited.

Shoshani was an obvious choice. He certainly had the requisite qualifications and experience; more importantly, he had a reputation for "getting the job done." In 1996, the State of Israel had given him national recognition by awarding him the David Rosolio Award for Public Service.[5] When Shoshani was approached by Steinhardt and Bronfman, he was not looking for a new position. His responsibilities at JAFI were broad, and he was more than satisfied with his position. Immediately, however, he understood that Birthright Israel had the potential to be a paramount project for the future of the Jewish people. He believed in the vision and relished challenges. In early 1999, he accepted the job and resigned from JAFI.

At Birthright Israel, Shoshani proceeded to create a nongovernmental organization that had the ability to work in both the public and private sectors. He recognized that an entirely new type of organization was needed. Shoshani was driven by his assessment that the organization needed to work with a range of stakeholders, including the Israeli government. He would have to balance the interests of Jewish organizations around the world with those of a group of philanthropists and a set of government agencies. World Jewish organizations had complex ways of doing business that were heavily dependent on consultative processes with lay and professional leaders. The philanthropists were entrepreneurs accustomed to getting things done their own way. Relationships with stakeholders notwithstanding, Birthright Israel also needed to be unconventional if it was going to attract large numbers of college-aged young adults who up until now had either been indifferent to or had avoided organized Jewish life.

Shoshani's practical seaman's sense of the task, tempered by his theoretical training, led him to organize Birthright Israel on a set of principles:

1. The organization itself would not run trips; instead, educational and logistic services would be outsourced to organizers and providers who would be required to meet detailed educational and logistical standards.
2. The core task of Birthright Israel would be to create a framework, including educational and logistical standards that would allow an open market to be developed.
3. The central organization would be compact and consist of a small staff of individuals with distinct skills (finance, education, marketing, public relations, organization, and administration). Additional expertise would be obtained by utilizing outside experts and advisers in critical areas (for example, legal publications).
4. The organization would function as an executive committee of key policymakers tasked with translating broad policy into action.

Shoshani's goal was to create a flexible, nonbureaucratic organization that could innovate and respond nimbly to challenges. He wanted to provide a new model of leadership for an educational venture that would engage world Jewry with Israel. His name and reputation as educator gave him a set of idiosyncrasy credits[6] that enabled him to create an innovative organizational structure. Shoshani had the skill to navigate the intricate sea of Israeli politics, bureaucracy, and law that was critical to obtain and sustain Israeli government support. His confidence, and his ability to deliver an educational product, also allowed him to gain the respect of the philanthropists and the cooperation of their staffs. Shoshani, despite his considerable experience leading public sector organizations, was neither an Israeli government bureaucrat nor a typical North American Jewish professional.

Partnering

When he began his job at Birthright Israel, Shoshani believed that he needed to develop an organization unlike others, and he was wary of following the McKinsey report recommendations. He recognized that the State of Israel would need to be a partner in the project and did not believe that an American-based consulting firm could appreciate the nature and complexity of that task. The Birthright Israel organization would need to operate as a public entity, subject to Israeli government standards, including detailed contracts, and elaborate documentation, and be sensitive to the ever-changing political environment. As much as the new organization needed flexibility, Birthright Israel could not be totally freewheeling.

Part of Shoshani's initial task was to convince the founding philanthropists of the importance of the government's role. At the point when Shoshani was hired, only five philanthropists had signed on, so only a fraction of the money necessary for the project had been raised. Even more problematic, the United Jewish Communities (UJC), which serves as the umbrella organization for Jewish community federations throughout North America, had raised serious reservations about the project's structure and implementation plan. Without adequate resources, it was not going to be possible to accomplish the task.

In addition, JAFI, which should have been a supporter, was initially opposed to the creation of a new entity. The leadership viewed the task of bringing Diaspora Jews to Israel as their exclusive domain and felt that Birthright Israel could undermine their programs. Yet, Shoshani reasoned, Birthright Israel needed resources and achieving the Israeli government's participation would demonstrate to philanthropists, as well as to Jewish communities around the world, that the project was important and worthy of support. Those Jewish organizations whose support was vital but who were currently uninterested might reconsider if the government endorsed the nascent effort and helped to fund the program.

Partnering with the Israeli government was not without drawbacks. Aside from nontrivial bureaucratic requirements, the political environment was volatile and there were a host of potential complications, even though the educational goals of the program were unassailable. Israeli politics is a contact sport, and the Birthright Israel organization would be very much in the public eye. Any politician who wanted to could stir things up or attempt to block the process. On a pragmatic level, if public money were involved, Birthright Israel's management would never be far from external scrutiny. Israel's government bureaucracy was highly centralized; even if the political path were clear, it would be a formidable task to receive and to implement a government contract to support the program. On the positive side, however, once an agreement was finalized, the government could be counted on to fulfill its promises.

The philanthropists, who were accustomed to quick results in their companies and private foundations, were not accustomed to the give-and-take of Israeli politics, nor of working under the degree of political scrutiny that would be required. Shoshani would have to educate the program's supporters and make clear that Birthright Israel, while nonbureaucratic, could not be run like an American nonprofit organization. It was an Israeli organization with different norms and constrainsts.

Shoshani began his educational effort by arranging a meeting between Michael Steinhardt and Israel's minister of finance, Avraham (Beiga) Shohat. He arranged a subsequent meeting with Israel's prime minister, Ehud Barak. But Barak's assent was not sufficient; the Israeli governmental system dictated a more complex, multistep process. An agreement would have to go through the Ministry of Finance, the Budget Division, the Knesset's Finance Committee, and finally back to the prime minister's office to be scrutinized by a legal team. Normally, such a process required two years. Shoshani's familiarity with the process, and his connections to key political figures enabled Birthright Israel to get a contract in the record time of only six months.

Staff

Shoshani's success was, in part, due to his own accomplishments as an educator and organizational expert. Nevertheless, he recognized that one of the keys to being an effective leader was having a highly competent and motivated staff. The small Israeli staff team he organized encompassed four spheres of activity. The first was financial. He needed a chief financial officer who could manage both government and nongovernment funds and whose integrity was beyond reproach. He selected a talented economist, Ehud Afek, who already worked for one of the sponsoring philanthropic foundations and had experience in a broad range of financial issues. As well, Afek had experience with both the Israeli government and Jewish life abroad. Shoshani's selection was a rigorously honest and strict CFO who, in his spare time, studied Jewish texts at one of the new institutes of study for secular Jews.

The second sphere was a chief operating officer (COO) whose job was to create the organizational structure for this heretofore nonexistent kind of operation. The COO position encompassed everything from negotiating with airlines over prices; arranging flights for thousands of participants; overseeing the implementation of standards and sanctions, office management; financial oversight, relations with trip organizers, and insurance. The first COO, Ze'ev Boneh, had been a senior officer in the IDF and worked with the Jewish community in the former Soviet Union. He created the structures and brought discipline to what could have been a chaotic organization. Later, Boneh waas succeeded by Meir Krauss, a senior Israeli educator. He was firmly rooted in Jewish traditional life, but equally at home in the world of secular education and Israeli realpolitik.

The third area was public relations and marketing—although, given Birthright Israel's mandate and structure, the position was more that of a "foreign minister." The responsibilities included recruitment, communication with philanthropists and partners, and public relations, both in Israel, and in the Diaspora communities that sent participants. Gidi Mark had been a talented Israeli diplomat. He decided that serving this cause was as significant as wearing formal ambassadorial garb and representing Israel in the world. His diplomatic skills would be useful as he helped to manage Birthright Israel's relations with supporters, skeptics, and the participants who were at the core of the organization's mission. Over time, he took on other roles.

The fourth area was education and the initial critical task of creating a program that had never existed before: a ten-day experience for young adults that was educationally rich, spoke to this age group, and that was fun. The educational tasks also included establishing a long-term research program; an oversight and evaluation process; and an ongoing in-service training program as well as personal connections with trip organizers. The incumbent in this area was a senior educational figure of one of the sponsoring foundations who was both a university academic in education and who had had decades of experience as an informal educator and expert in the Israel experience.[7]

Along with the core administrative areas, a variety of specialized skills were needed: legal, accounting, financial and fund-raising, event planning, and public relations. A variety of consultants were engaged to provide these services. Essential were the program's legal advisers, Tzali Reshef and Jonathan Shiff, who were involved in all aspects of the program and served both to protect the organization and ensure that it acted according to the highest ethical standards.

Another component of the organization requires special note: the North American offices and operations. Although an Israeli educational venture, most of the participants in the program were expected to be from North America. A New York office was established to handle communications with participants and financial issues, as well as liaise with Jewish organizations in the United States and Canada.[8] The New York office was administrated, almost from its inception, by a seasoned manager, Barbara Aronson. As the program evolved, perhaps the most critical job—vice president for operations—was assigned to a Canadian, Elizabeth Sokolsky. Working out of an office in Toronto, Sokolsky developed the registration system for North American participants and implemented eligibility standards for prospective participants. By 2006, the system Sokolsky oversaw was registering more than twenty-five thousand individuals per round of Birthright Israel trips and handling thousands of e-mail and telephone calls.

Two committees of experts oversaw the work of the staff. The Logistics Committee included representatives of the Israeli government, the Jewish Agency, philanthropists, and the public. The Education Committee included representatives of the government, JAFI, the UJC, worldwide Jewish communities, and leading Jewish educators. The Education Committee was chaired by Yitz Greenberg, as noted earlier, the head of Steinhardt's foundation and one of the early shapers of Birthright Israel. Both groups enabled the program to inform and receive feedback from key stakeholders.

STEERING COMMITTEE

Its nimble structure notwithstanding, from the beginning, Birthright Israel was a complex organization. Its leadership and staff were responsible to a board of directors representing diverse interests. The fiduciaries are organized as a steering committee that meets quarterly: twice a year in New York City and twice in Jerusalem. Chaired by a representative of the Israeli government, it has been co-chaired since its inception by the two founding philanthropists. The members of the Steering Committee include additional philanthropic funders, the government of Israel, and the Jewish communities.

Among the initial philanthropic members of the Steering Committee was a representative of Hadassah, the Women's Zionist Organization of America, Marlene Post. Hadassah is the largest American women's organization and was an early supporter of Birthright Israel. Post, a nurse by training and, when Birthright Israel began, at the end of her term as president of Hadassah, was an enthusiastic booster for the program. She argued, "by giving our youth a gift of Israel, we are enabling them to deepen their attachment to Judaism and seal an unwavering commitment to the Jewish people."[9]

The tone and focus of the Steering Committee was set early on. At one of the first meetings of the Steering Committee held in Jerusalem in early 2000, the mood was both upbeat and anxious. The group was elated because the program had been launched a few days earlier, and more than six thousand young Jewish adults were now in Israel, dispersed throughout the country from north to south, east to west. Despite early skepticism and resistance, their vision had received the support it needed. The committee was also pleased because Israel's minister of Diaspora and social affairs, Rabbi Michael Melchior, had announced a few months earlier that the State of Israel would contribute $70 million to the program over the next five years.

Although board members welcomed news of the successful launch, they were not complacent. The organizers had been working diligently on an agreement since the time of former Prime Minister Benjamin Netanyahu's administration, when the program was first conceived.[10] More worrisome, the overall five-year budget was $210 million, and they were still trying to put together an additional $140 million by recruiting additional philanthropists and soliciting funds from Jewish communities.

Charles Bronfman and Michael Steinhardt opened the meeting by thanking everyone who had worked so hard to make the launch happen. They asked Gidi Mark, the international director of marketing, to brief members of the steering committee about press coverage. He reported that the coverage had been extensive and positive. It was a welcome contrast with initial press coverage of the program, some of which had been scathingly critical of the fundamental plan (see chapter 1).

Initial opposition to Birthright Israel was not confined to critics in the United States. Some objected in Israel as well, even though eight hundred dollars would be spent locally for each participant, strengthening the economy. For example, a member of Knesset, Naomi Blumenthal of the Likud Party, was strongly opposed to the program. This was the first time in the history of the State of Israel that the country had allocated significant funds for a program to benefit Diaspora Jews; while she favored the effort in principle, she felt strongly that the money should be spent on Israelis. Said Blumenthal: "It is not imaginable that a youth from Kiryat Malachi can't go on a school trip because of a lack of money while Israel is willing to help finance a trip to Israel for a kid from Beverly Hills."[11]

Although a commitment had indeed been made by the State of Israel, the contract had not been signed, and only one million dollars had been paid. The board members asked for an update. Shimshon Shoshani explained that funds would be transferred once the contract was signed, probably in another two or three months. It had been a long process, and what they had been asking for was unprecedented in Israel's history. Finance ministry bureaucrats were holding things up, but supporters in the prime minister's office were working to remove the obstacles. Knesset Speaker Avraham Burg was especially supportive.

Discussion in the meeting focused on the program, but the financial issues hovered like the sword of Damocles over the proceedings. About three to four thousand young adults were expected to apply for the spring trips—would the government funds and money from the philanthropists be available in time? Seats needed to be reserved on El Al for the trips—did they have the money in hand to book the tickets? Philanthropists had made commitments to support the program—were they actually going to follow through with funds?

Discussion then turned to the contributions of Jewish communities. Shimshon Shoshani reported that there were no problems with funding from communities outside the United States, despite the fact that some were in a poor economic condition. The launch had included participants from India, Russia, and South American countries, in addition to the United States and Canada. There seemed to be no problem in funding further trips from outside North America.

Trips from North America were, however, in jeopardy because an agreement had had not yet been finalized with the UJC. Charles Bronfman, chairperson of the UJC board, discussed how local federations, particularly in the United States, were unhappy with the fact that participants were not paying any portion of the cost of their trips. Federation leaders insisted that participants make some type of financial commitment. It was a major point of contention because, from the point of view of Birthright Israel's founders, that insistence went against the program's fundamental idea: that it was every Jew's "birthright" to be able to visit and learn about his or her homeland. That ideology necessitated that the trip should be a gift—by definition, "free."

The situation was complicated because of the structure of the North American Jewish federations. Although UJC was their central body, local federations were autonomous, and each needed approval from its own board to contribute to the program. Some federation boards balked; as they viewed it, their local needs were pressing and, to some extent, they saw prospective Birthright Israel participants as the children of community members who did not contribute to the federation. Furthermore, the federations raised a host of jurisdictional issues. Who, for example, should be responsible for a New Yorker who attends college in Boston: the Boston Federation (Combined Jewish Philanthropies) or the New York Federation (UJA Federation of New York)? Whatever had been accomplished in creating the Birthright Israel organization, it was a skeleton structure and the details of program implementation were formidable. Much more had to be done to develop workable program policies that were acceptable to multiple stakeholders. Without such policies, securing funding so that one hundred thousand participants could visit Israel over the next five years would remain a dream.

Although the rationale for the organizational and educational approach taken by Birthright Israel was well explicated, it was unconventional. As described earlier, it was a novel approach to Israel experience programs and Jewish education. Perhaps it was not surprising then that the Jewish establishment found it threatening. The structure denied any one establishment group a key decision-making role. If Birthright Israel were successful, critics of these organizations would have additional ammunition about the establishment's inabilty to reach the next generation of Jews. Both of the central organizations responsible for the Jewish community—UJC and JAFI—while they later became partners, were initially opposed to the program.

Even some in the federation orbit who believed in the idea of Birthright Israel were miffed at the implementation process. They felt that their interests and goodwill were not taken seriously and that they were being "bulldozed" rather than being brought on board as true partners. At a meeting between federation executives and lay leaders with Charles Bronfman in the second year of the program (and in the midst of the intifada), the issue of the problematic partnership was raised by a lay leader. Bronfman was quick to accept responsibility for moving hastily and without thorough consultation with federations. He said that he was genuinely apologetic. But Bronfman asked, "In light of the intifada, would the program ever have been started if we had not done so?" The room was silent.

That Birthright Israel would be under Israeli government oversight dictated the parameters of how the trip organizers would be selected. It would have to be an open process and subject to multiple levels of review. The Birthright Israel organization was sophisticated in dealing with government agencies, and they recognized that outsourcing had potential legal liability. Because public money was involved, any aspiring trip provider could sue Birthright Israel if it felt that it did not have a fair chance to submit a proposal. Thus, a great deal of effort was expended in setting stringent educational and logistical standards, which were then scrutinized by legal advisers.

The document outlining these standards was unprecedented in its level of detail. There were obvious areas in which standards were set: types of sites to be visited, concepts to be discussed, qualifications of trip staff, and lodging requirements. There were also requirements for the mundane: contents of first aid kits, size and material of the signs on buses, dessert choices at meals, ownership of weapons carried by armed escorts. There was even a regulation that specified the quantity of soup to be provided each participant at meals.

Probably the most important organizational decision made by the Birthright Israel leadership was to, in effect, subcontract the running of trips to more than twenty-five trip organizers. Despite Shoshani's experience at JAFI and its track record of bringing thousands of young Jews to Israel, he did not necessarily want to replicate existing patterns. He was concerned that the denominational groups that dominated marketing of most existing programs could not attract broader audiences. He recognized that prior efforts to bring young people to Israel had largely focused on those who were already positively involved in Jewish life and Israel. The target population for Birthright Israel, however, was different. They were those who were unaffiliated, unengaged, and currently unconnected to the Jewish community. Another model would be needed to attract those were relatively uneducated Jewishly and only decided to travel to Israel because the trip was free.

This redirection resulted in Birthright Israel organizing itself out of the responsibility for planning itineraries, arranging for food and lodging, contracting for buses, hiring and managing tour educators, or doing any of the other operational tasks involved in leading a group around Israel. Rather, it would remain behind the scenes, setting policy, determining educational content, establishing standards, and engaging in budgeting and planning. Recruitment would be the responsibility of trip organizers; the trips themselves would be conducted by qualified educational organizations from North America and Israel willing to adhere to Birthright Israel's standards. Organizers would have to apply to Birthright Israel for authority to recruit and run trips.

Outsourcing solved two potential problems related to Birthright Israel's structure. First, outsourcing would minimize overhead and eliminate the need for a large implementation staff. Second, by offering applicants a range of trip choices, Birthright Israel would attract a broader range of participants, including those who did not have contact with traditional Jewish educational and communal organizations. The more trip choices available for applicants, and the more groups recruiting participants, the more likely it was that applicants would learn about trips—and—in turn, the more likely that they would find a match with a trip provider.

Once the initial "tender" (request for proposals) was publicized, 175 organizations applied to be trip providers. To ensure fairness in the review process, Birthright Israel staff did not do the actual evaluation. This task was outsourced to a consulting firm that had helped to articulate and formulate the standards. There were no legal complaints from any of the applying organizations. Nearly seventy applications were accepted; in the end, approximately forty organizations were authorized to recruit participants. The organizers ranged in size from groups that ran dozens of buses in any given round (Hillel International; Oranim tours) to those that ran fewer than a dozen (Kesher [the Reform movement] and Sachlav) to those that ran only a few (one to three) each round (JCCA [Jewish Community Centers Association] and SPNI [Society for the Protection of Nature in Israel]). The applicants varied in terms of whether they were nonprofits (for example, International March of the Living) or private sector organizations (for example, Tlalim, Israel Outdoors!), whether they were part of a religious group or movement (for example, KOACH, a college outreach arm of the Conservative movement), and whether they had a specific focus (for example, Shorashim, which emphasized mifgashim with Israeli peers). Interestingly, the heretofore largest purveyors of Israel youth travel in the 1980s and 1990s—the denominations and national educational organizations—were among the smallest of the Birthright Israel trip organizers.

Organizational theories notwithstanding, the outsourcing strategy could not have succeeded had Birthright Israel not attracted knowledgeable and dedicated educational leaders. In fact, their success in doing so seems the critical, albeit less visible, outcome of the structure that evolved. The directors of these trip organizations are a diverse and extraordinary group. They differ from one another in background, personality, and ideology. Some are seasoned formal educators with a passion for teaching about Israel, while others are informal educators experienced in dealing with Israeli and overseas youth trips. Some are part of large nonprofit organizations, while others are private tour company directors who have an educational or ideological commitment—and who recognize a potentially profitable market. Some of these trip organizers are essentially administrators who have little day-to-day contact with the trips or with participants. Others are "hands-on" figures who meet every group.

There is the dignified rabbi invariably dressed neatly in a suit who speaks with a gentle voice and exudes openness. There is the vivacious director of Hillel activities who combines great efficiency with a religious sensibility, and the passion of one who has settled in Israel and is still enthralled by it all. There is the charismatic mother of three who has committed her life to the mifgash (shared experiencing) of Jewish peoplehood by Israelis and young people from abroad; this woman is a combination of a caring social worker and a Hebrew language–obsessed Eliezer Ben Yehuda.[12] Then, there is the clean-shaven Canadian who runs a massive organization but remains accessible to every group and participant. And there is the tall Philadelphia-born cowboy-American who immigrated to Israel at age fifteen and has devoted his life to sharing the land and its people, in the hope that it will speak to others as it spoke to him. Directors are not with participants every day, and they do not have the direct impact of their staff. But they set the tone and are the conduit between Birthright Israel and the programs on the ground. Several are people whose name or messages shape hundreds and thousands of participants.

Momo

As each participant on an Oranim trip makes his or her way from the passport control booth through the gate to baggage claim at Ben-Gurion Airport, they are greeted by a booming "Welcome home." The voice belongs to Momo (nickname for Shlomo) Lifshitz, forty-something and burly. It does not take much imagination to see him as a tank commander—his former military occupation—and some of those he welcomes may feel that they are being inducted into his army. Momo is the founder and president of Oranim Educational Initiatives, a for-profit educational travel organization based in Kfar Saba. Oranim is a licensed travel agency that, for many years before Birthright Israel, ran educational touring programs for North American youth.

When Birthright Israel opened the process for organizations to apply to conduct trips, it required them to document their capacity to meet the battery of educational and logistical standards. Oranim applied, was accepted, and very shortly became one of the largest Birthright Israel trip providers. Oranim was successful because of an aggressive and innovative marketing plan, its use of Oranim alumni to recruit, a pioneering approach toward program packaging, its ability to reach out to markets beyond North America, and its use of nonconventional selling techniques.

Some have been amazed at Oranim's success and others, including its tour organizer competitors, have questioned the ability of for-profit travel agencies to provide serious educational programming. The organization's ability to recruit staff-educators, provide trips that are more than fun, and be dedicated to an educational credo have been challenged. One result is that Oranim has been under substantial scrutiny, including close monitoring by Birthright Israel regarding the degree to which their trips meet the educational and logistical standards. Oranim has been successful in fulfilling all educational and logistic requirements and has successfully demonstrated that its mixture of fun and Zionist education meets the program's standards. Its ability to do so validates not only the program's methodology, but Shoshani's open-market approach.

Key to Oranim's success is its founder, Momo. He is the living definition of a "hands-on" trip organizer. By 2004, Momo was bringing an average of fifty to sixty buses (two to three thousand participants) per Birthright Israel cycle. Along with his airport greeting, he meets personally with every group at least twice: a middle-of-the-trip meeting and a summary discussion. The discussions are not the American style of group processing; rather, they are done

Momo-style. One does not speak in a relaxed manner with Momo; instead, one waits for that brief moment when there is an opportunity to interject a comment or question. Momo passionately challenges, provides vision, and invites, even demands, reactions. His main declamations revolve around the centrality of being Jewish; the centrality of Israel to being Jewish, the need to commit oneself. Without even a hint of immodesty, his mantra calls for participation in "the Momo Revolution." The underlying theme is quite simple: love of Israel and infatuation with being Jewish.

Momo is a sabra; his father came to Israel as a young child in 1921. A discussion of Momo's background consists in part of personal biography but also much about the development of the State of Israel. He describes with passion what it was like to grow up in the shadow of the Holocaust, knowing that his life was a direct result of his grandparents' decision to leave Europe. Momo grew up in Tel Aviv and his adult life was shaped by his army service. He entered just after the Yom Kippur War and served as an officer. As Momo describes it, "getting leadership experience in combat" prepared him to do almost anything. He was an officer during the 1980s conflict in Lebanon and he quipped that he got to know "Beirut better than Boston."

Although the CEO of a large organization, Momo is known for the personal way in which he deals with everyone. His "pelephone" (mobile phone) is attached to him, almost like an umbilical cord, and it rings constantly—whether he is in Israel or abroad, whether it is daytime or night. Often, when trips are under way, he spends considerable time talking with parents or participants. Even though some of the questions he fields seem silly to an observer (one parent called to ask if her child could "plant a tree in Israel"), he treats each call as if it were of utmost importance. He is direct, in the way you might expect from a military officer, but it is not a cold, officious presentation. To the contrary, his warmth, indeed love, comes through with each of his loud, impassioned reactions.

Almost as soon as each trip season ends, Momo is on an airplane to North America and beyond to meet with alumni and encourage them to recruit participants for future trips. Like his "in your face" bearing as a super–tour leader, so too do his recruiting efforts display his unique approach. Frequently, he will rent out the hottest discotheque in a community and, along with food and music, will offer his message of Jewish engagement and commitment to Israel. Many times, the participants in these outreach efforts are his alumni. As he "sells" new particpants on Israel and participation in Birthright Israel, he works his alumni, encouraging them to come back to live or study in Israel. Like a great politician, he seems to have a mental Rolodex of people and programs—and each person is greeted as if he/she were a child that had only briefly been away from home.

Joe Perlov

Perlov is tall, has a deep voice, and easily goes back and forth between his native English and fast-spoken Hebrew. Like many of his tour operator colleagues, Joe has a standard "costume": jeans, a blue short-sleeve polo shirt, and a leather cowboy hat. One might think he was dressing up as a kibbutznik—which he *was* for fifteen years. But today he is an educator and a politically savvy trip organizer. Perlov is founder and director of Israel Experts, Inc., an independent educational tour company. He established the company in 1999, just before the launch of Birthright Israel. Perlov is from Philadelphia and came to Israel in 1970 at the age of fifteen. He has lived in Israel ever since. Until 1985, he was a kibbutznik; then, for three years he was *shaliach* (emissary) in the United Kingdom. For the next seven years, he headed the B'nai Brith Youth Organization (BBYO) in Israel. Although there is no question that he is an entrepreneur, like his fellow organizer Momo, Joe is an educator whose heart, soul, and life have been about the meaning and place of Israel in the lives of Jews—from wherever they live.

When asked, Perlov has a ready description of Israel Experts, Inc. The organization, he explains, "is about contemporary Israel. It is about a modern state rooted in a history and a culture. I want to show that Israel is not a museum, even though it is linked to great legacies of the past, but a living entity." Thus, it is no surprise that Israel Experts advertises itself—and creates programs—aimed at outdoor, contemporary Israel, and bicycling. In short, Perlov presents Israel as a very modern, dynamic state.

Although he did not create Israel Experts specifically to work with Birthright Israel, Perlov was involved in the program from its inception. Initially, he was skeptical about whether Birthright Israel would work. Perlov was not sure that a program of the scale envisioned by its founders could be successful, and he did not believe that a short-term program—ten days, compared to the six to eight weeks that were the norm for high school trips—could have the kind of impact envisioned by its founders. But the "massiveness" of the program's vision appealed to him, and he was attracted by the fact that the program targeted young adults, rather than adolescents. He committed his company to involvement with Birthright Israel, but viewed the venture as highly risky.

When talking with Perlov, one sees that the Israeli part of his identity clearly trumps his American roots. He is very direct and, when asked, is very clear about how his view of Birthright Israel changed. He explains, "I was proven wrong. . . . Ten days can make a difference. Ten days with this age group can be like thirty days with high school participants. This is a different youth culture—and one that is primed and ripe for what ten rich days in an exciting twenty-first century country has to offer." He also admits he was wrong in doubting the program's viability; Birthright Israel proved to be a significant business opportunity for him. By 2005, it was 50 percent of his total business and preoccupied him more and more. It is an endeavor that matters to him.

Given his entrepreneurial spirit, one wonders how Perlov views Birthright Israel as an organization. A brief conversation with him makes clear that he has strong views; one suspects that he would chafe at having to follow standards created by others. Somewhat surprisingly, his comments about Birthright Israel's structure are a veritable psalm of praise. His simple answer to a question about the organization is:

> The system works. The organization works. It is run by professionals who know what they are doing. In fact, I'm amazed that so few people can manage such a huge system. In the beginning it was tough to figure out how to deal with the system, but it became a workable, easy, accountable system—better than any I have worked with. It fulfills its commitments and it is good—finally—to have educational and logistical standards in this field . . . Actually, Birthright Israel has created a twenty-first century framework that is not "business as usual" and its organizational structure has forced me to be a better organizer and educator in my other programs. It has changed the way this field works, only for the better.

Perlov uses the kind of straight, concise, clear, and analytical language that suggests he has legal training. Joe Perlov is a lovely person who can also be *dugri* (very direct), "telling it like it is." His praise is all the more impressive as a result.

Of course, Perlov adds, no organization is worry-free and each has its own *mishegas* (crazy elements). In the case of Birthright Israel, he thinks that the organization is obsessed with branding: from the size of the letters that go on banners for every bus, to the placement of the tag line, to the color of shirts that are given to participants. He quotes sociologist Erving Goffman: "It [Birthright Israel] is very concerned with its presentation of self in everyday life."[13] But however demanding those requirements are, Perlov maintains his perspective. He believes that the oversight team and its work are very important and that its results are important for his staff—even when he cannot see the correlation between what they claim to see and the conclusions that they draw. Regardless, he believes that they are asking important questions. His "biggest gripe" with Birthright Israel has to do with oversight of recruitment processes. He likes competition, but he thinks that the ethics and sense of propriety concerning other issues should extend to recruiting. Gripes notwithstanding, this former Philadelphian is one of Birthright Israel's staunchest advocates.

Perlov, although his background is unique, is typical of many who work as part of the Birthright Israel program. He participates in the program not only because doing so constitutes a profitable occupation, but also because of his commitment to the goals. In a conversation about the future, Perlov makes clear that he wants to be part of the program for the long term. In his own words, "it enables me to educate. And from age fifteen, I was, am, and always wanted to be an educator. Birthright Israel lets me do it. It lets me do it because it's not simply big words but it has created an alternative to the usual way business in this field has been done—politics, long delays, and amateurism. Birthright Israel shows that education and business can work." Perlov doesn't use the word "blessed," but even to a nonreligious person, that seems an apt description of how he views his work experiences.

Rabbi Shlomo Gestetner

If there is a contrast in presentation and style to Momo Lifshiz and Joe Perlov, it is Rabbi Shlomo Gestetner. He is the director of Mayanot, one of the Birthright Israel tour organizers since the program's inception. In the program's first five years, it brought nearly twenty-five thousand participants on Birthright Israel trips. Although Mayanot is an independent organization, it is affiliated with the worldwide Lubavitcher-Chabad movement, a Hasidic movement, with headquarters in Brooklyn, New York.

Rabbi Gestetner dresses in a stylish black suit; even on a hot July day in Jerusalem, his only deference to the weather is a slightly loosened tie. He has a trimmed beard and a modest kippah; if one looked closely, one would probably catch a glimpse of *tzizit* (the four fringes that traditional Jews wear under their shirts). He radiates calm, gentleness, and ease. Although dressed the part of an aloof cleric, Rabbi Gestetner is highly approachable. He personifies the Hebrew phrase *"ish eshkolot"* (a man of virtue and grace).

Shlomo Gestetner was born in Australia to an observant Hungarian immigrant family. At age sixteen, he began attending the yeshiva day school in Melbourne, a secondary school affiliated with the Chabad movement. Since then, he has been associated with, and a leader of, Chabad education abroad and in Israel. He also directs the Mayanot School, has a congregation in the Nachlaot section of Jerusalem, and flies abroad regularly to fund-raise on behalf of his organization. Nevertheless, Rabbi Gestetner participates in some way in all Mayanot trips while they are in Israel. He has a large family and, typical of his Chabad colleagues, a very supportive wife.

To talk with Shlomo Gestetner is to enter into the middle of a long, perhaps never-ending discussion, about the large and small issues of life. One moment, conversation may be focused on the classic magnum opus of Chabad Hasidism—the *Tanya*—but, then, almost imperceptibly, the focus shifts to a discussion about education or life. It is not difficult to engage him in a conversation about Birthright Israel. He starts by saying that he was involved well before the program became Birthright Israel. He explains that one of Mayanot's missions is to reach out to young adults who are at a crossroads in their lives and excite them about Israel and about being Jewish. Like the program's founders, he believes that the eighteen to twenty-six age group is critical. He loves working with the participants and tells anyone who asks that "Birthright Israel made the work that was at the heart of my life possible."

In 1995, Rabbi Gestetner created a program called "Israel Express," a ten-day educational seminar program in Israel for college students and young adults. He took groups of ten, twenty, and thirty people to experience Israel and their Jewishness. Birthright Israel enabled him to implement, on a large scale, what was the core of his work. One hears a similar story from many Birthright Israel trip organizers. Aharon Botzer founded Livnot U'lehibanot in 1981 and since then has regularly conducted powerful educational experiences in Israel for postcollege young adults. Anne Lanski created Shorashim in 1983 and since then has devoted her life to bringing teens and young adults on Israel experiences rooted in the mifgash between Israelis and youth from abroad. Dovi Paritsky, general director of Yeladim-Netivot has been involved for many years, initially as a shaliach to South Africa, Australia, and North America. The Conservative and Reform movements have been conducting Israel educational programs (mostly for high schoolers but also for young adults) since the 1950s. Although Birthright Israel did not create the vision of educational trips to Israel, its funding and organizational vision enabled it to scale up what others had been trying to accomplish in this area.

Gestetner's take on the skeptic's question "Can ten days make a difference?" is instructive. As he often does in conversation, he refers to teachings of the late Lubavitcher Rebbe Schneerson. For emphasis, he pulls a book called *Challenge,* published in 1965, out of his bag. He excitedly points to a quote ascribed to the late Rebbe: "every day that goes by is a tremendous loss [for Jewish involvement]. What it takes ten years to do in the Diaspora can be done in ten days in the Land of Israel." Gestetner firmly believes that ten days can make a huge difference. He echoes the findings of the evaluation research team that indicated the ten days are indeed transformative: they create a new beginning for unaffiliated Jews and are like "sun and water that enable a flower to blossom" for the already connected. Parenthetically, and again referring to the Rebbe, he rejects the term "unaffiliated." "All Jews are affiliated," he says, "but they need to be recharged so that the inherent *nitzoz* [spark of Godliness] can emerge."

One of the interesting, albeit controversial, aspects of Mayanot's involvement in Birthright Israel, is the organization's focus on "those in need of re-

charging," the "least affiliated," in normal parlance. Some suspect that Mayanot's trips are about missionizing and cultism—that their aim is to turn these
unaffiliated young people into Orthodox Jews. Gestetner, when asked, responds warmly and firmly that they are not missionaries, are not trying to
convert, and are not trying to turn Conservative, Reform, and "just Jewish"
Jews into Orthodox or Lubavitchers. He tells the questioner, "We want to
touch their souls, we want to bring them closer to Israel and the Jewish
people, and we want to move them up a Jewish ladder." Indeed, Gestetner is
quite clear in distancing himself from the word *kiruv* (to bring closer), which
is the term sometimes used to describe outreach efforts to make Jews more
observant.[14] The one issue that Gestetner says is primary to Mayanot is the
"fight against intermarriage," one of the most serious problems faced by the
Jewish community.

Given his particular brand of Jewish universalism, how are Mayanot's trips
different than others? From Gestetner's modest perspective, he sees more
similarities than differences. Because of Birthright Israel, curriculum standards ensure that all groups visit the same set of places. What he thinks
Mayanot does differently is to raise spiritual issues—not, he explains, to "im-
pose our answers, but to raise questions." The educators pose a number of
questions: What is the meaning of God, Israel, and Judaism? What are Jewish
values? Mayanot's trips differ from others in that their leaders try to create
unique Shabbat experiences, particularly for those who have not observed rituals in the past. Gestetner's groups go to the Kotel on Friday night and learn
Shabbat songs. Mayanot leaders "suggest" Shabbat morning synagogue options. In his warm but firm way, Gestetner points out that no one is forced to
attend religious services and, in fact, most sleep in. But his group leaders
arrange for participants to have Shabbat lunch at homes with observant families so that participants can experience the beauty of Shabbat and breathe
what Gestetner calls "Shabbat oxygen."

Like Perlov, Gestetner only has praise for the Birthright Israel organization.
From the philanthropists (whom he regards as "great people") to the Birthright Israel staff (whom he touts for their dedication and diligence), he is uniformly positive. He states the obvious: "In the 'olden' days, every one made
Shabbos for themselves [each provider had all the responsibility]. We were always concerned for safety, we never slept when we had overseas participants
here, and we sought good food and places to sleep." He appreciates Birthright
Israel's commitment to these principles and sharing the burden of these
efforts. At the same time, he wishes that there were not quite so many bureaucratic requirements. The logistics have been particularly difficult for his organization, given that none of his staff travel on Shabbat or holidays. He wishes
that he could devote more resources to the program rather than to Birthright

Israel mandates. There's a hint of resentment at the time he spends on administration, although he does not really complain. That would be inconsistent with who he is. Rather, he describes the issues simply as part of life. Birthright Israel turned a labor of love into a professional field. At the same time, it made a labor of love a huge labor—and sometimes a term of servitude.

Nevertheless, there is no question that Rabbi Gestetner will continue to be a partner with Birthright Israel. As he explains, "Birthright Israel is only part of Mayanot and my life, but it is central. I want to be part of it forever. I want more and more and more seats [on planes]. How many more will I get? I want more seats because I believe that this is one of the most important Jewish educational ventures there is. More seats will be more forms. More forms will be more staff. More staff means I have to raise more money. But I want more seats."

Hillel

As noted, Birthright Israel trips are actually conducted by organizers, represented by the organizations that are run by Momo, Joe Perlov, and Shlomo Gestetner, as well twenty other groups. Organizers recruit their own participants in diverse ways. Over the years, Hillel International has been one of the largest Birthright Israel trip organizers. Hillel has a physical presence on more than one hundred college and university campuses in North America. Typically, it has a building (Beit Hillel), a staff (rabbis, adminstrators), and an elaborate network of student-run activities. Its mission is to serve Jewish college students and is the central address for Jewish life on campuses.[15]

Before the program began, one model proposed was that Hillel be the sole sponsor. But that was rejected in favor of an open-market approach. The concern was that Hillel only attracted a minority of the Jewish students on campus and that other organizations might be able to engage other segments of the community. For some, Hillel is associated with religious Judaism, and the program wanted in particular to engage those who were not religiously involved.

According to both of Hillel's leaders, Joel and Infeld, Birthright Israel was not only a gift for the participants, but for Hillel. It gave campus organizations a highly attractive program capable of engaging students who might otherwise not step over their threshold. From its headquarters in Washington and its Jerusalem office, staff such as Esther Abramowitz, Arye Furst, and Keith Kravitsky provided key support and oversight. In practice, Hillel established a different relationship between staff and students. As one student told interviewers after participating in a trip led by her campus rabbi, "Spending two weeks with my rabbi—who wore jeans—made me realize that I could talk with rabbis and that they understood me."

Hillel sees the trip as part of its engagement efforts and one element of a set of interactions. Thus, Hillel trips do not start and end at the airport. Instead, staff meet with students in advance to brief them on what to expect, facilitate the building of a group, and prepare them for longer-term engagement with Hillel. One or more campus staff accompany each trip. The theory is that these staff members will be able to maintain a connection with students once they return. Hillel trips are also are run somewhat differently. Regardless of who provides the logistic support for the trips (Hillel uses several providers), they all include several structured conversations on core themes that are critical to Hillel. Indeed, Hillel is exquisitively sensitive to its constituency. Because formal education is a part of Hillel's culture, it can use traditional didactic techniques, as well as informal educational programs to engage its participants intellectually.

In the early phases of Birthright Israel, Hillel-sponsored buses were mostly homogenous; that is, most participants on the bus came from the same campus. In recent years, this has changed and campuses are often mixed (usually, with those in geographic proximity); in addition, Hillel runs "theme" trips (for example, those that focus on outdoors). As a result, Hillel's trips are now more like those of other organizers that draw their participants from multiple campuses. Also, Hillel's rabbinic staff members are currently less likely to join trips. How these changes in the trip structure have affected participants is difficut to discern at this point; we may not yet have sufficient historical distance. As Infeld notes, the "wow" factor is so great—regardless of the specific factors on any trip—that it is hard to detect the impact of these variables. Perhaps the most interesting question is how Birthright Israel affects Jewish life on campus and the evolution of Hillel.

THE BEST OF PUBLIC AND PRIVATE ORGANIZATIONS

The Taglit–Birthright Israel organization created by Shimshon Shoshani, and implemented by a diverse array of passionate educators and entrepreneurs seems unique in the educational world. In some ways, it is like a public educational agency (ministry) with a set of formal rules and a headquarters that does not try to run the programs in the field. In other ways, however, it is like an entrepreneurial organization. It has changed and adapted as conditions have changed and exhibits far more elasticity than one would expect from a government body. It has faced almost constant financial pressure, as well as pressure from both local and worldwide terrorism.

That Birthright Israel, in its first eight years, successfully brought more than 150,000 young adults to Israel for ten-day educational tours is evidence of the organization's effectiveness. Yet, like balancing the financial books, just bringing participants to Israel is not in itself enough. Some of the answers to questions about the effectiveness of Birthright Israel in terms of its goals are suggested in the next chapter, which details evaluative research studies of Birthright Israel participants.

8

Participants and Evaluation

*Among the intellectual virtues are science, which is the knowledge
of proximate and ultimate causes, which one must investigate
if one is to know anything.*
—Maimonides

In fall 1999, two months before the first group of Birthright Israel
participants began their journey, a presentation was made in the boardroom
of the Andrea and Charles Bronfman Philanthropies on Park Avenue in New
York City. Researchers from Brandeis University presented a proposal to conduct an evaluation study of the nascent program.[1] Their audience included
the co-founders of the program along with nearly a dozen professional staff
members from the philanthropists' foundations and the newly organized
Birthright Israel. The Brandeis research team made clear that they thought
that the program idea was important and demanded a rigorous evaluation. It
presented a unique opportunity to study the development of Jewish identity
among young adults as well.

The researchers proposed an evaluation of the impact of the program on
participants. This evaluation of satisfaction with the program would have
two key elements. First, that impact would be measured not simply while the
program was under way, but also after participants returned home (a minimum of three to six months after they were in Israel). Second, they argued
that the study should focus on a comparison between individuals who participated in the program with those who did not.

Initially, the research proposal garnered a cool response. Several participants in the meeting were concerned that the effects would not be apparent
until months after the program. Critical comments, however, centered on the
comparison group design. Charles Bronfman, the cautious corporate leader
and investor asked, "Why should I put my money into studying people
who *don't* go on the program that I'm funding?" Michael Steinhardt, the risk-
taker, asked an even more charged question: "Isn't it likely that the proposed

[experimental] design will make it more difficult to show that the program is effective? Why should I invest in finding out that the program may not work?"

The researchers' responses were quick: indeed, the design was rigorous and the comparative postprogram evaluation lowered the probability of finding significant effects that could be attributed to Birthright Israel. But, one of the researchers pointedly asked Steinhardt, "If you are going to invest millions of dollars in this program, don't you want to have an accurate answer as to whether the investment was worthwhile? Why shouldn't interventions in the Jewish world be assessed with the same rigor that medical and, indeed, educational experiments are evaluated?" The researcher continued, in response to Bronfman's question, "Although the comparison subjects would serve as a 'control group,' in the context of Birthright Israel, those who do not go on the program at one point in time are your target audience for subsequent trips." The focus of the evaluation design was not merely to provide ammunition that the program could use to promote itself, but to develop answers to fundamental questions about whether the program had achieved its objectives. The evaluation was to be an independent investigation that used state-of-the-art methods to produce convincing answers.

As a result of the presentation in New York that fall, Birthright Israel awarded a contract to the Cohen Center of Brandeis University; evaluation was launched that has continued for more than seven years.[2] The evaluation has focused on a quantitative assessment, using what researchers call a quasi-experimental design;[3] it has also included field-based observations that allow investigators to see the program from the inside and link outcomes to processes. By 2007, more than a hundred thousand Birthright Israel participants and applicants to the program from North America have been surveyed[4]—before the program, and at intervals ranging from three months to four years after the program. Nearly one hundred groups have been the focus of participant observations, typically involving researchers (trained undergraduate and graduate students, as well as senior researchers) who join a group for an entire ten-day experience.[5] In addition, observations have been conducted at Birthright Israel sites and events. The surveys have been reported in nearly a dozen reports, and more than one hundred presentations.

Overall, the evaluation research conducted to assess Birthright Israel paints an extremely positive and consistent portrait. Throughout Birthright Israel's first six years—and independent of the changing conditions in Israel—participants returned home changed as a result of their experience. Responses to the program, itself, were almost uniformly positive: the experience was seen by virtually all of its participants as educational, fun, and meaningful. Furthermore, on virtually every comparative measure (partici-

pants compared to nonparticipants), program alumni had more positive attitudes about Israel, their Jewish identities, and about being part of *Klal Yisrael*
(community of Israel). The impact seemed to last over time; no matter
whether evaluations were conducted three months or a year or more after the
program, similar results were found. The key qualifier to these positive effects
is that the attitudinal changes produced by the program were not matched by
the level of behavioral changes. That is, effects of the program on actual engagement in Jewish life were far more modest than the attitudes expressed by
participants.

In considering the evaluation findings, the estimates of program impact
are relatively conservative. Although the focus of the program was on the least
engaged, the pool of Birthright Israel applicants—including both those who
did and did not eventually participate—has consistently represented a more
highly engaged group of young adults. Applicants and participants were likely
engaged more highly both in terms of their interest in Israel and their Jewish
identity. In a 2004–2005 study of American Jewish college students, for example, only 34 percent indicated a strong connection with Israel and at least
25 percent regularly participated in religious services.[6] As described below,
Birthright Israel applicants, at least up to 2007, report somewhat stronger
connections regardless of participation in the program. Thus, by comparing
Birthright Israel participants and applicant nonparticipants, the study challenges Birthright Israel to increase the Jewish engagement of many who are already, relatively at least, among the more highly engaged. This may change,
however, as the program expands and is able to provide the experience to a
wider group. Thus, for example, in 2007 the program was able to offer trips to
more than 30,000 participants (a nearly 50 percent increase from 2006).

2006 FOLLOW-UP EVALUATIONS

In June 2006, Birthright Israel marked an important milestone when the
100,000th participant—a twenty-six-year-old New York woman, Stephanie
Lowenthal—arrived in Israel (see chapter 10). As part of an assessment of the
program as it reached its initial target of program participants, nearly three
thousand North American Birthright Israel alumni and another one thousand nonparticipant applicants were surveyed and interviewed. The respondents for this phase of the evaluation came from cohorts that had applied to /
traveled with the program between 2002 and 2005. The goal was to conduct
an assessment of the impact of Birthright Israel on North American Jewish
young adults, not just in the short term, but in terms of the degree to which it
had affected participants' trajectories of engagement. Given the goals of the

program, the focus was on the program's impact on individuals' attachment to Israel, the Jewish community, and the Jewish people. The overall aim was to understand whether, and how, program participants were affected by the program.

Those sampled as part of the 2006 evaluation were drawn from three cohorts: Winter 2002–03, Winter 2003–04, and Summer 2005. In all cases, prior data about the individuals who were surveyed were compared; for participants, in particular, their experience on a Birthright Israel trip was part of the comparison. In the "oldest" cohorts, comparable data were taken from surveys conducted before and shortly after the trip. For the Summer 2005 cohort, the new data were compared with evaluations that the participants had completed at the end of their trips.

Similar to results from earlier surveys of Birthright Israel participants, the findings of the 2006 study are dramatic in the extent to which they yield consistently positive evaluations. Alumni from all three cohorts report strongly favorable recollections of their Birthright Israel experience. Interestingly, reviews of the program are as unequivocally positive for those who were participants more than three years ago as they are for participants last summer. Furthermore, participants are nearly unanimous in regarding their Birthright Israel experience as fostering their connection to Israel and to their Jewish identity. For many, the experience is a catalyst for engaging on a Jewish journey—to see themselves as part of the Jewish community, to be interested in Israel, and for some, to involve themselves in Jewish study.

THE BIRTHRIGHT ISRAEL EXPERIENCE

The 2006 evaluation data make clear that Birthright Israel alumni remain extremely enthusiastic about their experiences, even several years after they return home. As shown in figure 1, which summarizes evaluation data from the three cohorts, the vast majority of respondents recall the trip as fun and meaningful and as a highly educational and spiritual experience. In almost all cases, shortly after the trip and even several years later, respondents use the most positive choice on the scale (very much) to describe their reactions. A measure of participants' enthusiasm is that they become the program's most important recruiters; almost all "talk up" Birthright Israel with friends and relatives, encouraging them to participate.

Early skeptics about Birthright Israel, once they realized that it was highly popular, attributed the program's success to the fact that it offers a "fun vacation" for free. Given the security situation in Israel during recent years, this explanation might seem, on its face, implausible. The evaluation data support

FIGURE 1

Overall Evaluation of the Trip: Percent Responding "Very Much"

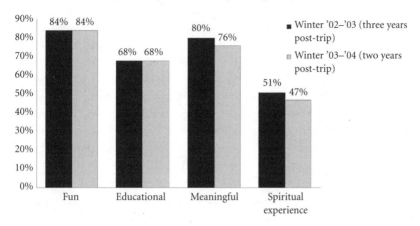

this view. With the perspective of one, two, and three years, only 16 to 20 percent of program alumni describe the trip as mostly a "fun vacation" (see figure 2). In contrast, between 38 and 46 percent described the experience as mostly about Jewish peoplehood ("A group Jewish experience"). The next largest group, between 30 and 34 percent of alumni, described the experience in terms

FIGURE 2

Meaning of the Trip

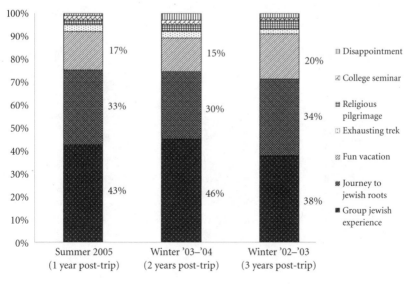

of their individual Jewish journeys ("A journey to my Jewish roots"). Thus, for the vast majority of Birthright Israel participants, the experience is not primarily about "fun"; rather, it is about much more serious engagement with their Jewishness. That the program is fun is not unimportant, but it likely explains more about how it achieves its goals than about its achievements.

The central mission of Birthright Israel is to cultivate Jewish identity and attachment to Israel and the Jewish people. The program was established to pursue these goals both as ends in themselves, and as steps toward promoting Jewish continuity. As found in each of the prior Birthright Israel evaluation studies, the strongest single attitudinal effect of the experience is on participants' sense of connection to Israel. Across all three cohorts surveyed in 2006, participants were significantly more likely than nonparticipants to indicate a strong attachment to Israel (see figure 3). These differences are obtained even two and three years after the trip for the earlier cohorts that include nonparticipants who have subsequently visited Israel—although not on a Birthright Israel program. The uniformity of the responses is striking, although (as one would expect) the most recent cohort shows the strongest connection.

Participants are also more likely than their counterparts who applied to the program but did not participate, to indicate a strong sense of connection to the Jewish people (see figure 4). Again, the pattern is identical across cohorts, although the strongest connection level of peoplehood connection is evidenced by the more recent cohort.

FIGURE 3

Jewish Identity: Connection to Israel. Percent Responding "Very Much/ To a Great Extent"

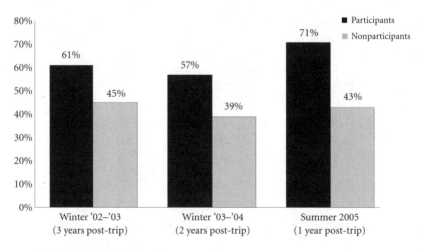

FIGURE 4

Jewish Identity: Connection to the Jewish People. Percent Responding "Very Much/To a Great Extent"

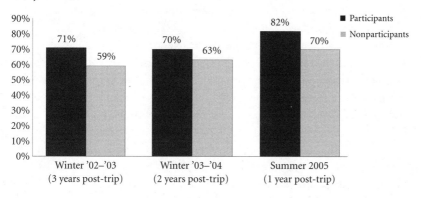

The evaluation also assessed behavioral measures of participants' Jewish identity and ties to the community. One set of questions inquires about marriage and family decision-making. The results indicate that program alumni, compared to nonalumni participants, report a greater commitment to marrying and to raising future children as Jewish (see figure 5). The differences between participants and nonparticipants are very large.

FIGURE 5

Jewish Continuity: Raising Jewish Children. Percent Responding "Very Much/To a Great Extent"

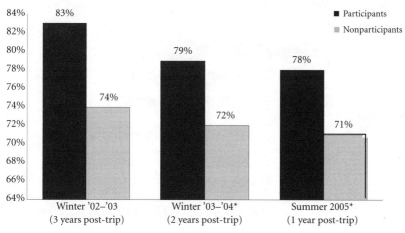

*$p < 0$

As an educational program, Birthright Israel seeks to reach program participants both cognitively and affectively; it aspires to teach young Jews about the history, culture, and social mores of contemporary Israel, and to cultivate attachments to the Jewish community, Israel, and the Jewish people (see chapter 4). As described earlier, the program seeks to expose participants to a broad range of views about Israel and to provide a balanced perspective about modern Israel. The broader context for this vision is the increasingly politicized and polemical quality of information about Israel in the participants' home contexts.[7] How well does Birthright Israel teach about modern Israel? One set of answers to this question contains participants' evaluations of their learning.

Beginning in 2005, participants were asked about the degree to which they learned about a number of specific areas concerned with the modern state of Israel—from social problems and conflicts to culture and natural environment. Overall, participants reported high levels of learning (see figure 6), but there were differences. Participants felt that they learned more about Israel's culture and environment as compared to learning about social problems and the Arab-Israeli conflict. It is difficult to know whether the complexity and fluidity of the social problems and the Palestinian conflict made it more difficult for respondents to feel that they learned as much, or whether those are areas to which the program needs to devote more attention.

The evaluation (for the 2005 cohort) also assessed learning about Israel by

FIGURE 6

Learning: Participants Evaluation. Percent Responding "Very Much/ To a Great Extent"

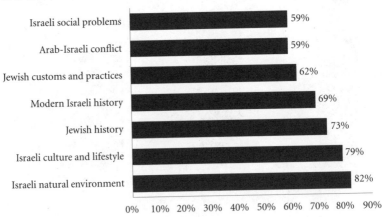

FIGURE 7

I think of Israel as a . . .

Israel Education: Democracy and Multiculturalism. Percent Responding "Strongly Agree"

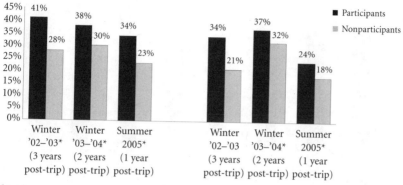

■ Participants
▨ Nonparticipants

| | Winter '02–'03* (3 years post-trip) | Winter '03–'04* (2 years post-trip) | Summer 2005* (1 year post-trip) | | Winter '02–'03 (3 years post-trip) | Winter '03–'04* (2 years post-trip) | Summer 2005* (1 year post-trip) |

*p < 0

asking participants and nonparticipants about their views of Israel. There is no objectively correct way to answer any of these questions—about Israel as a democracy, as a technology center, as a society in conflict—but a comparison of the participants and nonparticipants helps explicate how Birthright Israel affects judgments of the society. Without exception, following the program, participants perceive Israel in more positive terms than do nonparticipants. Thus, for example, participants are more likely than their counterparts who did not go to perceive Israel as a "lively democratic society" and a "multicultural society" (see figure 7). Participants are also more likely than their nonparticipant peers to perceive Israel as a "refuge for the Jewish people" and a "technological powerhouse" (see figure 8). It should be noted that the comparison group consists of individuals who applied to go on a Birthright Israel trip; in many cases, these individuals will eventually participate in the program. They are, most likely, predisposed to be positive.

A similar pattern is evident when one examines endorsement of statements describing Israel unfavorably (see figure 9). For those who traveled in the Summer 2005 program, participants are less likely than nonparticipants to view Israel as strife-ridden, militaristic, or religiously fundamentalist. In the earlier cohorts, participants and nonparticipants differed in their "positive" images of Israel (as noted above) but not necessarily in their endorsement of "unfavorable" images. To the extent that rosier images of Israel come closer to the truth, Birthright Israel appears to be succeeding remarkably well.

Analysis of the responses to the evaluation survey indicate that Birthright

Participants and Evaluation 145

FIGURE 8

I think of Israel as a . . .
Israel Education: Refuge and Technological Powerhouse. Percent Responding
"Strongly Agree"

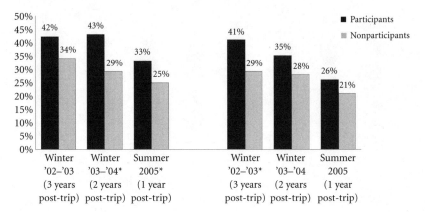

*p < 0

FIGURE 9

I think of Israel as a . . .
Israel Education: Unfavorable Images (Summer 2005). Percent Responding
"Strongly Agree"

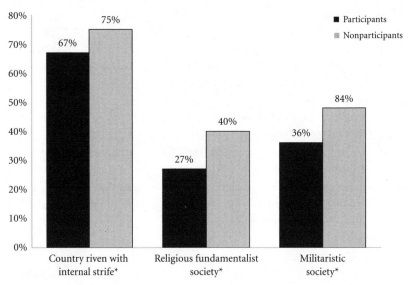

*p < 0

FIGURE 10

I think of Israel as a. . . . Percent Responding "Strongly Agree"

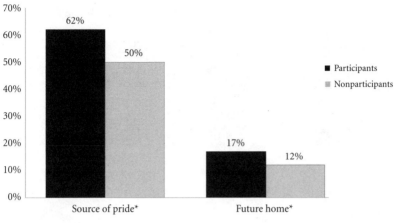

*p < 0

Israel participants become more positive in their views of Israel as a result of their exposure to Israel, to Israelis, and through the opportunity to learn about the country beyond the headlines reported about the Arab-Israeli conflict. But it is also clear that they develop an emotional attachment. Thus, for example, birthright alumni are more likely to feel strongly that Israel is a source of pride (see figure 10). Also, while it's probably unrealistic that many will chose to live in Israel, participants are also significantly more likely to consider Israel as a possible future home.

JEWISH ENGAGEMENT AFTER BIRTHRIGHT ISRAEL

Evaluation data consistently show dramatic attitudinal changes as a result of program participation; nevertheless, initial evaluation studies (in 2002 and 2004) reported only weak or ambiguous behavioral effects of the trip. The 2004 report concluded, for example, that "the trip has little effect on ethical behavior, religious behavior, or participation in organized Jewish life." As described below, this picture has become somewhat more complex, with specific behavioral impacts increasingly evident. As in these earlier studies, the 2006 survey found no consistent evidence of differences between participants and nonparticipants in Jewish activities in the community. However, with regard to on-campus involvement, the findings of the 2006 surveys depart substantially from those reported in the past.

FIGURE 11

Participation in Hillel. Percent Responding "3 Times or More in Past Year"

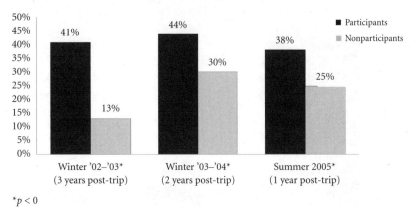

*p < 0

There is consistent evidence from the 2006 surveys that Birthright Israel catalyzed increased involvement in on-campus Jewish activities. Responses to the surveys indicate that current students who were participants are more likely than nonparticipant students to join in Jewish and Israel-related activities on campus. The finding was obtained across all cohorts (see figures 11 and 12). Particularly noteworthy is that the differences in results are largest for the 2002–03 cohort. If they are still on campus, they were freshmen or sophomores at the time of participation. Perhaps they were more highly mo-

FIGURE 12

Participation in Israel-Related Activities on Campus. Percent Responding "3 Times or More in Past Year"

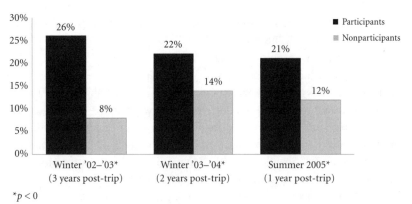

*p < 0

tivated (leading them to go early in their college career and at a time when Israel was considered unsafe), but they also had more time to engage in Jewish life on campus. It suggests that the impact of the program is magnified by being in an environment that allows the group lessons of the program to be followed through.

These findings about participation in Hillel and Israel activities on campus provide validation for the program theory that, as an identity-building experience, it alters young adults' trajectory of involvement with the community. The key question, of course, is whether this involvement continues post-college and in an environment where it may be more difficult (and *will* be more costly) to participate in communal events.

UNDERSTANDING BIRTHRIGHT ISRAEL

Evaluation studies are research studies, but have the specific goal of being designed to aid decision-making. The essence of evaluation is to understand, not merely to document, the impact of the program.[8] It is important to know whether or not the program has had impact, but it is also important to try to understand the nature of that impact on Birthright Israel's alumni. Specifically in the case of Birthright Israel, how is it that a ten-day program makes such a lasting impression? The 2006 surveys asked clusters of questions about three key dimensions of the trip experience: the tour guide/educator (madrich), the tour group, and the mifgash with Israeli peers.

As described earlier (chapter 4), tour guides convey the major themes that constitute Birthright Israel's core curriculum. They are educators but, like Udi and Francis, they are not dispassionate about their subject matter. Much of our observational data suggests that the program's success depends heavily on the way in which these educators conduct themselves and share their knowledge. Our hypothesis is that guides play a powerful role, not only because they are responsible for framing the experience, but also because they model the love of land and people that is at the core of Birthright Israel's message.

Our observations also make clear that even when guides make errors, ignore teachable moments, and present material in unbalanced ways, the impact of the trip does not necessarily suffer. Participants acknowledge that their guide was sometimes ineffective but say that it did not affect the trip experience overall. The second key is the tour group itself. Although the group climate is not disconnected from the skill of the guide, if the group is good, the experience is good. Previous research stressing the importance of the "group experience" has argued that tour groups serve as a proxy for the Jewish people as a whole. Thus, being part of a group is an essential part of the experience of learning about Israel, learning about one's Jewish heritage, and feeling a connection with the Jewish people.

A third element of Birthright Israel programs—the mifgashim—has come to distinguish it as a heritage educational experience, enabling it to succeed with participants who vary widely in their backgrounds, their knowledge, and their motivation. As described earlier (see chapter 5), the encounter with Israeli peers, in most cases soldiers, is a profound experience for participants. No matter how well the madrich models love of Israel and Klal Yisrael, no matter how much they enjoy being part of a group, peer role models provide a unique way for participants to identify with Israel and the Jewish people. The mifgash experience enables participants to see themselves in the mirror: to imagine what they would be like if, at least metaphorically, their grandparents had ended up in Tel Aviv rather than New York City.

The roles of these program elements were assessed as part of the later evaluation surveys. Analysis of the survey results from the 2005 cohort showed participants' responses to questions about each of these program components to be highly correlated. The individual questions were therefore combined into scales. As summarized in figure 13, respondents' evaluations of guides, group experience, and mifgash fell between the two most positive ratings. Only the average for the scale "Personal bus experience"—a measure of the individual respondent's personal sense of connection to others on the bus—was slightly lower. Thus, on the whole, trip participants reported strongly favorable feelings about their guides, groups, and mifgash. We conclude, then, that these elements are the cornerstones of a successful Birthright Israel experience.

FIGURE 13
Understanding Success (Summer 2005)

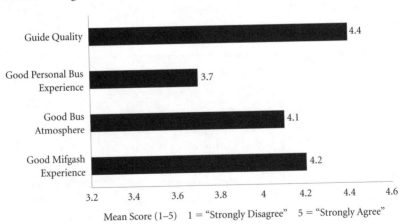

150 *Ten Days of Birthright Israel*

For the future, the central question is whether the impact of the program is sustained or ephemeral. It would not be surprising if the impact of the program deteriorated over time and if participants came to look more and more like nonparticipants. This result would be especially likely if participants fail to engage themselves with the Jewish community, return to Israel, seek out Jewish education, and maintain friendships built on their Birthright Israel trip. The alternative hypothesis is that the Birthright Israel experience is a milestone on a journey and fundamentally alters the participant's trajectory of Jewish involvement.

In some respects, the data can be interpreted to support both possibilities. Thus, there is some tendency for the impact of the trip to deteriorate over time. Although the 2006 study only provides three points of comparison (see figure 14), on the measure that assessed feelings of connection to Israel, the strongest differences between participants and nonparticipants appear in the period three to four months after the trip (Time 2). In the most recent survey, two to three years after the trip (Time 3), the difference between participants and nonparticipant respondents has narrowed. The implication is that, for some dimensions of the Birthright Israel experience, effects persist but diminish in robustness over time. A similar pattern, although not so pronounced, is observed for another measure: connection to the Jewish people (see figure 15).

It is difficult to know if these effects reflect "regression to the mean" (that is, the natural tendency for differences to attrit to the average) or whether it

FIGURE 14

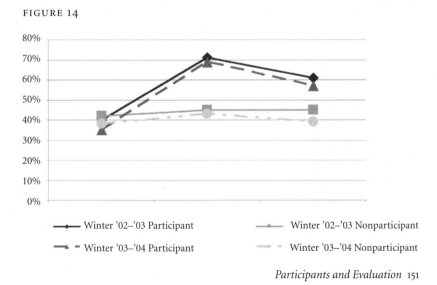

- Winter '02–'03 Participant
- Winter '02–'03 Nonparticipant
- Winter '03–'04 Participant
- Winter '03–'04 Nonparticipant

FIGURE 15

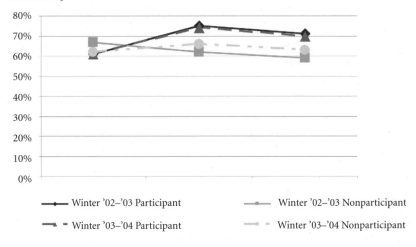

reflects some other factors. Thus, for example, at the time of the survey (spring 2006) Israel was the focus of negative publicity in the United States.[9] But there may also be a methodological issue. Over time (the three administrations of the survey), it became more difficult to locate and engage nonparticipants in the survey. The differences may be due to the fact that the willing nonparticipant respondents are more engaged than those who are unwilling to respond. Nevertheless, even with the observed diminution of effect, there remain statistically significant differences between participants and nonparticipants even two to three years after their trip.

As one implication, the long-term impact of the program is dynamic and, methodological issues aside, it is difficult to assess such effects without assessing the kinds of follow-up programming available to participants. The data from college participants who took part in birthright early in their campus careers suggest that, when post-programs are easily accessible, the impact will be cumulative. Whether that works with older participants is, however, hard to know at this point.

The survey data on participation in follow-up activities suggests that most participants, particularly those who are post-college, have not yet found a Jewish community in which to participate. The survey assessed whether alumni participate in activities sponsored by Birthright Israel or tour providers. In both cases, more than 80 percent of trip alumni (from the Summer 2005 cohort) report no participation in such activities, while 10 percent report having participated once. More than half of trip alumni (55 percent), however, report having been invited by the Birthright Israel Alumni Association to join in an activity. The impact of the program is likely to be different if participation rates increase. One suspects that participation in these activities depends both on participants and the quality of available programs.

The size of the alumni group is a potential further issue. As noted earlier, a large number of applicants are not being served by the program.[10] Although the size of the waiting list is relevant for the scope of the future program, it is also the case that increasing the number served has implications beyond the reach of the program. If the waiting list were reduced, it would likely magnify the impact of the program. Participants who return to communities with a much larger cohort of fellow participants are more likely to find Jewish peers with whom they have much in common and therefore have the social network foundation necessary for creating strong Jewish communities.

SUMMING UP

The focus of the Birthright Israel evaluation—in line with the program goals—was to capture the impact of the program on Jewish identity, continuity, learning, and engagement. On most measures, the findings are stable over time for particular individuals, consistent across the three cohorts—and impressive. In relation to both attitudes and behaviors, feelings and actions, Birthright Israel alumni are clearly different from their peers who applied to the program but did not go on a trip. Specifically, the evaluation documents that

- participants have a stronger connection to Israel, the Jewish people, and their Jewish identity
- participants are more likely to want to marry and to raise their children Jewish
- participants evince a greater understanding of Israeli society and history
- participants are more directly involved in Jewish activities on their college campuses

By comparing the responses of Birthright Israel participants to applicant nonparticipants, the study design sets an especially high hurdle for establishing program effects. The group of applicant nonparticipants is already "primed"—by their contemplation of participation and their execution of an application—to think in relatively positive terms about Israel and their Jewish identities. In addition, the nonparticipants who responded to the request to participate in follow-up surveys, though indistinguishable in terms of background characteristics from other nonparticipants, might very well hold distinctively positive feelings about Israel and their Jewishness. Estimates of program effects deriving from comparisons between participants and nonparticipants are, thus, conservative.

Along with assessing impact, we also examined the reasons for Birthright Israel's success. Our data indicate that program participants consistently provide high rankings to three program components: the tour guide, the bus community, and the mifgash with Israeli peers. The guides, their bus group, and interaction with Israeli peers provide the emotional and intellectual momentum behind the Birthright Israel experience. Taken as a whole, they help to explain how a relatively short experience can make such a striking difference in the lives of its alumni.

What challenges and opportunities for Birthright Israel lie on the horizon? Two specific challenges are obvious. First, although attitudinal effects of the Birthright Israel experience show surprisingly strong durability, there is evidence that for some specific types of impact the effect deteriorates over time. Second, whether or not the program achieves its distal goals may depend on whether or not compelling post-trip activities can be created for alumni who are diverse in age, background, and geography. There is no question that Birthright Israel touches souls and triggers a broad range of positive responses. Whether it is stimulus for a change in the trajectory of Jewish involvement, or just a wonderful experience, is explored further in the next chapter.

Participants' Voices

9

An individual is a person, when and because he knows himself as such;
a group is a people, when and because it knows itself as such.
—Mordechai Kaplan

It does not rain during the summer in Israel, but in the midst of the July heat of 2006—from Kyriat Shmona at the most northern tip of the country, to the coastal city of Haifa, to the Tiberias, along the Sea of Galilee—Israel experienced daily missile showers delivered by Hezbollah guerillas in Lebanon. By the time a mid-August cease-fire was arranged and United Nations' forces were poised to enter Lebanon, nearly 50 Israeli civilians had been killed, along with 119 Israeli soldiers and more than 1,100 Lebanese. No calculus can be performed to equate the killing of human beings with the destruction of property, but along with deaths and injuries, the thousands of Katusha rockets that were fired at Israel were returned by an even greater number of bombs delivered by the Israeli air force. The bombs wreaked physical havoc and immeasurable grief in both countries.

When Hezbollah initiated the violence by a cross-border raid to kidnap two Israeli soldiers on July 12, 2006, only a small number of Birthright Israel groups were in Israel. Very few of the groups were close to the northern border and only a handful of participants were scheduled to arrive in what remained of the summer. The war, nevertheless, had important implications for Birthright Israel and its participants. For the program, the war raised a new set of concerns about participants' physical safety and the program's responsibilities. More profoundly, the war affected participants' sense of their relationship to Israel. Undoubtedly, the experience of being inside Israel—however close one was to the missle attacks—was far different than the experience outside of the country. But at least for some program alumni, the sense of Jewish peoplehood that the program fostered linked them to the issues being faced by Israelis. Birthright Israel is a pilgrimage to a land with deep symbolic meaning for participants,[1] and the war was a reminder of how alumni were connected. That Israel was threatened, and that Diaspora Jewry had a direct connection to the events, enhanced the purely educational and ethnic-identity goals of the program.

Although the 2006 Lebanon War may have only intensified existing beliefs and feelings, the threat to Israel underscored the importance of Diaspora Jewry's involvement with the Jewish homeland. One theme of Birthright Israel is that the long history of the Jewish people, having roots that span more than three thousand years, included a host of challenges. Jewish history is replete with threats to Jewish existence: from the escape from slavery in Egypt, to the destruction of the Temple and exile to Bablyonia, to the Spanish Inquisition, to the Nazi Holocaust. The narratives of these events are one key element of Jewish education, and Birthright Israel educators unabashedly reinforce their meaning by connecting these historical events to the Land of Israel that participants experience. Many Birthright Israel participants come away believing that the establishment and flourishing of the modern State of Israel in Judaism's ancient homeland is nothing short of "amazing." As madrichim often emphasize, it is up to participants to decide what role they want to play in assuring Israel's future. Such attitudes provide an unsubtle reminder that Israeli Jews have a different set of obligations than Jews from the Diaspora.

The events of the summer of 2006 brought Jewish insecurity into sharp relief for Birthright Israel participants; indeed, the war was deeply distressing to Jews around the world. Although the calm that pervaded the border and northern area throughout 2007 has diminished the intensity of the distress, the threat posed by the missile attacks seemed at the time to have long-term impact. Inflammatory rhetoric and calls for Israel's destruction have long been a feature of Middle East discourse,[2] but few believed that Israel could not repel any attack. Israel, after all, is one of the most advanced technological societies in the world and has one of the most modern, battle-tested, and effective armies. Prior to the summer of 2006, Israel's military was seen as near-invincible. The events of 2006 suggested a crack in this invincibility, even as the war reinforced views of Israel's awesome military power. The war did bring into sharp relief debates about how to achieve peace. Although only the perspective of history will enable one to determine whether or not 2006 marked a turning point in Israeli history—in parallel with the cataclysmic events of 1956, 1967, and 1973—it has undoubtedly affected perceptions of Israel, including how Israel is seen by Diaspora Jewry.

UNDERSTANDING THE WAR'S IMPACT

Birthright Israel alumni have a unique perspective on the events of the summer of 2007, with important implications for their ongoing involvement with the Jewish community and Israel. Will the threat to Israel's security reinforce the importance of the Diaspora's support, or will the danger push them away? Will the Diaspora Jews who participated in Birthright Israel see themselves as having a stake in how Israel deals with the Arab world? Will they see Israel as central to their Jewish identities? And, perhaps even more important, will Birthright Israel alumni become unabashed advocates for Israel, knowledgable critics, or simply distant observers?

There were obvious signs that the 2006 war had profound effects on Birthright Israel participants—not just those in the country during the summer that missiles fell in the north of Israel, but on all of the alumni. One understanding of the impact of the war is suggested by the evaluation data discussed in chapter 8. The data indicate that Birthright Israel alumni have a very different understanding of Israel than their peers. They are much more likely than those who do not participate in Birthright Israel to think about Israel as a democracy and multicultural state; at the same time, they are less likely to see it as a militaristic and religious fundamentalist society.

ASSESSING REACTIONS TO THE WAR

At the end of the summer of 2006, the Cohen Center at Brandeis undertook an assessment of reactions to the war among U.S. college students, Birthright Israel alumni, and others.[3] Although the study was not designed to evaluate and undertand Birthright Israel per se, understanding the reactions of American young adults to the 2006 Lebanon War is useful in assessing the long-term impact of the program. The study attempted to understand how Jewish college students viewed Israel during and after the war: in particular, the study compared those who participated in Birthright Israel and similar programs, with those who had not traveled to Israel on a peer program. Data were gathered through online surveys of Birthright Israel participants, and applicants to the program who had not participated, along with a sample of Jewish students at three large universities in the United States.

The survey included questions about how respondents monitored the summer's events, their attitudes to Israel, Hezbollah, the Palestinians, and their view of current events in general. The goal was to try to understand how the program, and knowledge of Israel, affected attitudes. In general, the responses from Birthright Israel participants (along with other alumni of Israel experience programs) stood in sharp contrast to the responses of and those who had not been to Israel. The differences persisted even when the study controlled statistically for differences in background between the groups.

One difference, which perhaps underlies other findings, is that those who had traveled to Israel on a peer educational program[4] tended to obtain their information about the war from different sources than those who had not been on an Israel educational program. Although all of the survey respondents paid attention to the U.S. electronic media (in particular, CNN and the major network news programs), those who had been to Israel on a peer program also paid attention to Israeli media. Nearly half of the Israel program alumni indicated that, during the Lebanon War, they sought news on a daily basis from Israeli media outlets, including English versions of Israeli newspapers available on-line (*Haaretz, Yediot Achranot,* and the *Jerusalem Post*). Alumni were also more likely to have gotten information directly (e-mail and telephone) from Israeli peers and even educators that they met on their trips. Overall, having visited Israel on a peer educational program was significantly related to greater motivation and activity in seeking news about the conflict.[5]

The impact of an Israel experience was also evident regarding views of Israel's conduct in the context of the war. A number of items on the survey, which were elements of a construct labeled, "Israel was justified," showed significant differences between those who had been to Israel and those who had not. The items included such questions as, "Israel strived to minimize civilian deaths" and "Israel was wrong to target roads, bridges and the airport in Lebanon." Not surprisingly, those who had been on a trip were more likely to view Israel's conduct as more justified. The trip effect was manifest independently of general political orientation or specific views on the future of the West Bank. That said, respondents' political orientation also shaped responses to the war, above and beyond a high baseline level of support for Israel's position. Those who described themselves as politically conservative (linked with opposition to dismantling of Jewish settlements in the West Bank) were more likely to believe that Israel was fully justified in its war-related conduct.

Learning about the respondents' level of interest in and support for Israel is important. It is also important, however, to learn how and to what extent their interest and feelings were translated into action. One would expect that Birthright Israel alumni have connections to organizations and individuals that enable them to put their attitudes into action, much more so than those who have not been on an Israel educational program. The survey assessed several dimensions of actions respondents might have taken in response to the war, including attending lectures about the conflict, contributing money to Israel, and attending meetings or rallies about the war. Having visited Israel on a peer program such as Birthright Israel was, as expected, significantly related to engaging in action. Other factors, such as age and Jewish denomination, were also related to taking action (younger, Orthodox respondents were more likely to report engagement), but participation in an Israel program had an independent effect.

The bottom line in terms of reactions to the war is that the Birthright Israel experience appeared to give participants a different perspective on the situation, perhaps fueled by their ability to get information from Israeli sources. Program alumni were motivated and had connections with Israel and Israelis that enabled them to understand the war, as it unfolded, differently than did college students who did not have their experience. Although other factors, including gender, age, and Jewish education background were influential with respect to one or another of these responses to the war, only visiting Israel on a peer program—primarily, Birthright Israel—was consistently influential across the full range of responses.

The impact of Birthright Israel, although not unexpected, is all the more remarkable against a backdrop of heightened concern among most respondents to the survey. Indeed, the overall level of attachment, engagement, and support among those who had not been to Israel was quite high. Previous research assessing the overall American Jewish community suggests that support for Israel peaks during periods when Israel is perceived to be under threat.[6] The war between Israel and Hezbollah during the summer of 2006 was clearly an example of such a threat, much like the missile attack from Iran during 1991. The high overall level of concern and support for Israel expressed by the majority of all respondents was, thus, to be expected. But the fact that Israel program alumni were obtaining information directly from Israel and were more likely than their counterparts to have acted in support of Israel, is of particular note. It suggests the contours of a different relationship between Diaspora and Israeli Jews over time.

One might say, simply, that travel to Israel is stimulating; the findings described in this chapter, however, point to something potentially more significant. This population acquires what might be described as a new "data and affect processing system" vis-à-vis Israel. Because of a combination of factors—the age of the participants, the central role of Israelis, the specifics of the program content, the emphasis on personal and group processing—participants learn a new style or methodology of accessing and processing facts and attitudes toward Israel. CNN and newspaper headlines now became replaced by logging on to Israeli newspapers on the Internet or by e-mailing Israelis on one's trip. Within the short span of ten days, Birthright Israel participants began to acquire the skill to understand and process information about Israel differently. The ten-day trip did not simply show them Israel; it gave them a skill, a predisposition, and a frame for interpreting Israel events upon their return home. The experience of summer 2006, in particular, suggests that Birthright Israel participants did not just go home with pictures of Israel; they also went home with the new skill of holding a different "camera" and "lens" through which interpret subsequent Israel events. If this finding is true, it points to a potentially revolutionary way of educating people in how to interpret Israeli dynamics.

One question about the impact of Birthright Israel on reactions to the war is how the program's short—ten-day—duration affects attitudes and behavior. Do longer programs change attitudes more effectively? Although most of the respondents to the survey were, in fact, Birthright Israel alumni, there were a considerable number who had attended longer-term programs, including study abroad at a university, volunteer programs, and yeshiva study. Respondents who attended both Birthright Israel and long-term programs were assigned to the latter category. Although one would expect that longer programs would be likely to produce stronger effects, the results indicate that on several key parameters there were no systematic differences between those who had participated in Birthright Israel and those who had spent significantly more time in Israel. Common sense and anecdotal evidence suggest that longer-term programs create different kinds of experiences. It would be simplistic to suggest that Birthright Israel is the definitive and singular model of israel experience for the twenty-first century. Indeed, the nuanced differences among diverse kinds of trips offer an important arena of study in the years to come.

HOW DOES ISRAEL AFFECT PARTICIPANTS?

The lingering question underlying our assessment of the outcomes of Birthright Israel participants is, how can a brief program produce so much change? And why is its impact felt in similar ways among individuals from vastly different backgrounds and motivations for participation? The consistency of reactions and their stability over time seem remarkable in the context of an educational program. Only time will tell if the program fundamentally alters how Diaspora Jewry relate to Israel and their Jewish identity, but it is already clear that profound changes were produced by the program.

At this point, we can only hypothesize about the mechanisms of program impact, but an important set of clues is provided by what participants say as they prepare to leave Israel. We have already described some of the scenes as participants take leave of their group at the airport (see chapter 6). The airport experience is invariably emotional, but perhaps more telling is the closing *sicha* (discussion), a feature of all trips. The format of the closing discussion gives participants a chance to reflect on their ten days. What is evident, as will be described below, is that the the Birthright Israel experience gives participants new language and a new way of thinking of themselves. It is transformative, because it enables highly thoughtful young adults to reframe how they think of themselves in relationship to others.

We have observed dozens of these closing sessions and, although they vary,

depending on the trip organizer and the educators, the responses of participants are remarkably consistent. The experience seems to overwhelm group,
and even individual, differences. Described below are two such sessions, conducted in 2007 at the end of two different trips with Canadian participants.[7]

Hotel Conference Room

The sicha is held at a hotel outside Jerusalem, close to the main highway to
the airport. The sicha is run at night, after the group spent their last exhaust-
ing day in Jerusalem. Shortly after the session, they head to their overnight
flight home. The group of nearly forty young adults from Canada, five Israeli
soldiers, their Israeli madrich, and Canadian staff have assembled in a hotel
conference room. The room is just large enough to hold all of the members of
the group, but small enough so that it feels very intimate. The members of the
group are clearly exhausted, but they are as attentive as if they are awaiting instructions on final examination.

Among the first to speak are several young male college students. Each describes his upbringing in a Jewish household, the prerequisite Hebrew
schools, and the bar mitzvah. But, as each one describes his life as a college
student, he notes that Jewishness was not a central identity—until he participated on Birthright Israel. One, in a comment that is echoed by others, discusses how his experience today at the Har Herzl brought it "together" for
him. His group had been guided by a staffer who discussed his brother, lost in
a military operation and buried at the cemetery. Although hearing such a
story might be expected to make the distance between Diaspora and Israeli
Jews seem even greater, it had the opposite effect on these participants. The
mechanism was simply to make history personal—less about events and
more about families and relationships.

The sense of personal connection is reinforced by several of the next participants to speak. One, also a college student, shares that although her prior
Jewish experiences had been positive, it took participation in the program
over the last ten days to make clear to her how important her Jewish identity
is and how close she feels to Israel. It is, she declares, the chance to get to know
her fellow Birthright Israel participants and the opportunity to meet
soldiers—peers who are very much like her, but carry the additional responsibility of protecting "our" country. Her closing declaration summarizes what
others had tried to say less articulately: "I came [to Israel] knowing that I was
Jewish. I leave knowing what that means." Participation in an experiential
educational program appears to make ideas about identity concrete and
seems to be mediated by personal connections.

The group's educator is a presence throughout the discussion, alternately
thanking those who speak for their comments and encouraging them to elab-

orate. Relationship issues form a substrate of the conversation and there is occasional banter about those who had formed couples. As tired as the participants seem to be, the discussion never flags, and more than half of the group speak. The reaction part of the agenda continues for more than an hour.

Most of the participants who speak are typical of North American Jewish young adults, alumni of Hebrew schools, and participants in typical ways in their community. But these factors are not universal. One participant is a young man who says that he had never considered himself Jewish. His mother is Asian and, due to his appearance, others considered him non-Jewish. He knew about Judaism, but Birthright Israel had opened him up to what it meant to be part of the Jewish community. He proudly reveals his Magen David (Star of David) pendant and says that he now sees himself as a Jew. It is clearly difficult for him to speak about his newly acquired identity; in some ways, it is easier to display it with a pendant than to talk about it. The group clearly has had a powerful influence on him, and their full acceptance of him made his Birthright Israel experience life-changing.

Perhaps at the opposite end of the continuum to that participant are two women who were born or had lived in Israel. Both have Israeli parents who left Israel for jobs abroad when they were very young. They describe how exciting it is to return to Israel with a group of peers, but also how scary. They speak about how meaningful it is to see Israel through the eyes of people who are the same, save for where they live. One of the young women ends by saying, "I know that I am home. I'm not sure yet how I am going to return or what I am going to do, but I know that this is where I belong." Clearly, the idea of returning to Israel is something on the minds of both of these participants. The Birthright Israel experience had allowed them to test their interest.

The closing comments from participants come from soldiers. The officer begins by saying that he was charged with speaking on behalf of all of the soldiers. The educator interrupts and asks him to speak for himself. For some reason, it's difficult for the officer to do so, but when he arrives at his substantive comments, he discusses how incredible the experience had been. He reveals that he did not realize until now how much he had in common with his Diaspora kin, and notably, that the program has helped him understand why he serves as a soldier for Israel. Knowing that he is protecting the Jewish people and helping to ensure that the Jewish life continues has given meaning and purpose to the last four years of his life. For the soldiers, like the participants from North America, participation in Birthright Israel has made concrete and palpable something that they knew but had not felt. By the time the session comes to a close, the group is emotionally spent and clearly in need of time to recharge before they go to the airport.

What the closing sicha demonstrates is that Birthright Israel achieves its aims by making identity and abstract concepts of peoplehood concrete and personal. Being with a group of peers for ten days—eating, sleeping, studying, talking together—creates an experience that may not be easily duplicated in any other manner. Regardless of their starting point, the program appears to affect individuals in similar ways. What is also clear is that the program is, in some ways, unique to Israel. Although the mechanisms may be universal, the context is important.

At the Port

Yaffo, the old port area of Tel Aviv is strikingly beautiful and, on a summer night, a hub of social activity. Couples about to be married come to Yaffo to be photographed, while youth groups and tourists mingle. Despite Yaffo's busyness, the Birthright Israel group that had been on one of the specially organized outdoor adventure trips, visits and holds their closing discussion. Despite the environment, the outdoor meeting is surprisingly intimate— much as the crowded hotel conference room had been.

The participants do not need much prompting to get started and, in contrast to the hotel group where the focus was on getting deep reflections from those who spoke, the goal of the port discussion is to hear something from all of the participants. Discussion starts off on a relatively mundane level. A number of participants talk about their outdoor adventures. One participant, for example, talks about how putting himself to the test physically had deepened and strengthened the experience. He will never forget the the activity run by the Israeli soldiers at the Ramon Crater and their two nights in the field.

Another participant seems to capture the sense of the group when she says, "Every day I thought, 'Today is the best day' . . . and then the next day was even better." Another responds, "This trip changed my life." She then cries and does not even finish her sentence to explain how and why the trip changed her. The sense that something, difficult to explain, occurred that changed participants is an ongoing theme. One participant says, "This was my first visit in Israel. I had a strong experience that changed my life. I changed my opinion about IDF soldiers: they are human beings just like me; they are special people who share their personal experiences . . . every day, they endanger their lives, they have values."

An Israel participant, whose parents actually live in North America, notes that the experience strengthened the choice she made. Another Israeli solider says, "I didn't know anything about the Jews of Canada . . . I discovered a world that is special and different from my own." Another soldier says, "It will be very difficult to get back to routine. The strongest thing you gave me is a reason to smile. I have come to know each one of you well. I had a strong experience, like I have never had before."

The mutual impact of the experience of Israeli and North American peers getting to know another reverberates through the conversations. A participant remarks, "My life changed, I will miss everyone and I want to thank my Israeli soldiers for everything you do . . . You deal with things that are not easy." Another says, "I have traveled in many places in the world, but I have never yet had an experience like this . . . to live with Israeli soldiers for ten days is amazing . . . I'm taking you home with me . . . I am going to look for meaning in my life." Yet another admits, "There was a debate on my campus between an Israeli and a Palestinian and I supported the Palestinian . . . the soldiers on the program gave me a broader perspective." Perhaps the most telling comment is made by one of the soldiers, who says simply, "I didn't believe it would be possible to create such strong friendships in such a short period of time." His comments are met with nods and, interestingly, with the participants looking at one another—almost as if to capture a mental picture of their experience.

As observers of these closing sessions, we are struck by several consistent elements of what participants say. First, how articulate the participants are in explaining how the program has given them a new way to see themselves and their community. Second, it is often striking how difficult it is to discern the background of individual participants until they explain their background. Even more remarkable, were it not for distinct accents (and, sometimes, their uniforms), by the time of a closing session, it is difficult to distinguish the Israeli soliders from the North American visitors. It is also remarkable how, without prompting, participants are open about their reactions and willing to share them with others.

Veteran observers of Israel educational trips will rightly comment that all closing sessions are full of emotion, pathos, and great affect. What has seemed unique in the thousands of closing session of the Birthright Israel trips is not the fact of the affect in itself but a particular linguistic and conceptual terminology that seems to predominate. It is a language composed of such words or phrases as "transcendent," "life-changing," "unique," "unlike any Jewish experience I ever had before," and "I'll never be the same." This language is a symbolic system of young, emerging adults, who talk in terms related to life patterns and their imminent entry into adulhood. The tens of thousands of letters, along with comments made at tie-in sessions reinforce our view that the program has caught participants at a particularly important moment in their development. Later research will yield better answers to the long-term meaning of the experience, but their language makes clear that their participation in Birthright Israel has been transformative.

How Birthright Israel experiences alter the way in which young adult Jews view their relationship with Israel is only one part of the assessment of the program. Equally important is how participation in the program alters the Jewish identity of particpants and their motivation for involvement in the Jewish community. The issues of participants' relationship to Israel and their Jewish trajectories are, perhaps separate (even though it is their experience in Israel that is the catalyst for the change in the Jewish identity). Consider how several program alumni describe their experience and what happened to them afterwards.

Audrey was a relatively young participant when she joined a Birthright Israel trip in the summer of 2006, just after her freshman year at a small college in the Northeast. Her family was a member of a Conservative synagogue, where she went to Hebrew school from kindergarten to seventh grade. She celebrated her bat mitzvah at the synagogue and participated in the synagogue's youth program. But she came away from these experiences not feeling "very Jewish." For her, Birthright Israel was an "Israel trip," not a Jewish trip. She was among those who were in Israel just before the Lebanon War. Although she was never in any danger, she had been in the Negev when the Israeli soldier Gilad Shalit was kidnapped.[8] At the time of the interview several months after the trip, she was still not sure who she was Jewishly. In terms of Israel, however there was no ambiguity: Audrey felt connected and "obligated" to be part of what was happening in her people's land.

Another participant, Ellen, traveled on a Birthright Israel trip in 2001. She was the product of a nonreligious household and, in some respects, her history was opposite to that of Audrey. Ellen's mother was Jewish, but her father was not. She described Birthright Israel as her first real Jewish experience: it gave her the first "real" synagogue experience, her first Shabbat dinner. These experiences profoundly changed her life. Directly after her trip, she returned to her university on the West Coast and took courses in Middle East history and politics. The courses frustrated her, however, and her professors seemed biased against Israel. That, in turn, led her to return to Israel to study. By 2005, she decided that *her* Jewish community was in Israel, and she decided to make aliyah. Ellen now lives in Tel Aviv. She is part of only a small group of North Americans for whom Birthright Israel was the springboard for aliyah, but her feeling that she had found a home is not unique.

Daniel also participated in a Birthright Israel trip in 2001. At the time of the interview, he is twenty-six and works as a government researcher in a relatively isolated community. Both of his parents are Jewish: his mother was raised as a Reform Jew and his father's background is Orthodox. Daniel attended some Hebrew school as a child and celebrated his bar mitzvah, but he admits that he never took his Jewishness very seriously. His Birthright Israel experience was very important and profoundly affected him, but he has a hard time articulating the impact. Daniel says that he tries to go to a Conservative synagogue and has also met a Chabad rabbi who has invited him to take part in Shabbat dinners. But he does not feel as if he has found his place in the Jewish community. He does not see it as a place that welcomes young people like himself. Israel, however, is very much on his mind. He hopes to return to Israel and has considered aliyah. Clearly, the program precipitated a different frame of mind regarding Daniel's Jewish identity.

A different story, yet consistent with the themes of the others, is the experience of Abe, a twenty-year-old college student who went on Birthright Israel during early 2006. Abe and his family were members of a Reconstructionist synagogue. He describes his father as a "nonbeliever," but active in the Jewish community and supportive of the family engaging in Jewish ritual. Abe attended Hebrew school but doing so did not make him feel very connected to Jewish culture. He decided to go on Birthright Israel because it was "free" and was not sure what to expect. He tells the interviewer that the experience surprised him: it showed Judaism as a rich culture and Israel as an extraordinary society. He came to believe that Israel was part of his heritage. Abe's goal is to return to Israel to study, and he sees himself for the first time as someone interested in finding a Jewish woman to be his life partner. Israel and his Jewishness are now inseparable from who he is.

Another alumna, Rachel, is a recent college graduate who participated in an early 2006 Birthright Israel trip. Rachel grew up culturally Jewish. Her family lit Shabbat candles on Friday nights, and Rachel attended a Conservative synagogue on the High Holidays. But her father is not Jewish, and she also celebrated Christian holidays with the paternal side of the family. Rachel was given a choice about Hebrew school and decided not to participate. Unlike the other alumni who went with secular Birthright Israel providers, Rachel decided to go with Mayanot, the Chabad group. Although her trip itinerary was much like the others, a rabbi served as one of her guides, and the trip had an implicit religious focus. The impact of the trip on Rachel was profound. She came away with a clearer sense of herself Jewishly and a strong desire to learn more about Judaism and her own history. For her, the program was primarily about her fellow Birthright Israel participants and, in particular, the Israeli peers who were part of her group. But the effect of the trip centered on her sense of feeling part of Judaism and being connected to the Jews of Israel.

Not every participant reported the kinds of impact that Audrey, Ellen, Daniel, Abe, and Rachel experienced, but even among those for whom it did not have profound impact, it deeply affected how they view Israel. One participant, David, who went on a 2001 trip, reported in 2006 that although he still has good memories of the experience, it did not change his life in discernible ways. For him, a typical North American young adult who lives in a fast-paced, rarefied world, Birthright Israel was an interesting experience. Striking, however, is that while he professes an almost blasé attitude about what the program meant for him, his affect and engagement changes when the conversation turns to Israel. He says that his experience makes him pay attention to the news in a different way and feel a connection to what is going on—even though it is five thousand miles and a completely different language away.

There is another kind of reaction to the program, one that is not specifically Jewish- or Israel-focused, but that suggests the program's broad impact. Annette is a tall, compelling model of a young professional. She works at a public relations firm and is enthusiastic and articulate in talking about her Birthright Israel experience. She starts by explaining, "Our household was Reform, my brother had a bar mitzvah, and we had 'Jewishness' but didn't overly care about it either." Her eyes lit up as she talks about her grandfather who *did* care and symbolized Judaism for her. Judaism did not play a prominent role in her life; it was not "negative," she says, but Judaism simply was not on her radar screen.

The conversation with Annette becomes extended when she talks about how Birthright Israel is affecting her life plans. In graduate school she met a man five years older than her. She describes him as driven, like her, to achieve and proudly talks about him as the love of her life and soul mate. He is not, however, Jewish. They have been together for several years and plan to get married. But, the interviewer asks, what about the fact that that your future husband is not Jewish? She answers indirectly by telling how she decided to participate in Birthright Israel. She says, "One day my best friend called and said 'let's go on birthright.' I had no idea what birthright was but when she told me the details, I said 'I'm in.' It was cool to travel with my friend, my grandfather would be so proud, and Israel was not off the moon for me." She found herself on a bus for ten days, drinking in everything she saw and heard, and having an experience of a lifetime. Israel, she says, "showed me who we are as a people. It resonated. It ignited me." She came back, if not transformed, engaged in a different way. She says, "It made me care more about Jewish holidays." Moving closer to answering the question about her marriage, she continues, "We talk about Israel and we talk about living a life of two faiths. Ours will be an interfaith marriage. But it is important to me that the kids be Jewish, and he agrees. He enjoys Jewishness and is taken by its warmth, family-centeredness, and values. The kids will go to Hebrew school and have bar and bat mitzvah. He goes to church, but he is happy with my Jewishness." Annette's story is just an anecdote about how Birthright Israel mattered. Yet, in several respects, her story suggests what may become a central chapter in the next decades of American Jewish life. How her children will be brought up remains to be seen, but ten days in Israel seems to have changed how she frames her life. The ten days came at the right time developmentally and affected her deeply. We do not know what makes an adult an identified Jew, but it appears to put some on a different Jewish trajectory.

Although the individual stories of the impact of participating in Birthright Israel are as varied as the sizes and shapes of participants, what seems common is that it had an important impact on some part of their life. To return to a term discucssed earlier (see chapter 4), participants come away with new "schema"—new frameworks for understanding who they are. The behaviorial manifestitations are slightly different: from changing levels of engagement with religious aspects of Judaism, to engagement in Israel advocacy, to simply seeing Jewishness as central to one's identity and essential to how one wants to raise children. Some participants—like Ellen who made aliyah—make profound behavioral changes. Some return to take a leadership role with their campus Hillel; others change career paths and decide to work in the Jewish community. One, who changed his name to Shaul after participating in Birthright Israel in 2000, grew up in a Reform household and had what he described as minimal Jewish education. For Shaul, his Birthright Israel experience became the "first rung on a ladder" of engagement. On his return, he became more religiously observant and eventually returned to Israel to study in a yeshiva.

A description of the impact of the program in participants' voices would not be complete without mention of those participants who began the program already highly knowledgeable about Israel or enmeshed in family ties. A fair number of these participants were immigrants or first-generation North Americans. The largest group came from the former Soviet Union (FSU) and many had close family ties in Israel. For some of the FSU participants, the meetings with their family were poignant. On a 2004 trip, Igor, a young man who had emigrated from the FSU to the southern United States with his mother more than a decade earlier was reunited with his father. Igor's parents separated at the time they left the FSU, and his Birthright Israel trip gave him the first chance he had had in a decade to see his father. He learned that his father had remarried and that he had a new family in Israel. As he described the scene shortly after returning from the reunion, meeting his new siblings swept away a decade of bitter feelings. Part of the reason that the visit was successful was that Birthright Israel made it normative to reconnect with family and made everyone feel as if they were at a reunion. Igor was not simply a son meeting a lost father.

Another group of participants were children of Israeli parents. To be eligible for Birthright Israel they could not have lived in the country after age twelve; while they may have visited relatives many times, many had little formal education about Israel. Most had not gone to the key historical sites and, even if they could speak fluent Hebrew, they had little knowledge of their parents' land. One of these birthrighters, Avi, described later on what it felt like to be a participant. "At first, I felt odd, since Israel was a place I thought I knew and I was clearly different than the other members of my group. But as many times as I had visited *saba* [grandfather] and *safta* [grandmother], I had never been to the Kotel, and Israel did not feel like home. Now it does and, while I don't know what that means for my future, I know it's going to be important."

ISRAEL AS CONTEXT

The context for Birthright Israel is the modern State of Israel. The educational program is unique due to Jews' historical connection to the land and the extraordinary circumstances of the birth of the state. For program participants, the conflict that Israel has faced with its Arab neighbors (and, as a result, the view of Israel in their home countries) is clearly central to the program. Yet it is hard to know in what way. To be sure, the conflict makes traveling to Israel seem dangerous, and security is a constant concern of program staff. One issue is that Israel remains a country under threat. The program does not explicitly train its educators to engage participants as advocates for Israel and discourages educators from promoting any particular internal Israeli political view. But there is no question that participants come away as advocates. Even the soldiers who participate in the mifgashim come away as more supportive of Israel's need to defend itself. We suspect that, in the same way that the program allows participants to reframe their identities, it allows them to see Israel in a different way—from the inside out, instead of newspaper headlines' outside in.

How the education of Diaspora young adults about Israel will affect future support for the country is not easy to document. Perhaps the most important sign is that program alumni, as a result of their Birthright Israel experience, have new ways to understand Israel and to gather information. Although Israel is a focus of Western news coverage, much of the coverage is sensational and, for someone without much historical or background knowledge, may be uninterpretable.[9] The situation is fluid and to be well informed means that one has to have access and pay attention to a variety of sources.

In terms of the changes under way, only the perspective of history will enable us to understand the impact of the Israel-Hezbollah War of 2006. In the short term, the war wrought death and destruction and led to intervention from Western armies. Whether or not the war will lead to stability and peace or to an increase in tension between Israel and her neighbors is yet to be answered. Clearly, Diaspora Jews have a different stake in the resolution of the conflict than their Israeli peers, many of whom were combatants or had families who were targets of missile attacks. Nevertheless, as a result of Birthright Israel, a new generation of Diaspora Jews has a direct connection to those who were affected and a level of knowledge that no one—no matter how addicted to CNN or the BBC or how well read—could appreciate.

Whether this connection and level of knowledge will lead program alumni, over the long term, to increase their level of engagement with Israel and their Jewish identities cannot yet be evaluated. As noted in chapter 8, there is substantial evidence of impact in attitude changes. There is evidence, as well, of Birthright Israel alumni who feel so connected that they returned to Israel to help in the war reconstruction effort.[10] The initial signs are that program alumni will have a very different kind of interest in Israel than do their American peers. At the foundation of that increased interest and involvement is a different understanding of Israel, made palpable by their personal connections with Israelis.

If Birthright Israel alumni are very different, having not only different attitudes but a different relationship with Israel, it will be a powerful confirmation of the program's effectiveness in meeting its goals. Typically, researchers assume that a person's current environment has a much more powerful impact on his or her attitudes and behavior than historical experiences. Whether the impact of the program can be sustained once participants return to their home community is the key issue for the future. Its importance is magnified by the increasingly hostile views of Israel, even its right to exist. If Birthright Israel alumni can remain knowledgable supporters of Israel—not advocates per se, but individuals who care about the society because they see themselves as part of it and have a stake—the program will more than have justified its creation and the substantial resources necessary to maintin it.

Israel identification notwithstanding, the underlying issue is how participation in the program (including identification with Israel) affects the extent to which Jewish young adults identify with their ethnic and religious heritage. As much as individuals may be able to separate political and religious views, the support for Israel by organized Jewry—from communal institutions such as federations, to synagogues and Hillels—makes the link with Jewish identity inescapable. If the implicit assumption—that education is key—is correct then Birthright Israel alumni should be in a better position than their peers to navigate between their views of Israel and their identity as Jews.

If the Birthright Israel experiment has "worked," participants should return to their home communities eager to continue to learn about Israel and their Jewish roots. They will come to see their Birthright Israel experience as only one chapter in their journey to engage with their heritage. Most important, they will have been transformed in how they understand and feel about Israel and their Jewish heritage.

The Tenth Day WHAT WE LEARNED

10

Learning in old age is like writing on sand;
learning in youth is like engraving.
—Solomon Ibn Gabriol
Everyone is kneaded out of the same dough, not baked in the same oven.
—Yiddish proverb

As the sun sets, the beat of a single drum, then a set of drums slices through the clamor of the eager crowd. The percussion is amplified and soon every one of the more than seven thousand souls in the amphitheater can feel the drums, not just hear their beat. The stage lights pulsate with the same level of energy as the music. When the dance troupe of at least one hundred young Israelis appears on stage, the atmosphere consumes the audience. It is early June 2006; the audience is made up of Birthright Israel participants from more than a dozen countries around the world: the United States and Canada primarily but also from Argentina, Australia, France, Germany, Russia, Ukraine, and elsewhere. These groups of young adults, previously strangers to one another, are unified now as they sit riveted by the largest-scale Jewish performance they have ever seen.

The participants are gathered in the amphitheater as part of the now-ritualized Birthright Israel mega-event. Part rock concert, part revival meeting, with features of an Israeli political rally, the mega-event brings six thousand non-Israeli Jews and nearly a thousand young Israelis together to share an experience of Jewish peoplehood. The site of the June mega-event is the amphitheater in Latrun, alongside the Tel Aviv–Jerusalem Highway, the key connector of Israel's business and government centers. As the site of a major battle in the 1948 War of Independence, Latrun occupies a central place in Israel's history. The 1948 battle pit the fledgling Israeli defense forces against the Arab Legion and ultimately helped prevent the Jewish-settled part of Jerusalem from being isolated and occupied by Arab armies. For American Jews, Latrun has special significance. It is the battleground where the American Jewish military hero Mickey Marcus was accidentally killed by friendly fire.[1] Today, the site is both an amphitheater used for military and civilian ceremonies, and the location of the Israel Defense Forces' Armored Corps Museum.

During winter trips, mega-events are held inside at the Jerusalem Convention Center, but in the summer, they are held outdoors. On this day, the buses began rolling into the parking area shortly after 5:00 P.M. The then newly elected prime minister of Israel, Ehud Olmert, was initially scheduled to speak at the event but was required to make a diplomatic trip to Europe instead. Had he been able to appear, the buses would have come several hours earlier to enable security checks, a fact of life even for an event such as this. The buses streaming into the lots arrived from all over Israel; by 7:30 P.M., thousands of the Birthright Israel participants fill the amphitheater. The groups are seated according to their buses. The participants wave flags and banners from their respective countries and exercise their vocal cords. At 7:55 P.M., the VIPs, as their seats are labeled, begin to arrive: philanthropists, leaders of the supporting Jewish organizations, government and army officials, Knesset members, and other international influentials. Even with the open sky as the ceiling, there is a constant din of voices, noise, and singing. Just before the show commences, a spotlight reaches out to the last dignitary to arrive, Deputy Prime Minister Shimon Peres—eighty-two years old, a Nobel Peace Laureate, former prime minister, and current president of Israel. Flanked by his security staff, and cheered on by the crowd, Peres makes his way into the arena. Birthright Israel participants along his route reach out to him while camera flashes accompany him to his seat.

Participants report that when they arrived at the mega-event, they could not believe that everyone was Jewish, and that they were actually going to hear from the prime minister and the philanthropists—people they had only heard about before their trips. For most of the participants, this was the first time they experienced a gathering of young Jewish adults of this nature. Some may have been at High Holiday religious services with a thousand members of their community. Those settings, however, had been formal occasions: it may not have been their choice to participate; they would have been wearing suits, ties, and dresses; and they would have been a small part of a large group of older adults. The Birthright Israel mega-event is the antithesis to those experiences. As one participant described the encounter: "Even now [three years later], I remember the event. It was spectacular—an auditorium full of Jews my age from all over the world. I don't know what Ariel Sharon [the prime minister] said. He talked for a long time, but it was amazing that he came to talk to us and that he thought we were important. I have thought about that night every time I hear the news about his stroke. We partied late into the night and all of sudden I forgot how tired I was. It didn't really hit me until I got home how amazing the experience had been."[2]

In the case of the Latrun mega-event, Birthright Israel T-shirts, energy, and exuberance dominate. The end of the opening act of drumming and dance is punctuated by fireworks shooting up into the darkening Israeli night sky. Further adding to the rock concert–like atmosphere, the emcee for the evening is an Israeli former MTV host, Becky Griffin. Griffin begins by recognizing all those who make Birthright Israel a reality: the Israeli government, the United Jewish Communities, the Jewish Agency for Israel, and a long list of philanthropists, benefactors, and members of the Israeli Knesset. The volume of cheers thanking each of the organizations and people who fund and enable the trip reverberates throughout the amphitheater. From the expressions on the faces of many of the VIPs, the message of appreciation is clearly welcome.

Following a video clip that shows some of the participants—from ten different cities across the world—preparing to come on their trip, Shimon Peres makes his way to the podium. Peres is joined on the stage by three of the founding philanthropists, Charles Bronfman, Lynn Schusterman, and Michael Steinhardt, along with Birthright Israel's symbolic 100,000th participant, Stephanie Lowenthal. Peres, in his soft-mannered yet emphatic way, begins his address by speaking about the meaning and importance of being Jewish and of supporting Israel: "To be Jewish is to be together. To be Jewish is to love Israel. To be Jewish is, for Israelis, to love the Jewish people. To be Jewish is to love peace. To be Jewish means never to forget the greatest contribution of the Jewish people—the moral code. To be Jewish is to make Israel strong, open, scientific, and promising."

Following Peres's welcome, Michael Steinhardt echoes the need for all Birthright Israel participants to maintain the ties with Israel that they have developed. After acknowledging and thanking Shimshon Shoshani, Lynn Schusterman tells the audience that if they want to "put a face on Jewish identity—individually and collectively—look around at yourselves." Charles Bronfman chooses not to speak. In lieu of his speech, organizers debut a short tribute film to Bronfman's late wife, Andrea, who had died tragically earlier in the year. "Andy" Bronfman, as noted in chapter 1, had been intimately involved with her husband in planning Birthright Israel and a range of their philanthropic work.

The sound of a shofar—the traditional instrument used to "awaken" Jews—is sounded. It pierces the night sky, calling everyone to attention and signaling, even to the most Jewishly detached participants, that this is a Jewish moment. The dancers again flood the stage. Slowly but surely, the rock concert, this time originating from a blast of the ancient shofar, returns. The star of this segment of the show is a Canadian-born musician and rap artist,

Shai Hadad. Hadad made aliyah just six months after returning from his own Birthright Israel trip in 2001. His song, "Home," instructs the audience, "if you want to make it where you're going, you have to remember where you came from." Shai's message remains central to the rest of the evening's musical program as other musicians take the stage to lead the audience in a sing-along medley of Jewish and Israeli tunes.

The evening ends with the singing, in Hebrew, of *"Hatikva"* (Hope), Israel's national anthem:

> In the Jewish heart
> A Jewish spirit still sings,
> And the eyes look east toward Zion
> Our Hope is not lost,
> Our hope of thousands of years
> To be a free people in our Land,
> In the Land of Zion and Jerusalem

It is likely that many of the Birthright Israel participants came to Israel not knowing the words of the national anthem. But the strength of the singing and the evident passion make it difficult to tell. Even to trained observers, it is hard not to be caught up in the emotional power of the words and melody. Participants lock arms, hold hands, sway, and weep. "Hatikva" concerns the undying hope of the Jewish people that they will someday return to independence in their homeland. What was evident during that night of celebration was that the thousands of Jewish educational tourists who had arrived in Israel with little sense of their identities engaged in an intense experience of solidarity and peoplehood. They were alternately stirred emotionally, engaged behaviorially, and stimulated cognitively.

UNDERSTANDING EDUCATIONAL IMPACT

Anyone who has participated in a Birthright Israel mega-event senses that the critique of the program idea—that a ten-day trip to Israel is an expensive paid vacation, not an educational experience that could have lasting impact—is misinformed. Without question, Birthright Israel participants have a great deal of fun, but they are as attentive to the speeches by sponsors and political figures as they are exuberant in their responses to the music. And when one wanders around the educational booths that are part of a mega-event, one observes that the experience is something more than a rock concert. The point is illustrated further when participants begin to sing the Israeli national anthem as if their own lives are bound up with one another and in the fate of Israel.

The description of the impact of the program provided by participant observers bolsters and supports the findings of the evaluation studies (see chapter 8). But the observations and evaluation data do not necessarily answer the underlying question about the program. Why should a relatively brief experience, such as Birthright Israel, be so powerful? Is the program sui generis? Is the profound affect of the program linked to the unique history and status of Diaspora Jews? Is there something about how the program was designed or implemented that creates a special set of educational conditions? Or, is the impact of the program simply a function of sending young adults away in groups? Is the fact that the program is located in Israel and is based on an elaborate educational program unimportant?

Birthright Israel is neither a perfect nor a comprehensive social experiment. It was not designed to test whether the same effects would be achieved with different ethnic/religious groups, nor was it designed to test whether sending groups to settings other than Israel would lead to similar outcomes. Similarly, it is not clear whether other educational models might have been even more effective. As described in chapter 8, however, the program demonstrably influences the attitudes and behavior of participants. The observation of the mega-event provides some clues as to why it succeeds.

In important ways, the data validate the initial theory of the program: a Dewey-influenced approach that focuses attention on how individuals learn from experience and use multiple senses. Translating the quilted theory of experiential education into concrete terms, Birthright Israel is successful because it touches participants emotionally (affectively), intellectually (cognitively), and physically (behaviorally). Most educational approaches emphasize only one or two of these channels and engage only limited senses. Those limitations are particularly true of Jewish education delivered to Diaspora youth. Educational experiences that are emotionally engaging, intellectually rich, and physically demanding are rare. Such an approach, however, is the essence of the Birthright Israel experience.

Affect

That learning and self-discovery should be "joyous" is both self-evident and a contradiction. Learning about one's religious and ethnic identity is a solemn activity and, particularly for Jewish youth, learning an ancient language and tradition is hard work. For many of those who participate in Birthright Israel, their experience of Jewish education has been like that of the weekend athlete who practices sporadically and, thus, is always sore from being out of shape. Jewish tradition suggests a different approach. There is, for example, the tradition of giving young children candy when they first study Torah so that they will associate sweetness with Torah. Studying Torah, and grappling with its meaning, is supposed to be a difficult experience, but one that should be enjoyable and rewarding.

The emotional component of Birthright Israel, however, is not simply creating the association of pleasure with Jewish identity. The program stimulates emotional engagement (strong feelings) in a variety of ways. The mere fact of travel to a distant place that has been the focus of so much myth and ongoing attention is an omnipresent feature of the program. It is magnified for Birthright Israel participants by the range of experiences they are exposed to—from the the excitement of travel, to new foods, to meeting a cadre of soldier-peers, to becoming part of a large collective of young people. The Birthright Israel experience is intense, novel, and highly personal. For participants, it is invariably emotionally engaging.

The emotional experience of traveling to Israel with a group of peers is, perhaps, magnified for young adult contemporary Americans who live in a world dominated by social interaction that is mediated by e-mail, text messages, and mobile phones. It may be difficult for those raised in earlier eras to comprehend, but the experience of being with a group of peers—even in the bubble of a plane and bus, mostly disconnected from telephones and the Internet and "forced" to interact—is a novel experience. Aside from whatever participants learn from one another and from their Israeli peers in the mifgashim, the experience of being part of a group is essential to the program's emotional engagement. To be sure, group members do not form equally intense bonds with every member of their group, but they return home feeling that they are somehow bound to one another. Participants often report that they are unable to get back into their work: they cannot restrain themselves from e-mailing, calling, and seeing their fellow group participants and madrichim.

The emotional ties among members of the group are key to how participation in Birthright Israel enables effective education. Even so, ties to the group are only part of what trips are able to do. Each day of the journey brings participants into contact with new sites, novel experiences, and others not part of their group. What is unique about the experience is that, unlike typical touring—where the guide focuses on sharing information—Birthright Israel trips emphasize connecting visitors to the sites and experiences. Guides strive to show participants what sites mean to them and, through mechanisms such as "tie-in" discussions (see chapter 3), engage the travelers in understanding the meaning of the experience.

There is, as well, a rhythm to trips. Although each itinerary is different, all trips are organized around the Jewish calendar, and Jerusalem plays a central role. Often, groups are introduced to Israel by visiting the Haas Promenade and then the Kotel (see chapters 4 and 5), and each group spends at least one of their two Shabbat days in Jerusalem. Whether the tour organizer is secular or religious, activities are organized so as to allow participants to feel the onset of the Sabbath. The preparations begin early on Friday afternoon and lead toward celebration of Kabbalat Shabbat and enjoyment of the Sabbath itself. Groups like the Mayanot tour described in chapter 4 emphasize the experience to an even larger extent. Their goal is to change how participants feel about Shabbat—from an unwelcome intrusion, to a joyous and necessary respite from daily concerns.

Some tour organizers intentionally organize their itinerary in ways designed to enhance the emotional experience. Oranim, for example (see chapter 6), ends all of its trips in Jerusalem. On the last day, as their participants go from the Holocaust Memorial museum at Yad Vashem, to the national cemetery at Mount Herzl, to western Jerusalem and the Kotel, they experience the story of the Jewish people's near-destruction, the founding of the State of Israel, and its emergence as a Jewish democratic state. In a single day, the program is structured to allow them to confront the sadness and solemnity of Holocaust remembrance, public recognition of those who died in the service of the state, and the joyousness of Jewish religious life. Many leave Jersualem and arrive at the airport in tears.

The mega-event is the public representation of the program's emotional content and how it engages participants. Cynics might regard the mega-event simply as a rock concert/party, catering to the sybaritic side of contemporary youth, but, as noted above, its serious purposes are also evident. The mega-event adds an element of fun to the exploration of Jewish identity and peoplehood and provides participants with an experience that they can share with the adults who make the program possible. Just as universities understand that what goes on in extracurricular activities and dormitories is critical to their educational purposes, so too does Birthright Israel.

Cognition

If Birthright Israel were only an emotionally engaging (albeit fun) experience, it is unlikely that it would have the kind of long-term impact demonstrated by the evaluation data. It would also not elicit descriptions from participants that emphasize the personal meaning and educational import the program provided. Although the experiment has not been conducted, a ten-day stay in Cancún would be unlikely to serve as an equivalent. For most participants, a set of college lectures and seminars that run for sixteen hours per day is more akin to a Birthright Israel trip than a vacation on a resort island. Although assigned readings and papers are not a feature of the trips, the educational content is substantial.

On the front lines providing serious cognitive content are the guides. Earlier, we met Udi and Francis: two very different group leaders who, while passionate about their goal to spark Jewish and Israel engagement in their charges, are also dedicated to sharing knowledge about the Land of Israel (see chapter 4). They work hard to provide information and, as the description of guiding at Masada makes clear (see chapter 3), they try both to shape a story and make sure that alternative narratives are provided. If evaluated by strict academic accuracy criteria, the guides would receive high marks. Although there are differences among tour educators, and not all are expert at managing young adult groups, their government certifications ensure that they are well trained and knowledgeable. And, almost without exception, they are passionate about their subject.

Providing additional scaffolding for the cognitive content of the program are the multiple lecturers and public figures whom the participants get to hear and meet. From political figures such as Sharansky and Weisglass, to Jewish educators like Avraham Infeld, to academic experts (political scientists, historians), and ordinary Israelis (Holocaust survivors, kibbutzniks), participants are bombarded with information, analysis, and narratives about Jewish history and the Land of Israel. In some cases, they meet the leading contemporary figures who shape the news; in other cases, they hear from those whose job it is to track the news, understand it, and place it in context.

To be sure, there are differences across groups, both in terms of participants and the orientation of tour organizers. Observation suggests that groups made up of students from highly selective and academically rigorous institutions are, as one might expect, more interested and engaged in the intellectual content of the program. Compared to those from less select schools, these students have a wider base of knowledge from which to draw, ask more penetrating questions, and have more patience for intellectual analyses of the history and sites that they are seeing. There are, as well, differences among the groups, especially those that are composed of post-college participants.

The tour organizers also differ. Although some use the same lecturers, each has its own list of experts. Some organizers, like Hillel, use experts from outside their own organization. Others, such as Kesher and Aish HaTorah, have their own educational centers in Israel and utilize faculty who teach in these programs as supplemental educators. Across the groups, the best madrichim know how to adjust their styles to the temperament of the group. They know "when to walk and when to talk" and they also have a keen sense about the appropriate pitch level for their explanations.

From the outset, Birthright Israel's designers realized that they were dealing with an age and a socioeconomic demographic that was nurtured on the role of thinking and cognition in life. Moreover, a high percentage of this demographic was precisely at the age developmentally when the main business of their lives involved some, if not major, preoccupation with ideas. Thus, the content of these trips was overtly shaped by a reflective, dialectic, ideational frame.

Behavior

Many educational experiences have both emotional and cognitive components, but relatively few also include a behavioral component. What is unique about Birthright Israel is that it allows participants not only to be stimulated emotionally and learn about their heritage, but also to behave as members of the community: in effect, to try out what they are learning. In a superficial way, it is learning about Jewish history by experiencing historical and contemporary sites as part of a Jewish group. In a more profound way, it is about living as part of a Jewish community, being on a Jewish calendar, and hearing and seeing the language of the Jewish people, Hebrew, in active use.

As suggested earlier, North American Birthright Israel participants come out of a culture in which modern technology has assumed an ever-greater role in mediating interaction. Participating in group activities is not wholly novel, but learning about one's history, culture, and people in situ has a power that cannot be replicated by any amount of reading, watching DVDs, or viewing Powerpoint presentations. Evaluation data suggest that Birthright Israel has found a way to use Eretz Yisrael to teach young adults about their identity and connection to other Jews. For most Diaspora Jews, Eretz Yisrael is an idealized concept, not reality. There may not be an equivalent educational substitute to being in Israel in order to learn about Israel.

At the core of the behavioral experience of a Birthright Israel trip is being part of a group. From the moment a participant arrives at the Kennedy airport or one of the other points of embarkation, he or she is drawn into a group. Symbolically, the sense of groupness is reinforced by the logo T-shirt and name badge for each participant, but for the next ten-plus days, the participant's social identity is the bus group. Membership in the bus group becomes a metaphor for belonging to the Jewish People, being part of Klal Yisrael. In Israel, the participant travels with his or her bus group, but periodically joins with other buses to visit particular sites, to hear lectures, and so on.

The inclusion of Israeli peers on the trip extends the group's boundaries. Participants no longer experience Israel primarily as outsiders, as Diaspora Jews, but rather as a group containing diverse members, including Israeli Jews. When Birthright Israel alumni are interviewed after their trip, one of the comments that is often made is that the experience with Israeli peers was surprising. Until they actually engaged in interaction with their soldier-peers, they could not have imagined that it would be as rewarding as it was. As described by one participant, Leah:

The biggest surprise to me . . . was how interesting it was to meet the Israeli soldiers whose lives are so much different and harder than ours. . . . When we were first meeting them I assumed that they would think that their lives were so much harder than ours, and that we were pampered and spoiled and didn't know what it truly meant to feel any type of pride in your country. And I just thought it would be "we're fighting for something over here and we are in danger at all times." But, honestly, they had no preconceived notions. They didn't think that we were any better or worse. It was just so much easier to find a common ground than I thought. We are so similar even though we'd experienced such different lifestyles. These people were our friends; they weren't people who happened to be our age that were in the army and it was just a really big surprise to me that they were so non-judgmental.[3]

The success of the mifgashim with Israeli peers is an indicator of how powerful this extension of identification can be. Regardless of the sites they visit— early Zionist settlements or religious icons in Jerusalem—this sense of groupness extends even further, to the generations who preceded them. To watch the process unfold is to see a fast-forward version of identity development. It is difficult to imagine that it could take place outside of Israel and, perhaps more important, without the physical engagement of participants.

The same process was true for other elements of the program. Whether it was singing together in Hebrew at the mega-event or spending a Shabbat walking in Jerusalem and talking about the meaning of texts, participants did not come with a schema for understanding these experiences. The actual "doing" was what tied together the affective and cognitive. Birthright Israel participants were confronted with people, issues, and settings in which Judaism was defined in behavioral rather than exclusively spiritual or metaphysical terms. Israel is about the responsibility and complexities of using power. It is about the actual behavior of holding a rifle, serving a country for three years, making tough moral decisions. For many Birthright Israel participants, they came face-to-face for the first time with being Jewish as a behavioral system. They confronted a Judaism of daily life. They may have known that it existed, but they had never had a chance to experience it and see it played out in mundane and profound ways.

BIRTHRIGHT ISRAEL IN PERSPECTIVE

Lee Shulman, one of the most distinguished contemporary educators and president of the Carnegie Foundation for the Advancement of Teaching, describes three habits that form the essence of effective education: "habits of mind, hand, and heart."[4] Shulman's conception of education in terms of cognitive understanding, physical engagement, and concern for others is, while not isomorphic with the affective-behavioral-cognitive explanation for Birthright Israel's effectiveness, very similar. The explanatory framework provided here for Birthright Israel places more emphasis on emotional engagement, rather than our "concern for others." That said, perhaps developing concern for others (habits of heart) does form the core of the overall program goal. To be part of Klal Yisrael is to be concerned about others: to be concerned about where and how one "fits" with others. It is a process of meaning-making, but it is very specific as to meaningfulness in relation to others.

Birthright Israel, however, creates a very specific kind of connection among its participants. In the language of social capital (see chapter 1), it builds "bonding social capital"; that is, connections among (relatively) homogeneous individuals. To participate in Birthright Israel, one must declare oneself Jewish and building Jewish social capital is central to the program's goals. Is that a good outcome? To use *New York Times* columnist Thomas Friedman's term, we live in an increasingly "flat world."[5] In such a world, what is the role of an educational effort that fosters in-group identification? In a world filled with strife, what is the impact of increasing the identification of group members with a particular religion and ethnicity? These questions are critical, in particular because Israel is frequently the brunt of negative attention by dint of its ongoing conflict with the Palestinians. At the same time, anti-Semitism and hatred of Jews appears across the world.

As we suggested at the outset (see chapter 1), bonding social capital, rather than being negative, seems necessary if individuals are to develop bridging social capital (connections with those who are different). Learning how to commit to similar others is, in this formulation, a basic building block of learning how to express concern for those who are different. Long-standing Jewish tradition has linked self-interest with support of others. One of the most famous pieces of Jewish wisdom, recorded in *Pirke Avot* (Ethics of our Fathers)[6] and attributed to Hillel, captures this attitude: "If I am not for myself, then who will be for me? And if I am only for myself, then what am I?"

We do not as yet have good data about the impact of Birthright Israel on the extent to which alumni provide *tzedakah* (charity) and feel responsibility not only to fellow Jews, but to others as well. Our hypothesis is that the experience of being part of a group and getting to know another culture translates broadly to concern with others. Although it is possible that the program's Jewish-centricness will lead to an exclusive concern with the Jewish community, our understanding of the participants makes that highly unlikely. Most return to their secular American lives changed, but still committed to life as

Americans and expecting to participate fully in American life. We suspect that one impact of Birthright Israel is that participants are inspired by Israelis, staff and peers, whom they meet. The Israelis demonstrate a level of communal commitment that the Diaspora Jews may not have seen before. The Israelis' efforts to reach out to the Americans (and perhaps that most of them are soldiers, putting their life plans on hold in order to defend their country) suggests to the North Americans that individual acquisitions and success are not the most important goals.

At the root of the issue over bonding and bridging social capital is the question of whether ethnicity and religion have a positive role to play in postmodern society. The ongoing violence in the Middle East, to some extent fanned by fundamentalism of different religious stripes, suggests to some that we need to find nonsectarian identity solutions. Jewish tradition, in particular, is a three-thousand-year-old culture of debate about ethical and moral issues.[7] It is a tradition that has renewed and reinvented itself repeatedly, even while remembering its history. If anything, postmodern societies need to be reminded of ethical imperatives and the inherent interconnections among people. In that respect, fostering Jewish identity and connections seems not only a worthy goal, but a critical task in an era of anomie and individualism.

FOSTERING CHANGE

One measure of the success of Birthright Israel will be whether it enters the "DNA" of Diaspora Jewry and becomes institutionalized. Certain rituals, such as bar or bat mitzvah ceremonies for thirteen-year-olds to mark their transition to adult reseponsibilities, have become a natural part of the upbringing of any who considers themselves Jewish. Whether or not educational trips to Israel for young adults become normative for the next generation of emerging adults is a key test for the program. For the moment, the question seems mostly about resources: will the Jewish communities of the world provide the resources to allow the program to serve a wider group of participants? There seems an ever-larger group of young adults interested in the program and eager to learn about their heritage. Will the current generation of funders be replaced by a new cohort of philanthropists? And will Jewish communities around the world see Birthright Israel as essential to their mission?

Particularly interesting in this regard is an experimental effort under way in Boston, home to one of the largest groups of college and post-college young adults. The local Jewish Federation, Combined Jewish Philanthropies, is working with Birthright Israel to increase the number of participants by focusing on a select number of campuses.[8] At each of these campuses they are trying to eliminate waiting lists for Birthright Israel and bring larger groups. The idea is to test a "tipping point,"[9] to see what happens if a critical mass from the same community participates in the program. It may not change the program itself but may open a range of possibilities for posttrip activities.

The engagement of Birthright Israel participants after they return to their home communities is the next frontier of the program. How the participants fare once they come home, whether they choose to engage with the Jewish community and maintain their connection to their Jewish identity and to Israel, will tell us much about the educational processes of the program and will also suggest directions for the future of the Diaspora Jewish community. Whether their home experiences can ever match the novelty and intensity of their Birthright Israel experience is unlikely; the issue is whether the depth of engagement with individuals at home can come to represent something as important as their pilgrimage experience in Israel.

Birthright Israel Organization

The future of the organization that supports the program is also an open question. It has been so successful that, perhaps naturally, it has been asked to take on additional responsibilities. During the 2006 Lebanon War, for example, Birthright Israel was given responsibility to help thousands of those who were evacuated from northern Israel. One of its responsibilities was to provide trips and tours for the youngsters as a way to keep them out of harm's way and to engage them in meaningful activities. Birthright Israel's expertise in logistics and standard-setting allowed them to develop, almost overnight, educational programs that served more than five thousand youth.

Regardless of whether the organization expands, contracts, or becomes part of a larger entity, it has left a legacy that will no doubt influence Israeli education and Jewish education throughout the Diaspora. It has been a model of public-private partnership and a trailblazer in its use of educational standards to shape its program. Shimshon Shoshani, CEO of the organization, is an exceptional educator who assembled a lean, but stellar team of educational and logistical experts. He and his staff did not do it alone; they had access, particularly with the philanthropists and their staffs, to an extraordinary group of advisors and consultants. Although the role of professionals at the philanthropies that supported the program, including Rabbi Yitz Greenberg and Jeffrey Solomon, was sometimes to cajole and direct, mostly they served as sounding boards and advocates.[10] Perhaps the unique team that developed the program explains its success. But the techniques used by Birthright Israel have wide applicability and can be emulated by others.

Educational Applications

Birthright Israel's success suggests a new model of education that, despite its unique focus on Israel and the particularistic elements of educating young adults about their ethnicity and ties to a homeland, has broad applicability. The program philosophy, percolated from decades of experimentation on the education of Diaspora youth about Israel, was made possible by two philanthropists who were willing to ignore the rest of the Establishment. It was made a reality by educators committed to new ways of thinking. Undoubtedly, the most important outcomes concern the development of ethnic and religious identity, particularly Jewish identity and *ahavat Yisrael* (love of Israel); nonetheless, they include broader secular and religious goals as well.

Jewish education in the Diaspora is, perhaps, forever changed as a result of Birthright Israel. The program has created new norms about educational intensity that set a standard for other programs. Retreats, shabbatonim, and camp programs will all undoubtedly benefit by the comparison to Birthright Israel. Hebrew school and other formal education programs will be challenged to show how they can match Birthright Israel's intensity. Perhaps most important, the program will serve as a reminder that education is not simply about "pouring information into empty vessels." Education, and Jewish education in particular, is about stimulating minds, about stirring emotions, and about giving individuals a chance to "walk and talk" in new ways. The program is a reminder that Jewish education should not be allowed to end, as it does for too many Diaspora youth, at the age of bar or bat mitzvah.[11] To the contrary, young adults are anxious to learn about their heritage and to be engaged in adult ways in the Jewish community. It seems more a question of providing engaging opportunities than of convincing them those are important.

It is unlikely that Birthright Israel will be seen as a revolutionary development by general educators, even though there has been great interest by other ethnic groups in replicating the model. The programmatic approaches by themselves are not untested or unfamiliar. But the scale of Birthright Israel is, nevertheless, a dramatic reminder of what can be accomplished by intensive education that involves all of the senses. Whether it has applications to other areas, such as the teaching of foreign languages and culture, remains to be seen. The program should be a reminder to educators, regardless of their content focus, that young adults are not simply minds that need to be stimulated with knowledge and given complex problems to solve. Good educators, of course, understand that they need to consider the "whole person," but in this age of high-stakes testing and performance standards, it is a lesson that is too often neglected. Young adults are complex emotional, rational, and physical beings. Their development as people with a sense of connection to others may be as important as anything else they can learn. Developing this sense may contribute to their intellectual evolution and to their emergence as concerned and socially responsible members of the community.

PALPABLE EFFECTS

The Birthright Israel initiative is, by a host of objective criteria, an extraordinarily successful educational venture and has been a singular success in the world of Jewish education. It is one of a small number of educational interventions that were developed and brought to scale in a short time and about which there is clear evidence of success. The program's initial goals—to promote Jewish identity, create a sense of Jewish Peoplehood, and to create love of Israel—have, at least in the short run, been met. Although the story of Birthright Israel's long-term impact is yet to be written, and can only be discerned over the next decade, its short-term effects have far exceeded what its founding philanthropists, Bronfman and Steinhardt, could have hoped.

At the same time as we tout the impact of the program, it is also true that Birthright Israel is neither a perfect educational program, nor a panacea for what ails Jewish education and educational efforts more broadly. The present account attempts to identify both strengths and weaknesses of how the program has been conceived and implemented. As powerful as the effects have been, not all educators are equally skilled; not all participants are transformed in major ways; and, perhaps most important, not all participants return ready to be engaged with the Jewish communities. That said, it would scarcely be believable if such a short-term program such as Birthright Israel were more effective.

Indeed, it would be shortsighted to reduce all notions of the Israel experience to the Birthright Israel model. Birthright Israel opens the door to the notion of many diverse models appropriate to different age groups and demographic sectors of contemporary Jewry. We do not want to fall into the exclusivist trap that co-opted Israel teen travel from the 1980s on as the only way. The lesson of Birthright Israel is that it is *a* way, not the only way, to engage young adult Jews with Israel and their religious-ethnic identity. It is, without question, an innovative approach to engaging those who inhabit a heterogeneous postmodern Jewish world. Perhaps the most important lesson is that innovation, and out-of-the box answers need to be stimulated and supported.

Even with these caveats, some might quibble that our account of Birthright Israel has not been totally objective. To be sure, our objectivity has been affected, possibly even compromised by our involvement in the program design. But the central reason that this account is so positive is that we have been able to participate in the program and watch thousands of young Jews take their journey through the Birthright Israel curriculum. Unapologetically, we acknowledge that we have been affected by the hundreds of participants we encountered who, with extraordinary consistency, report that their experience on a Birthright Israel trip was "amazing." The experience with participants reinforces our convictions that our description and assessment of the program is accurate.

FINAL THOUGHTS

That a short-term educational experience such as Birthright Israel could receive near-universal positive evaluations from a wide range of participants and appears to have long-lasting impact on intellectual and personal growth should be a cause for celebration. But, as social scientists and educators, we do not want to pause too long to celebrate. The program has an established platform to shape the next generation of Diaspora and Israeli Jews. Nevertheless, however important and effective the mechanisms of the program, they need to be refined and adapted for the future. The engagement of Jews around the world has a great deal at stake in the outcome of this effort.

Traditional Jewish wisdom links thinking with doing, studying with action. Metaphorically, Judaism is a contact sport: it is not, like other religions, based on the acceptance of faith. That linking is a part of the relationship of a Jew to his or her religion, but it is not the whole. To be Jewish is to be part of a Jewish community and requires more than cerebral activity. To be Jewish involves activity and interaction. It shapes how one thinks about oneself; more important, it is a way of being. Jewish tradition obligates one to engage in tasks without regard to their difficulty. As is expressed in a well-known text from the Pirke Avot, "We are not obligated to complete the task, but neither are we free to abandon it."[12] The effort to engage uneducated Jews in their heritage seems like one of those tasks that has no clear beginning or end.

Our efforts throughout this book to offer an objective account of Birthright Israel notwithstanding, our conclusion is that it is an extraordinary undertaking. It takes the ideas and ideals of Jewish forebears to heart and helps to ensure the continuity of a rich tradition. Birthright Israel is a laboratory for the development of an ethnic identity and community that transcends national and cultural borders. In the contemporary world, shrunk by modern communications and transportation systems but divided by cultural and ethnic conflict, how one creates connections—even within a homogeneous community—is a critical issue. It will take a generation to understand and measure fully Birthright Israel's impact. But even its early lessons seem clear and can help influence how we educate and socialize the next generation of those who will constitute the Jewish people throughout the world.

1. For legal reasons, initially, Birthright Israel was spelled with lowercase letters. In Hebrew, the program was called "Taglit" (discovery), and in 2003, the program changed its name to "Taglit–Birthright Israel." Throughout this book, the program will generally be referred to as "Birthright Israel."

2. The names of participants have been changed to protect their privacy. Except as noted, other names, however, are of the individuals who were part of the program and are being used with permission.

3. Ehud Olmert became interim prime minister of the State of Israel in 2006 when Prime Minister Ariel Sharon suffered a stroke. As a result of elections in April 2006, Olmert became prime minister. Yossi Beilin is the head of an opposition political party, Yachad.

4. Shoshoni 2006. Taglit–Birthright Israel CEO Report. Updated with information from Birthright Israel registration system and reports to Steering Committee.

5. Troen 1999.

6. Steinhardt 2001.

7. $1 invested in his first company in 1967 was $481 in 1995 when he left the market (see Steinhardt 2001, p. 243).

8. Steinhardt 2001.

9. Newman 1979.

10. Chazan 2002; Mittelberg 1999.

11. Wohlgelernter 2000. The arrival of an idea. *Jerusalem Post,* January 7, p. 5B.

12. Originally known as the CRB Foundation, the name was later changed to ACBP—Andrea and Charles Bronfman Philanthropies. ACBP operates and supports programs in the United States, Israel, and Canada to strengthen the unity of the Jewish people, to improve the quality of life in Israel and to promote Canadian heritage. Ultimately, ACBP seeks to span the separations created by geography, culture, and the requirements of daily life with a bridge built on the willingness of individuals in search of community, identity, and meaning (see http://www.acbp.net/overview.html).

13. Bayme 2002, p. 409.

14. Beilin 2004.

15. At the United Jewish Communities' General Assembly (GA) held in Denver, Colorado.

16. Beilin 2000. The idea for "birthright" had multiple roots. A group working with Beilin was considering a number of new ideas. The group included staff of the United Jewish Communities.

17. See Mittelberg 1999.

18. See Chazan 2002.

19. Chazan 1994.

20. Kelner 2002.

21. Breakstone 1986.

22. Leed 1991.

23. Cohen 2001, as cited in Chazan 2002, p. 6; Mittelberg 1999.

24. Dewey 1938.

25. Chazan 2002.

26. Heilman 1998.

27. Cohen 2003.

28. Bronfman 1996. Booklet in honor of the tenth anniversary of the CRB foundation. Retrieved November 28, 2006, from http://www.acbp.net/history.html.

29. Involvement in education 2005. Retrieved November 28, 2006, from http://www.acbp.net/involvement.html; Israel Experience Ltd. About us. Retrieved November 28, 2006, from http://www.israelexperience.org.il/newsite/index1.asp?PageID=51&DepIDMain=7&Language=english.

30. The majority of American Jews identify with one of three large denominations: Orthodox, which represents a broad spectrum of traditional beliefs; Conservative, which while traditional, tries to interpret Jewish life in modern ways; and Reform, which is considered the most liberal and the least bound to tradition. At present, more Jews identity as Reform (around 30 percent); fewer, Conservative (around 22 percent) and the smallest, Orthodox (8 percent). Increasingly though, Jews do not claim a denomination (see Kadushin, Phillips, and Saxe 2005). The official names of the youth movements of each denomination are: National Conference of Synagogue Youth (NCSY), United Synagogue Youth (USY), and North American Federation of Temple Youth (NFTY).

31. Sales and Saxe 2003.

32. Chazan, Cohen, and Wall 1996.

33. Mittelberg 1999.

34. London and Hirschfeld 1991; Mittelberg 1992.

35. Chazan 1997, p. 157.

36. Chazan 1997, p. 4.

37. NJPS 2000–01 indicates that 35 percent of the adults of the "broad" population of 5.2 million Jews and Jewish-connected people have been to Israel. According to the United Jewish Communities, the figure for the adults of the narrower 4.3 million population of Jews is 41 percent; however, the NJPS dataset underestimates the proportion of non-Orthodox Jews and, thus, likely overestimates participation/engagement (see Saxe, Tighe, Phillips, and Kadushin 2007).

38. Although it is difficult to estimate how many young people participate, prior to 2000, only a relatively small percentage of those under twenty-five had been on an Israel experience program. Analyses of data at the Steinhardt Social Research Institute at Brandeis Univeristy indicate that the proportion is likely less than 20 percent (see Saxe et al. 2007).

39. Chazan and Cohen 2000.

40. Wohlgelernter 2000, p. 6B. Birthright: So Far, So Good. *Jerusalem Post,* July 14:

"the two philanthropists were immediately laughed at and criticized—behind their backs and publicly."

41. Liebler 1999, Only in America! *Jerusalem Post,* November 8, p. 8.

42. See, for example, Bayme 2002: "Ten days is simply too short a time span to effect real change among those initially uncommitted to the Jewish collective experience" p. 409.

43. Philanthropic partners included the government of Israel, Diaspora Jewish communities (United Jewish Communities, United Israel Appeal, and the Jewish Agency for Israel), and individual philanthropists/philanthropies: S. Daniel Abraham, the Abramson Family Foundation, the AVI CHAI Foundation, Andrea and Charles Bronfman, Edgar Bronfman, Sr., Richard and Rhoda Goldman Foundation, the Harold Grinspoon Foundation, Hadassah–The Women's Zionist Organization of America, Ronald S. Lauder, the Marcus Foundation–Bernie Marcus, Marc Rich, the Samberg Family Foundation, Charles and Lynn Schusterman Family Foundation, Judy and Michael Steinhardt, the Wasserman Foundation, Leslie and Abigail Wexner and the Wexner Foundation, and Karen and Gary Winnick.

44. *Hillel Annual Report: Adding Value, Adding Values* 2003. Washington, D.C.: Hillel International, p. 1.

45. Rosen 2006.

46. Ibid.

47. Based in Jerusalem, the Israeli organization was called Taglit (see note 1).

48. In the initial cohort, 5 percent identified as Orthodox, 33 percent identified as Conservative, 32 percent identified as Reform, 1 percent identified as Reconstructionist, 21 percent identified as "just Jewish," and 5 percent identified as other. Saxe, Kadushin, Pakes, Kelner, Sternberg, Horowitz et al. 2000, pp. 17–18.

49. Shay 2004.

50. An international fact-finding commission, chaired by former U.S. Senator George Mitchell (Sharm el-Shek Fact-Finding Committee) concluded: "The Sharon visit did not cause the 'Al-Aqsa Initifada.'" Rather, the Mitchell committee pointed to the growing lack of trust between Israel and Palestinians and the inability of either side to "exercise restraint." For a discussion of the issues regarding the Temple Mount, see Gorenberg 2000; Demirel, S., et al. 2001.

51. Schiff 2004; see also an Israeli government account: "Since the beginning of the current conflict, September 29, 2000, more than three hundred kassam rockets have been launched into Israeli territory." As of July 24, 2004, there have been 889 attacks on Israelis in Israel proper since September 2000, and a total of 22,406 attacks when including attacks within the Gaza Strip and the West Bank. http://www1.idf.il.; editorial.

52. Cole 2007.

53. See Israel's Ministry of Foreign Affairs website, http://www.mfa.gov.il/mfa/ Links to terrorism before 2000. "Fatal Terrorist Attacks in Israel Since the Declaration of Principles": From the signing of the Declaration of Principles between Israel and the PLO on September 13, 1993 until September 2000, 256 [Israeli] civilians and soldiers were killed in terrorist attacks in Israel. Fatal terrorist attacks in Israel since the Declaration of Principles (September 24, 2000). Retrieved November 28, 2006 from

http://www.mfa.gov.il/MFA/Terrorism-%20Obstacle%20to%20Peace/Palestinian%20 terror%20before%202000/Fatal%20Terrorist%20Attacks%20in%20Israel%20Since %20the%20DOP%20-S.

54. Shay 2004.

55. Adelson and his wife, Miriam, through their foundation donated $27.5 million. It enabled the program to increase by more than 50 percent the number served by the program. Leyden 2007. Adelson donates $25 Million to Birthright Israel, Reinforces Economy. *Israel News Agency,* February 6. http://www.israelnewsagency.com/ birthrighttaglitisraeleconomyadelson48020607.html.

56. Cf. Taglit–Birthright Israel CEO status report, in preparation.

57. Greenberg 2004, 2006. See also Sales and Saxe 2006.

58. Bellah, Madsen, Sullivan, Swidler, and Tipton 1985, p. 221.

59. Putnam 2000; Etzioni 2003.

60. Saxe, Sasson, and Hecht 2006b.

CHAPTER TWO. DREAMS REALIZED AND SHATTERED: ISRAEL IN THE MIND OF AMERICAN JEWS (PAGES 19–32)

1. Agnon 2000.

2. Keinon and Zacharia 2001. Military Response Okayed by Cabinet. *Jerusalem Post,* June 3.

3. See Herzl 1976; Derfler 2002.

4. See Gilbert 1987.

5. Gilbert 1998.

6. See Hahn, Hecht, Leavitt, Saxe, Tighe, and Sales 2004.

7. Gilbert 1998; Elon 1983, p. 3.

8. Twain 1869/1996, pp. 606–608.

9. Heschel 1997.

10. *Tanakh: The Holy Scriptures, The New JPS Translation According to the Traditional Hebrew Text* 1985. Philadelphia: Jewish Publication Society. Genesis 12:1.

11. *Tanakh: The Holy Scriptures, The New JPS Translation According to the Traditional Hebrew Text* 1985. Deuteronomy 26:9.

12. Segal 2001, pp. 1372–1375.

13. Segal 1987.

14. Sarna 1996.

15. Brandeis 1942.

16. See Rawidowicz 1986, p. 197.

17. Ibid., pp. 194–204.

18. See AJC website. Israeli Premier's first official declaration clarifying relationships between Israel and Jews in the United States hailed by Blaustein as "document of historic significance" (1950, September 10). American Jewish Committee.

19. Sarna 2004, pp. 334–335.

20. Marans and Bell 2006.

21. Fishman 2004; Phillips and Fishman 2006; Saxe and Chertok 2007.

22. For general overviews, see Elazar 1995; also, Sarna 2004.

23. See Leshem and Shuval 1998; Guttman 2006. A.B. Yehoshua sparks uproar by saying only Israel can ensure Jewish survival. *Jerusalem Post,* May 4.

24. Wertheimer 1997, p. 19 ff. See also Gal and Gottschalk 2000; Tobin, Solomon, and Karp 2003.

25. Phillips, Lengyel, and Saxe 2002.

26. Ibid.

27. Kosmin 1991.

28. Fishman 2000; Cohen and Wertheimer 2006.

29. Fishman 2004.

30. Mittelberg 1992.

31. Cohen 1975; Urofsky 1979; Urofsky 1995.

32. Chazan 2002.

33. See Kaplan, E. H. 2002, p. 8. Competing risks and realities. *Jerusalem Post,* January 8. According to Kaplan, a professor of management at Yale University, during the first year and half of the intifada (October 2000 through December 2001), the risk of highway deaths in Israel was four times that of terrorism inside of Israel. Of note, highway death rates during this period were one-half the rate in the United States (see also Liebman 1974).

34. See, for example, Hingson, Heeren, Winter, and Wechsler 2005. Magnitude of alcohol-related mortality and morbidity among U.S. college students ages eighteen to twenty-four: changes from 1998 to 2001. This study indicates that among approximately eight million U.S. college students (ages 18 to 24), the death rate from alcohol-related incidents in 2001 was 1,700. In addition, according to Hingson et al. 2005: "More than 500,000 fulltime 4-year-college students were unintentionally injured under the influence of alcohol, and more than 600,000 were hit or assaulted by and more than 70,000 experienced a date rape caused by another student who had been drinking" (260).

35. Kelner 2002, p. 44.

36. See Mittelberg 1999 (see also Tobin et al. 1995).

37. Tobin et al. 1995.

38. Saxe et al. 2000, pp. 17–18.

39. Fishman 2004, pp. 1–13.

40. Phillips 1997.

41. Among recent applicants to Birthright Israel, 20 percent cannot distinguish the letters of the alphabet ("aleph" from "bet") and approximately another 50 percent can read (prayerbooks, etc.), but do not understand what they are reading (see Saxe, Sasson, Phillips, Hecht, and Wright 2007).

42. Kosmin et al. 1991.

43. Mittelberg 1994.

44. See Wertheimer 1997.

CHAPTER THREE. SITES AND SIGHTS (PAGES 33–51)

1. Jewish National Fund: celebrating one hundred years as caretaker of the land of Israel. Retrieved November 28, 2006, from http://www.jnf.org/site/PageServer? pagename=history#JNF%20100TH%20ANNIVERSARY.

2. Murphy 2003.

3. This translation of the Amichai poem was given by a guide. Published English translations (see, e.g., Amichai 1994) use different words for "obligate."

4. Cohen 1979; Cohen 1984; Cohen 1997; Leed 1991; Turner 1974; Van Gennep 1960.

5. Leed 1991.

6. This quote is taken from responses to an optional question on the Birthright Israel application (included since 2003) and analyzed by research staff at the Cohen Center for Modern Jewish Studies, Brandeis University.

7. Kelner 2004, p. 7.

8. Drawn from *Educational standards and program requirements*. 2005. March. Taglit–Birthright Israel.

9. Turner 1969.

10. Goldberg 2002; Heilman 2002.

11. See discussion of narratives by Kelner 2002 (see also Goldwater 2002).

12. Farmer 1960.

13. Zerubavel 1995.

14. Ben-Yehuda 1995; Laqueur 2003.

15. Minkin 1956.

16. Translations are by the guides, as recorded/remembered by observers.

17. Amichai 1994, p. 333.

18. David Ben-Gurion (Israel's first prime minister) is buried at his former home in Sde Boker, the Negev; and Chaim Weizman (Israel's first president) is buried in Rehovot.

19. Zvi 2004.

20. Telushkin 1991.

21. Laqueur 2003.

22. Goldwater 2002.

23. Kelner 2002.

CHAPTER FOUR. A PEOPLE REVOLUTION (PAGES 52–71)

1. Sharansky was the government's representative to Birthright Israel and in this capacity served as chair of the Steering Committee from 2004 to 2006.

2. See Sharansky 1998.

3. Sharansky and Dermer 2004.

4. Brandeis 1942 (see, for example, pp. 12–35).

5. Infeld, reportedly, met a woman at the Lisbon Airport who had heard his speech (a three pillar/three legs of a stool version). The woman was wearing a pendant she had made. It had the three legs of the Jewish peoplehood stool inside. It illustrates the impact of Infeld's teaching and the degree to which participants feel personally touched.

6. Saxe, Sasson, and Hecht 2006b.

7. Schwab 1978, p. 119.

8. Beginning in 2001, security considerations required that participants not travel unescorted and guides were required to follow elaborate rules to ensure participants' safety.

9. Goldwater 2002.

10. Taglit–Birthright Israel (2005, March). *Educational standards and program requirements.*

11. Heilman 2002; Goldberg 2002.

12. Kirshenblatt-Gimblett 2002 (see also Shapiro 2006).

13. Turner 1969.

14. Goffman 1961.

15. The original funding formula required that one-third of the program costs be provided by philanthropists, one-third from the State of Israel, and one-third from Jewish communities (through the United Jewish Communities and the Jewish Agency for Israel).

16. The Charles and Lynn Schusterman Family Foundation supports a leadership training and innovation initiative called ROI (return on investment) that brings Birthright Israel alumni (and others) to Israel for summit meetings designed to spur new programs and projects (see www.ROI120.com). The Schusterman Foundation supports a number of other initiatives that allow alumni to return to Israel to do social service projects and network with other alumni.

17. Steinhardt has a vacation home that newlyweds can use—but they have to get there on their own. Several couples have used it.

18. See Cooley 1964; Miller 1982.

19. In this sense, the program remained true to Beilin's initial vision of Birthright Israel (see Beilin 2000).

CHAPTER FIVE. SHARED ENCOUNTERS (PAGES 72–93)

1. An affectionate term, more akin to my brother/sister.

2. Ezrachi and Sutnick 1997.

3. We have already referred to Heilman's (2002) and Goldberg's (2002) ethnographic studies of Israel trips, which pointed to the power of the Israel experience but at the same time, to the striking absence of meeting real young Israelis.

4. See ten-year report and speech given by Charles Bronfman at Hebrew University in 1991.

5. *Taglit program requirements,* November 1999.

6. See Taglit CEO Status Report, 2007.

7. There were discussions prior to the Rabin assassination of a rabbinic dictate called *pulsa dnura,* which permitted removing a traitor to the Jewish cause; Dershowitz 2002.

8. The Sikarim (also spelled "siccari" or known in Hebrew as the "Canaenans") were revolutionaries who attempted to overthrow Roman rule (see Brandon 1967).

9. Haberman 2001. Gilo Waits for Deliverance as Middle East Violence Goes On. *New York Times,* August 30.

10. The U.N.-mediated agreement between Jordan and Israel stated that in regards to Jerusalem, "the status quo continued: the New City [would] remain in Jewish hands

and the Old City in Arab hands. The Jordanians promised the Israelis free access to the Hadassah hospital and the Hebrew University on Mount Scopus, and to the shrines and cemetaries on the Mount of Olives." Sachar 2006, p. 350.

11. Amichai 2004, p. 312.

12. Chafets 1986.

13. Amichai 2004, p. 333.

14. Jung 1983. See also Person 2001.

15. See, for example, http://www.asimon.co.il/personalLineArticle.aspx?AID= 2531&CID=5638.

16. Amichai 1996, p. 147.

CHAPTER SIX. PEDAGOGY FOR PEOPLE (PAGES 94–114)

1. Drawn from field notes by evaluators (in particular, Dr. Mark Rosen) from the Maurice and Marilyn Cohen Center for Modern Jewish Studies, Brandeis University.

2. See Oren 2002.

3. See Olmert Moves Office to Old City. 2000. *Ha'aretz*. December 28.

4. Chazan 2002.

5. See Saxe, Sasson, Phillips, Hecht, and Wright 2007.

6. Lewin 1951, p. 228 ff.

7. For debates on proselytizing, see e.g., Tugend 1996; Polish 1982; Kaellis 1987; Croner and Klenicki 1979.

8. By force of its founding mandate, JAFI is "committed to assuring the future of the Jewish people with a strong Israel at its center, through immigration to Israel, Jewish-Zionist education and partnership with and for Israel" (www.jafi.org.il). This mandate is sometimes seen as a point of contention because the manifest function of Birthright Israel is not promoting aliyah.

9. See Sales and Saxe, 2006.

10. Dewey, 1938, pp. 25–32; 1916, pp. 139–151; 1929, pp. 181–188.

11. See description and analysis of programs in: Mittelberg 1999, 1994; Israel and Mittelberg 1998; Mittelberg and Ari 1996; Kelner 2002; Shapiro 2006.

12. Gardner 1993.

13. Koren 2007a; 2007b (see also Bard 2006, 2004).

14. Turkle 1995.

15. Fishkoff 2003.

16. For a parallel example of the importance of an educational vision, see Lightfoot, S. L., 1983; Arum 2003; Arum and Beattie 2000.

17. For detailed descriptions of specific sites visited by Birthright Israel participants and discussed throughout this book, see *Carta's Official Guide to Israel and Complete Gazetteer to All Sites in the Holy Land* (2001). Jerusalem: Ministry of Defense: Carta. Yad Vashem is a Holocaust memorial located on Har Hazikaron (Mount of Remembrance) adjacent to Mount Herzl, in Jerusalem, and is named for "a memorial and a name" (Isaiah 56:5). The site is dedicated to documenting the history and preserving the memory of the Jewish people who perished in the Holocaust, as well as teaching the legacy of the Holocaust. The site houses museums and archives on Jewry in the

Holocaust, including an international school for Holocaust studies and an institute for Holocaust research. In 2005, a new museum opened that chronicles the rise of the Nazis and their systematic program of extermination applied to Jews across Europe.

18. These sites reflect Jewish values of compassion and care for the weak in the community. Yad Sarah is an Israel-wide network of volunteers aiding the sick, disabled, elderly, isolated, and housebound with a number of services dedicated to making home living more comfortable. Malben Hospital in Afula has social service programs for the elderly and handicapped. Eshel, the Association for the Planning and Development of Services for the Aged in Israel, is an offshoot of AJDC-Malben. Alyn Hospital is one of the world's leading hospitals and research centers in the active and intensive rehabilitation of children with physical disabilities.

19. Jerusalem, known in ancient times as the City of David, is the holiest city for the Jews. It is the focus of thousands of poems, books, and essays and is the heart of Zion. Synagogues around the world are designed so that their Torah is in an ark on the wall backing toward Jerusalem, so that worshipers face Jerusalem during prayer. Masada is an ancient mountaintop fortress in southeastern Israel, high above the Dead Sea. It is the site of the Jews' last stand against the Romans after the fall of Jerusalem in 70 C.E. Caeserea is an archeological marvel; a massive port city two thousand years ago in Roman times, much of the ancient city still remains, including an aqueduct, theater, excavated houses, mosaics, and palaces. Bet Shean, another ancient metropolis of the Roman era, was first settled in the fifth century B.C.E. and was ruled over by various groups of Jews, Christians, and pagans. It is in the Jordan River Valley, a fertile farming region, and today is an agricultural and textile manufacturing center.

20. Taglit–Birthright Israel. Jerusalem, Israel.

21. Moach Eser (Moach 10) is an Israeli educational evaluation firm that has worked with Birthright Israel and other educational organizations to monitor and assess programs. Using systems they developed and tested with other organizations, they developed a process for monitoring how individual Birthright Israel tour providers implement the program and meet program standards. For each round of trips, they conduct observations of a sample of programs and conduct surveys of participants. The findings are used to provide feedback to Taglit–Birthright Israel and to tour operators. The findings of Moach 10's work have been used to improve how tours are conducted and, on occasion, to sanction providers for failures to meet program standards. Since 2005, Moach 10's survey data have been integrated with the overall evaluation of Birthright Israel (see chapter 8).

22. Arnett 2004; 2000.

23. See Erikson 1968; 1950; 1963; 1959.

24. Erikson (1959) posited eight stages of psychosocial development, each with its own critical psychosocial crisis. He found that the central crisis within the adolescent stage was identity versus role confusion. However, he also believed that a prolonged adolescence in which identity was explored into the stage he titled "young adulthood" was allowed in industrialized societies (see also Arnett 2000).

25. Arnett and Jensen 2000.

26. See Cherry, DeBerg, and Porterfield 2001.

27. Blumer 1986.

28. Côté and Levine 2002.

29. Heilman 2002, p. 230.

30. Lewin 1935; 1936; 1951; Tajfel and Turner 1986.

31. *Talking about Tie-Ins: A Guide to Leading Tie-In Discussions* 2002. New York: Birthright Israel, p. 1.

32. Dewey 1916; 1938, pp. 357–358. Buber 1958, p. 114; Rogers 1969, pp. 284–285; Maslow 1964; 1994, pp. 24–28.

33. See Goldwater 2002.

34. For an example, see the discussion of how counselors function at summer camps in Sales and Saxe 2004, pp. 97–118.

35. For a particularly uncomfortable description of the failures of Jewish education, consider the characterization of Rabbi Eric Yoffie, leader of the Reform movement (the largest movement of American Jewry), who, at the Union of American Hebrew Congregations' 66th Biennial Convention in 2001, described the typical parental attitude toward after-school or Sunday religious education: "Many of our parents look upon religious school as a punishment for being young . . . It is the castor oil of Jewish life, a burden passed from parent to child with the following admonition: 'I hated it, you'll hate it, and after your bar mitzvah, you can quit.'" Yoffie 2001.

36. Bruner 1996, p. 22.

CHAPTER SEVEN. AN ORGANIZATIONAL CULTURE (PAGES 115–136)

1. In the Israeli system, the "director general" is the highest ranking nonpolitical position in a ministry (the equivalent of a cabinet department in the United States) and is designated for a highly regarded professional. Ministers are political figures and change frequently, while the director general typically serves a longer term.

2. One of Shoshani's models was fomer Harvard School of Education dean, Theodore Sizer (see Sizer 2004 [1984]).

3. Included was the coauthor of this book, Barry Chazan.

4. I. Greenberg is best known as the author of *The Jewish Way: Living the Holidays* (1993). More recently, Greenberg wrote *For the Sake of Heaven and Earth: The New Encounter between Judaism and Christianity* (2004).

5. Rosolio Prize for Outstanding Contribution to Israeli Public Administration.

6. Hollander 1964; pp. 12–13, 167 ff.

7. The education director from the inception of the project was Barry Chazan, coauthor of this book.

8. The New York/North American headquarters were directed by a number of individuals over the course of the program's first seven years: Michael Papo, Rabbi Sheldon Zimmerman, Simon Klarfeld, and Robert Aronson. The structure evolved and, currently, a separate organization, the Birthright Israel Foundation—headed by Jay Golan—works alongside Taglit–Birthright Israel in North America.

9. Post 1999. Don't bash birthright. *Jerusalem Report*, December 20, p. 54.

10. Gilbert 1999. Barak, Shohat OK $70M for birthright project. *Jerusalem Post*, October 13, p. 5.

11. Quoted in Wohlgelernter 2000. Birthright: So far, so good. *Jerusalem Post,* July 16.

12. Eliezer Ben Yehudah was an early Zionist who revived Hebrew as a modern language. See http://www.jafi.org.il/education/100/people/BIOS/beliezer.html.

13. Goffman 1959.

14. In a 1974 conversation with the then Chief Rabbi of Tel Aviv (Rabbi Yisrael Lau), Rabbi Menachem Mendel Schneerson (the Seventh Lubavitcher Rebbe) explicitly rejected the term "*kiruv*" to describe the educational work done by Chabad. Rabbi Lau described his conversation in an address in 27 July 1994 at South Head Synagogue in Sydney (see Solomon 2000). *The Education Teachings of Rabbi Menachem M. Schneerson.* Northvale, N.J.: Jason Aronson, p. 22.

15. See Sales and Saxe 2006, p. 9 (see also Rosen 2006).

CHAPTER EIGHT. PARTICIPANTS AND EVALUATION (PAGES 137–154)

1. The presentation was made by Leonard Saxe, with Charles Kadushin. Charles Kadushin was co–principal investigator with Saxe of the evaluation from 2000 through 2005. In 2005, Theodore Sasson joined the team and currently serves as co-principal investigator with Saxe.

2. The evaluation contract provided for an independent evaluation. Funded by Birthright Israel, it gave the investigators the responsibility to design the study and the authority to publish findings, regardless of whether they were positive or negative.

3. See Saxe and Fine 1981; Shadish, Cook, and Campbell 2002.

4. Separate evaluation of non-NA participants.

5. Participant observers have included faculty/research scholars from Brandeis University, including Charles Kadushin, Sylvia Barack Fishman, Mark Rosen, Shaul Kelner (currently at Vanderbilt University) and Theodore Sasson. As well, nearly a dozen Ph.D. candidates and a half-dozen undergraduate researchers have done participant observation.

6. Sales and Saxe 2006, pp. 16, 24.

7. Bard 2006; 2004.

8. See Rossi, Lipsey, and Freeman 2004; Saxe and Fine 1981.

9. See Massing 2006. The Storm over the Israel Lobby. *New York Review of Books* 53, no. 10, June 8; Peretz 2006. Oil and Vinegar. *New Republic,* April 10; Oren 2006. Quiet Riot. *New Republic,* April 10.

10. In the summer of 2006, there were more than 25,000 North American applicants for only 10,000 available slots. Registration was so high that the registration period was terminated weeks before it was scheduled to end.

CHAPTER NINE. PARTICIPANTS' VOICES (PAGES 155–170)

1. Kelner 2002.

2. Fathi 2005. Iranian President Stands By Call to Wipe Israel Off Map. *New York Times,* October 29.

3. Saxe, Sasson, and Hecht 2006a.

4. Peer-oriented programs include high school trips, Birthright Israel, college study

abroad, ulpan, volunteer programs, yeshiva, synagogue and federation trips, and youth movement programs. Roughly half of those in the Hillel sample who had been on an Israel program had gone on Birthright Israel. Others participated in a wide range of other programs, mostly longer in duration.

5. For all analyses, respondents on peer trips and others were made equivalent by statistically adjusting for age, gender, and political views (see Saxe, Sasson, and Hecht 2006a).

6. See Phillips, Lengyel, and Saxe 2002.

7. The report of these groups is an amalgam based on several observations by the authors and their colleagues. Because it was not possible to seek individual permission for discussion of these observations, identities of groups and participants have been disguised.

8. Corporal Gilad Shalit, age nineteen, was kidnapped on June 25, 2006, by Palestinians on the Israeli side of the Gaza Strip border, near Kerem Shalom. See Keinon and Siegel 2006. PM: Hamas to blame; top priority to save captured corporal. *Jerusalem Post,* June 26.

9. Dershowitz 2006. Blame the terrorists, not Israel. *Boston Globe,* July 24, p. A9.

10. Initiated in 2007, "Leading Up North" is a Joint Distribution Committee short-term service project. Sponsored by the Charles and Lynn Schusterman Family Foundation, its goal is to bring young Diaspora Jews from around the world to the north of Israel both to volunteer and to build their leadership, solidarity, and connection to the people of Israel. See http://www.jdc.org/p_is_ps_bld_upn.html.

CHAPTER TEN. THE TENTH DAY: WHAT WE LEARNED (PAGES 171–186)

1. Colonel David (Mickey) Marcus was killed accidentally by one of his own troops in the early morning hours of June 11, 1948, the day that the cease-fire was declared. Marcus, who had been wandering the grounds just outside the camp at Abu Ghosh, was mistaken for an intruder and killed. See Gilbert 1998, p. 209.

2. Interview conducted by the authors.

3. From a focus group transcript (2006), part of a community pilot study (of long-term outcomes). Sasson, Saxe, Rosen, Hecht, and Selinger-Abutbul 2007.

4. Shulman 2006; 2004.

5. Friedman 2005.

6. Kravitz and Olitzky 1993.

7. See, for example, Sacks 2007.

8. IACT: Inspired, Active, Committed, and Transformed Strategy. Combined Jewish Philanthropies, Boston, Massachusetts.

9. Gladwell 2000.

10. Along with Rabbi Greenberg (who headed Steinhardt's Foundation) and Jeffrey Solomon (who heads ACBP), several other key staff were involved. Connected with Steinhardt were Shula Navon and Rabbi David Gedzelman. Connected with Bronfman was Janet Aviad.

11. Kelner et al. 2001.

12. Pirke Avot 2:15.

BIBLIOGRAPHY

Agnon, S. Y. 2000. *Only yesterday (Tmol shilshom)*. Translated by B. Harshav. Princeton, N.J.: Princeton University Press.

Amichai, Y. 1994. *Yehuda Amichai: A life of poetry, 1948–1994*. Translated by B. Harshav and B. Harshav. New York: HarperCollins.

———. 1996. What a complicated mess. In *The selected poetry of Yehudah Amichai*. Translated by C. Bloch and S. Mitchell. Berkeley and Los Angeles: University of California Press. p. 147.

Arnett, J. J. 2000. Emerging adulthood: A theory of development from the late teens through the twenties. *American Psychologist* 55, no. 5:469–480.

———. 2004. *Emerging adulthood: The winding road from late teens through the twenties*. New York: Oxford University Press.

———, and L. A. Jensen. 2000. A congregation of one: Individualized religious beliefs among emerging adults. *Journal of Adolescent Research* 17, no. 5:451–467.

Arum, R. 2003. *Judging school discipline: The crisis of moral authority*. Cambridge, Mass.: Harvard University Press.

———, and I. R. Beattie, 2000. *The structure of schooling: Readings in the sociology of education*. Mountain View, Calif.: Mayfield Publishing.

Aviad, J. O. 1983. *Return to Judaism: Religious renewal in Israel*. Chicago: University of Chicago Press.

Bard, M. G. 2004. *Tenured or tenuous: Defining the role of faculty in supporting Israel on campus*. Washington, D.C.: Israel on Campus Coalition.

———. 2006. *In search of Israel Studies: A survey of Israel Studies on American college campuses*. Washington, D.C.: Israel on Campus Coalition.

Bayme, S. 2002. Roundtable on Yossi Beilin's *The death of the American uncle*. In *Jewish arguments and counterarguments*, edited by S. Bayme. Jersey City, N.J.: Ktav Publishers.

Beilin, Y. 2000. *His brother's keeper: Israel and Diaspora Jewry in the twenty-first century*. New York: Schocken Books.

———. 2004. *The path to Geneva: The quest for a permanent agreement, 1996–2004*. New York: RDV Books.

Bellah, R. N., R. Madsen, W. M. Sullivan, A. Swidler, and S. M. Tipton. 1985. *Habits of the heart: Individualism and commitment in American life*. New York: Harper and Row.

Ben-Yehuda, N. 1995. *The Masada myth: Collective memory and mythmaking in Israel*. Madison: University of Wisconsin Press.

Blumer, H. 1986. *Symbolic interactionism: Perspective and method*. Berkeley and Los Angeles: University of California Press.

Brandeis, L. D. 1942. *Brandeis on Zionism: A collection of addresses and statements.* Foreword by Justice Felix Frankfurter. Washington, D.C.: Zionist Organization of America.

Brandon, S. G. F. 1967. *Jesus and the zealots: A study of the political factor in primitive Christianity.* Manchester, U.K.: University of Manchester Press.

Breakstone, D. L. 1986. *The dynamics of Israel in American Jewish life: An analysis of educational means as cultural "texts."* Jerusalem: Department of Jewish Education, Hebrew University.

Bruner, J. S. 1996. *The culture of education.* Cambridge, Mass.: Harvard University Press.

Buber, M. 1958. *I and thou.* Translated by Ronald Gregor Smith. New York: Scribner.

Chafets, Z. 1986. *Heroes and hustlers, hard hats and holy men: Inside the new Israel.* New York: Morrow.

Chazan, B. 1994. The Israel trip: A new form of Jewish education. In *Youth trips to Israel: Rationale and rationalization.* New York: Jewish Education Service of North America.

———. (1997). *Does the teen Israel experience make a difference?* New York: Israel Experience.

———, ed. 2002. *The Israel experience: Studies in Jewish identity and youth culture.* Jerusalem: Andrea and Charles Bronfman Philanthropies.

———, and S. M. Cohen. 2000. What we know about American Jewish youth and young adults. *Journal of Jewish Communal Service* 77, no. 2:76–83.

Cherry, C., B. A. DeBerg, and A. Porterfield. 2001. *Religion on campus: What religion really means to today's undergraduates.* Chapel Hill: University of North Carolina Press.

Cohen, E. 1979. A phenomenology of tourist experiences. *Sociology* 13:179–201.

———. 1984. The sociology of tourism. *Annual reviews in anthropology* 10:373–392.

Cohen, E. H. (2003). Tourism and religion, a case study: Visiting students in Israeli Universities. *Journal of Travel Research* 42, no. 1:36–47.

Cohen, N. W. 1975. *American Jews and the Zionist idea.* Jersey City, N.J.: Ktav Publishers.

Cohen, S. M., and S. Wall. 1994. Excellence in youth trips to Israel. In *Youth trips to Israel: Rationale and rationalization.* New York: Jewish Educational Service of America.

Cohen, S. M., and J. Wertheimer. 2006. Whatever happened to the Jewish people? *Commentary* 121, no. 6:33–37.

Cooley, C. 1964 [1902]. *Human nature and the social order.* New York: Schocken.

Côté, J. E., and C. Levine. 2002. *Identity formation, agency, and culture: A social psychological synthesis.* Mahwah, N.J.: L. Erlbaum.

Croner, H. B., and L. Klenicki. 1979. *Issues in the Jewish-Christian dialogue: Jewish perspectives on covenant, mission and witness.* New York: Paulist Press.

Demirel, S. T. Jagland, G. Mitchell, W. Rudman, and J. Solana. 2001. *Sharm El-Sheikh Fact-Finding Committee Report.* April 30. Retrieved October 25, 2007 from http://www.state.gov/p/nea/rls/rpt/3060.html.

Derfler, L. 2002. *The Dreyfus affair.* Westport, Conn.: Greenwood.

Dershowitz, A. M. 2002. *Why terrorism works: Understanding the threat, responding to the challenge.* New Haven, Conn.: Yale University Press.

———. 2006. Blame the terrorists, not Israel. *Boston Globe.* July 24. A9.

Dewey, J. 1916. *Democracy and education.* New York: Macmillan.

———. 1922. *Human nature and conduct.* New York: Henry Holt.

———. 1938. *Experience and education.* New York: Macmillan.

Elazar, D. J. 1955. *Community and polity: The organizational dynamics of American Jewry.* Rev. ed. Philadelphia: Jewish Publication Society.

Elon, A. 1983. *The Israelis: Founders and sons.* New York: Penguin.

Erikson, E. H. 1950. *Childhood and society.* New York: Norton.

———. 1959. *Identity and the life cycle.* New York: Norton.

———, ed. 1963. *Youth: Change and challenge.* New York: Basic Books.

———. 1968. *Identity, youth, and crisis.* New York: Norton.

Etzioni, A. 2003. *My brother's keeper: A memoir and a message.* Lanham, Md.: Rowman and Littlefield.

Ezrachi, E., and B. Sutnick. 1997. *Israel in our lives: Israel education through encounters with Israelis.* Jerusalem: The CRB Foundation, the Joint Authority for Jewish Zionist Education, and the Charles R. Bronfman Centre for the Israel Experience: Mifgashim.

Farmer, W. R., ed. 1960. *Flavius Josephus: The great Roman-Jewish war: A.D. 66–70 (De bello Judaico).* New York: Harper.

Fathi, N. 2005. Iranian president stands by call to wipe Israel off map. *New York Times.* October 29. p. 3.

Fishkoff, S. 2003. *The Rebbe's army: Inside the world of Chabad-Lubavitch.* New York: Schocken Books.

Fishman, S. B. 2000. *Jewish life and American culture.* Albany: State University of New York.

———. 2004. *Double or nothing? Jewish families and mixed marriage.* Waltham, Mass.: Brandeis University Press.

Friedman, T. 2005. *The world is flat: A brief history of the twenty-first century.* New York: Farrar, Straus, and Giroux.

Gal, A., and A. Gottschalk, eds. 2000. *Beyond survival and philanthropy: American Jewry and Israel.* Cincinnati, Ohio: Hebrew Union College Press.

Gardner, H. 1993. *Frames of mind: The theory of multiple intelligences.* New York: Basic Books.

Gilbert, M. 1987. *The Holocaust: A history of the Jews of Europe during the Second World War.* New York: Owl Books.

———. 1998. *Israel: A history.* New York: Morrow.

Gilbert, N. 1999. Barak, Shohat OK $70M for birthright project. *Jerusalem Post.* October 13. p. 5.

Gladwell, M. 2000. *The tipping point: How little things can make a big difference.* Boston: Little, Brown.

Goffman, E. 1959. *The presentation of self in everyday life.* New York: Doubleday.

———. 1961. *Asylumns.* New York: Doubleday Anchor.

Goldberg, H. 2002. A summer on a NFTY safari. In *The Israel experience: Studies in Jewish identity and youth culture*, edited by B. Chazan. Jerusalem: Andrea and Charles Bronfman Philanthropies.

Goldwater, C. 2002. *Constructing the narrative of authenticity: Tour educators at work in the Israel experience.* Jerusalem: Hebrew University, Melton Centre for Jewish Education.

Gorenberg, G. 2000. *The end of days: Fundamentalism and the struggle for the Temple Mount.* New York: Free Press.

Greenberg, A. 2004. *OMG! How generation y is redefining faith in the iPod era.* New York: Reboot.

Greenberg, A. 2006. *"Grande soy vanilla latte with cinnamon, no foam . . ." Jewish identity and community in a time of unlimited choices.* New York: Reboot.

Greenberg, I. 1993. *The Jewish way: Living the holidays.* New York: Touchstone.

———. 2004. *For the sake of heaven and earth: The new encounter between Judaism and Christianity.* Philadelphia: Jewish Publication Society.

Guttman, N. 2006. A. B. Yehoshua sparks uproar by saying only Israel can ensure Jewish survival. *The Jerusalem Post.* May 4. p. 2.

Haberman, C. 2001. Gilo waits for deliverance as mideast violence goes on. *New York Times.* August 30. P. 8.

Hahn, A., S. Hecht, T. Leavitt, L. Saxe, E. Tighe, and A. Sales. 2004. *Jewish elderly Nazi victims: A synthesis of comparative information on hardship and need in the United States, Israel, and the Former Soviet Union.* Waltham, Mass.: Brandeis University, Maurice and Marilyn Cohen Center for Modern Jewish Studies.

Heilman, S. 1998. Judaism and Jewish identity: Changing interrelationships and differentiations in the Diaspora and Israel. In *Jewish survival: The identity problem at the close of the twentieth century*, edited by E. Krausz and G. Tulea. New Brunswick, N.J.: Transaction.

———. 2002. A Young Judea Israel discovery tour. In *The Israel experience: Studies in Jewish identity and youth culture*, edited by B. Chazan. Jerusalem: Andrea and Charles Bronfman Philanthropies.

Herzl, T. 1946 [1896]. *The Jewish state: An attempt at a modern solution of the Jewish question.* New York: American Zionist Emergency Council.

Heschel, A. J. 1969. *Israel: An echo of eternity.* New York: Farrar, Straus, and Giroux.

Hillel annual report: Adding value. Adding values. 2003. Hillel International: Washington, D.C.

Hingson, R., T. Heeren, M. Winter, and H. Wechsler. 2005. Magnitude of alcohol-related mortality and morbidity among U.S. college students ages 18–24: Changes from 1998 to 2001. *Annual Review of Public Health* 26:259–279.

Hollander, E. P. 1964. *Leaders, groups, and influence.* New York: Oxford University Press.

Israel, S., and D. Mittelberg. 1998. *The Israel visit—not just for teens: The characteristics and impact of college-age travel to Israel.* Waltham, Mass.: Brandeis University, Maurice and Marilyn Cohen Center for Modern Jewish Studies.

Jung, C. G. 1983. *The essential Jung.* Selected and introduced by Anthony Storr. Princeton, N.J.: Princeton University Press.

Kadushin, C., B. Phillips, and L. Saxe. 2005. National Jewish population survey, 2000–2001: A guide for the perplexed. *Contemporary Jewry* 25:1–32.

Kaellis, E. 1987. *Toward a Jewish America.* Edited by R. Kaellis. Lewiston, N.Y.: E. Mellen Press.

Kaplan, E. H. 2002. Competing risks and realities. *The Jerusalem Post.* January 8. p. 08.

Keinon, H., and J. Siegel. 2006. PM: Hamas to blame; top priority to save captured corporal. *The Jerusalem Post.* June 26. p. 01.

Keinon, H., and J. Zacharia. 2001. Militaty response okayed by cabinet. *The Jerusalem Post.* June 3. p. 01.

Kelner, S. 2002. *Almost pilgrims: Authenticity, identity, and the extraordinary on a Jewish tour of Israel.* New York: Department of Sociology, City University of New York.

———. 2004, June 20. "Somebody else's business: The attempt to influence individual belonging through Israel experience programs." Paper presented to the conference on Dynamic Belonging: Shifting Jewish Identities and Collective Involvements in Comparative Perspective. Institute for Advanced Studies, Hebrew University of Jerusalem, Israel.

———, L. Saxe, C. Kadushin, R. Canar, M. Lindholm, H. Ossman, J. Perloff, B. Phillips, R. Teres, M. Wolf, and M. Woocher. 2001. *Making meaning: Participants' experience of Birthright Israel.* Waltham, Mass.: Brandeis University, Maurice and Marilyn Cohen Center for Modern Jewish Studies.

Kirshenblatt-Gimblett, B. 2002. Learning from ethnography: Reflections on the nature and efficacy of youth tours to Israel. In *The Israel experience: Studies in Jewish identity and youth culture,* edited by B. Chazan, 263. Jerusalem: Andrea and Charles Bronfman Philanthropies.

Koren, A. 2007a. *Brandeis University's Summer Institute for Israel Studies: The first three years.* Waltham, Mass.: Brandeis University, Maurice and Marilyn Cohen Center for Modern Jewish Studies. Unpublished.

———. 2007b. *Israel scholar development fund: An evaluation.* Waltham, Mass.: Brandeis University, Maurice and Marilyn Cohen Center for Modern Jewish Studies. Unpublished.

Kosmin, B., S. Goldstein, J. Waksberg, N. Lerer, A. Keysar, and J. Scheckner. 1991. *Highlights of the CJF 1990 national Jewish population survey.* New York: Council of Jewish Federations.

Kotler-Berkowitz, L., S. Cohen, J. Ament, V. Klaff, F. Mott, and D. Peckerman-Neuman. 2004. *National Jewish population survey, 2000–01: Strength, challenge and diversity in the American Jewish population.* New York: United Jewish Communities.

Kravitz, L., and K. M. Olitzky. ed. 1993. *Pirke Avot: A modern commentary on Jewish ethics.* New York: URJ Press.

Laqueur, W. 2003. *A history of Zionism.* New York: Schocken Books.

Lassner, J., and S. I. Troen. 2007. *Jews and Muslims in the Arab world: Haunted by pasts real and imagined.* Lanham, Md.: Rowman & Littlefield.

Leed, E. J. 1991. *The mind of the traveler: From Gilgamesh to global tourism.* New York: Basic Books.

Leshem, E., and J. T. Shuval. ed. 1998. *Immigration to Israel: Sociological perspectives.* New Brunswick, N.J.: Transaction.

Lewin, K. 1935. *A dynamic theory of personality.* New York: McGraw-Hill.

———. 1936. *Principles of topological psychology.* New York: McGraw-Hill.

———. 1951. *Field theory in social science.* New York: Harper and Row.

Leyden, J. 2007. Adelson donates $25 million to Birthright Israel, reinforces economy. *Israel News Agency,* February 6. http://www.israelnewsagency.com/birthrighttaglit israeleconomyadelson48020607.html.

Liebler, I. 1999. Only in America! *The Jerusalem Post.* November 8. p. 08.

Liebman, C. S. 1974. Diaspora influence on Israel: The Ben-Gurion–Blaustein exchange and its aftermath. *Journal of Social Studies* 36:271–280.

Lightfoot, S. L. 1983. *The good high school: Portraits of character and culture.* New York: Basic Books.

London, B., and A. Hirschfield. 1991. The psychology of identity formation. In *Jewish Identity in America,* edited by D. M. Gordis and Y. Ben-Horin, 31–50. Los Angeles, Calif.: Susan and David Wilstein Institute of Jewish Policy Studies, University of Judaism.

Marans, N., and R. Bell ed. 2006. *The A. B. Yehoshua controversy: An Israel-diaspora dialogue on Jewishness, Israeliness, and identity.* New York: Dorothy and Julius Koppelman Institute on American Jewish-Israeli Relations, American Jewish Committee.

Maslow, A. 1994 [1964]. *Religions, values, and peak-experiences.* New York: Penguin.

Massing, M. 2006. The storm over the Israel lobby. *New York Review of Books* 53(10).

Mead, G. H. 1982. *The individual and the social self: Unpublished essays by G. H. Mead.*Edited by D. L. Miller. Chicago: University of Chicago Press.

Miller, D. L., ed. 1982. *The individual and the social self: Unpublished essays by G. H. Mead.* Chicago: University of Chicago Press.

Minkin, J. S. 1956 [1936]. *Herod: King of the Jews.* New York: Thomas Yoseloff.

Mintz, R. F., ed. And trans. 1966. *Modern Hebrew Poetry.* Berkeley and Los Angeles: University of California Press.

Mittelberg, D. 1992. The impact of Jewish education and the "Israel Experience" on the Jewish identity of American Jewish youth. *Studies in Contemporary Jewry* 8:194–218.

———. 1994. *The Israel visit and Jewish identification.* New York: American Jewish Committee.

———. 1999. *The Israel connection and American Jews.* Westport, Conn.: Praeger.

———, and L. L. Ari. 1996. *Jewish identity, Jewish education and experience of the kibbutz in Israel.* Haifa: Institute for Research and Study of the Kibbutz and the Cooperative Idea, University of Haifa.

Murphy, S. D., ed. 2003. Congressional effort to move U.S. embassy to Jerusalem. In Contemporary practice of the United States relating to international law. *American Journal of International Law* 91, no. 1:179–180.

National Jewish population survey 2000–2001: Strength, challenge and diversity in the American Jewish population. 2000. New York: United Jewish Communities.

Newman, P. C. 1979. *King of the castle: The making of a dynasty: Seagram's and the Bronfman empire.* New York: Atheneum.

Olitzky, K., and L. Kravitz. 2000. *Shemonah Perakim: A treatise on the soul.* New York: URJ Press.

Oren, M. B. 2002. *Six days of war: June 1967 and the making of the modern Middle East.* New York: Oxford University Press.

———. 2006. Quiet riot. *New Republic,* April 10.

Peretz, M. 2006. Oil and vinegar. *New Republic,* April 10.

Person, E. S., ed. 2001. *On Freud's "Group psychology and the analysis of the ego."* Hillsdale, N.J.: Analytic Press.

Phillips, B., and S. B. Fishman. 2006. Ethnic capital and intermarriage: A case study of American Jews. *Sociology of Religion* 67, no. 4: 487–505.

Phillips, B., E. Lengyel, and L. Saxe. 2002. *American attitudes toward Israel.* Waltham, Mass.: Brandeis University, Maurice and Marilyn Cohen Center for Modern Jewish Studies.

Phillips, B. A. 1997. *Re-examining intermarriage: Trends, textures and strategies.* Boston: Susan and David Wilstein Institue of Jewish Policy Studies and the American Jewish Committee, the William Petschek National Jewish Family Center.

Polish, D. F. 1982. Contemporary Jewish attitudes to mission and conversion. In *Christian mission—Jewish mission,* edited by M. A. Cohen and H. B. Croner. New York: Paulist Press.

Post, M. 1999. Don't bash birthright. *Jerusalem Report* 54, December 20.

Putnam, R. D. 2000. *Bowling alone: The collapse and revival of American community.* New York: Simon and Schuster.

Rawidowicz, S. 1997. Excerpts from a correspondence between David Ben-Gurion and Simon Rawidowicz on the State of Israel, the diaspora, and the unity of the Jewish people. In *State of Israel, diaspora, and Jewish continuity: essays on the "ever-dying people,"* edited by B. C. I. Ravid. Hanover, N.H.: University Press of New England.

Rogers, C. 1969. *Freedom to learn: A view of what education might become.* Columbus, Ohio: Merrill Publishing.

Rosen, M. I. 2006. *The remaking of Hillel: A case study on leadership and organizational transformation.* Waltham, Mass.: Brandeis University, Fisher-Bernstein Institute for Jewish Philanthropy and Leadership, Maurice and Marilyn Cohen Center for Modern Jewish Studies.

Rosenzweig, F. 2002. *On Jewish learning.* Edited by N. N. Glatzer. Madison, Wis.: University of Wisconsin Press.

Rossi, P., M. Lipsey, and H. Freeman. 2004. *Evaluation: A systematic approach.* Thousand Oaks, Calif.: Sage Publications.

Sachar, H. M. 2006. *A history of Israel from the rise of Zionism to our time.* New York: Knopf.

Sacks, J. 2007. *To heal a fractured world: The ethics of responsibility.* New York: Schocken Books.

Sales, A. L., and L. Saxe. 2004. *How goodly are thy tents: Summer camping as Jewish socializing experiences.* Hanover, N.H.: University Press of New England.

———. 2006. *Particularism in the university: Realities and opportunities for Jewish life on campus.* New York: The AVI CHAI Foundation.

Sarna, J. 1996. A projection of America as it ought to be: Zion in the mind's eye of American Jews. In *Envisioning Israel: The changing ideals and images of North American Jews,* edited by A. Gal, 41–59. Jerusalem and Detroit: Hebrew University Magnes Press and Wayne State University Press.

———. 2004. *American Judaism: A history.* New Haven, Conn.: Yale University Press.

Sasson, T., L. Saxe, M. Rosen, S. Hecht, and D. Selinger-Abutbul, 2007. *After birthright: Finding and seeking young adult Jewish community.* Waltham, Mass.: Brandeis University, Maurice and Marilyn Cohen Center for Modern Jewish Studies.

Saxe, L., and F. Chertok. 2007. Kishkes, kortex, and kinesthetics: Engaging young adults in Jewish life. *Reform Judaism,* 61–65.

Saxe, L., and M. Fine. 1981. *Social experiments: Methods for design and evaluation.* Beverly Hills, Calif.: Sage Publications.

Saxe, L., C. Kadushin, J. Pakes, S. Kelner, L. Sternberg, B. Horowitz, A. Sales, and A. Brodsky. 2000. *Birthright Israel launch evaluation: Preliminary findings.* Waltham, Mass.: Brandeis University, Maurice and Marilyn Cohen Center for Modern Jewish Studies.

Saxe, L., T. Sasson, and S. Hecht. 2006a. *Israel at war: The impact of peer-oriented Israel programs on responses of American young adults.* Waltham, Mass.: Brandeis University, Maurice and Marilyn Cohen Center for Modern Jewish Studies.

———. 2006b. *Taglit–Birthright Israel: Impact on Jewish identity, peoplehood, and connection to Israel.* Waltham, Mass.: Brandeis University, Maurice and Marilyn Cohen Center for Modern Jewish Studies.

Saxe, L., T. Sasson, B. Phillips, S. Hecht, and G. Wright. 2007. *Birthright Israel Evaluation: 2007 North American Cohorts.* Waltham, Mass.: Brandeis University, Maurice and Marilyn Cohen Center for Modern Jewish Studies.

Saxe, L., E. Tighe, B. Phillips, and C. Kadushin. 2007. *Reconsidering the size and characteristics of the American Jewish population: New estimates of a larger and more diverse community.* Waltham, Mass.: Brandeis University, Steinhardt Social Research Institute.

Schiff, Z. 2004. Israeli death toll in intifada higher than last two wars. *Ha'aretz.* August 24.

Schilpp, P. A., ed. 1949. *Albert Einstein: Philospher-Scientist.* Volume VII in *The Library of Living Philosophers.* Evanston, Ill: The Library of Living Philosophers.

Schwab, J. J. 1978. *Science, curriculum, and liberal education.* Chicago: University of Chicago Press.

Segal, B. J. 1987. *Returning: The land of Israel as focus in Jewish history.* Jerusalem: Department of Education and Culture of the World Zionist Organization.

Segal, B. J. 2001. Land of Israel. In *Etz hayim: Torah and commentary,* edited by D. Lieber, 191–200. Philadelphia: Jewish Publication Society.

Shadish, W. R., T. D. Cook, and D. T. Campbell. 2002. *Experimental and quasi-*

experimentation: Designs for generalized and analysis causal inference. Boston: Houghton Mifflin.

Shapiro, F. L. 2006. *Building Jewish roots: The Israel experience.* Montreal: McGill-Queens University Press.

Sharansky, N. 1998. *Fear no evil: The classic memoir of one man's triumph over a police state.* New York: Public Affairs.

———, and R. Dermer. 2004. *The case for democracy: The power of freedom to overcome tyranny and terror.* New York: Public Affairs.

Shay, S. 2004. "Ebb and flow" versus "the al-Aqsa intifada": The Israeli-Palestinian conflict, 2000–2003. In *A never-ending conflict: A guide to Israeli military history,* edited by M. Bar-On. Westport, Conn.: Praeger.

Shoshani, S. 2007. *Taglit-Birthright Israel CEO status report 2007.* Taglit–Birthright Israel.

Shulman, L. S. 2004. Professing the liberal arts. In *Teaching as community property: Essays on higher education.* San Francisco, Calif.: Jossey-Bass.

———. 2006. *Professing the liberal arts: The essential tension between liberal and professional studies in American higher education.* Lecture given at Brandeis University, Waltham, Massachusetts, February 27.

Sizer, T. 2004 [1984]. *Horace's compromise: The dilemma of the American high school.* Boston: Houghton Mifflin.

Steinhardt, M. 2001. *No bull: My life in and out of the markets.* New York: Wiley.

Tajfel, H., and J. C. Turner. 1986. The social identity theory of inter-group behavior. In *Psychology of intergroup relations,* edited by S. Worchel and L. W. Austin. Chicago: Nelson-Hall.

Tanakh: The holy scriptures, the new JPS translation according to the traditional Hebrew text. 1985. Philadelphia: The Jewish Publication Society.

Telushkin, J. 1991. *Jewish literacy: The most important things to know about the Jewish religion, its people and its history.* New York: Morrow.

Tobin, G. 1995. *Teen trips to Israel: Cost, price & marketing.* Waltham, Mass.: Brandeis University, Maurice and Marilyn Cohen Center for Modern Jewish Studies.

Tobin, G., J. Solomon, and A. C. Karp. 2003. *Mega-gifts in American philanthropy: General & Jewish giving patterns between 1995 and 2000.* San Francisco, Calif.: Institute for Jewish & Community Research.

Troen, S. I. 1999. The post-Holocaust dynamics of Jewish centers and peripheries. In *Jewish centers and peripheries: Europe between America and Israel 50 years after World War Two,* edited by S. I. Troen. New Brunswick, N.J.: Transaction.

Troy, Gil. 2006. *Why I am a Zionist: Israel, Jewish identity, and the challenges of today.* Montreal: Bonfman Jewish Education Centre.

Tugend, T. 1996. Should Jews actively seek Christian converts? *The Jerusalem Post.* November 8. p. 10.

Turkle, S. 1995. *Life on the screen: Identity in the age of the Internet.* New York: Simon and Schuster.

Turner, V. W. 1969. *The ritual process: Structure and anti-structure.* Chicago: Aldine.

———. 1974. *Dramas, fields, and metaphors: Symbolic action in human society.* Ithaca: Cornell University Press.

Twain, M. 1996 [1869]. *The innocents abroad; Or, The new pilgrims' progress.* New York: Oxford University Press.

Urofsky, M. 1978. Essays in American Zionism, 1917–1948. New York: Herzl Press.

———. 1995. *American Zionism from Herzl to the Holocaust.* Lincoln: University of Nebraska Press.

van Gennep, A. 1960. *The rites of passage.* Translated by M. B. Vizedom and G. L. Caffee. Chicago: University of Chicago Press.

Wertheimer, J. 1997. *Current trends in American Jewish philanthropy.* American Jewish Yearbook. New York: American Jewish Committee.

Wohlgelernter, E. 2000a. The arrival of an idea. *The Jerusalem Post.* January 7. p. 05B.

———. 2000b. Birthright: So far, so good. *The Jerusalem Post.* July 14. p. 06B.

Yad Izhak Ben Zvi. 2004. *A nation's memories and hopes: Mount Herzl and the military cemetery.* Taglit–Birthright Israel.

Yehoshua, A. B. 2006. The meaning of homeland. In *The A. B. Yehoshua controversy: An Israel-diaspora dialogue on Jewishness, Israeliness, and identity,* edited by N. Marans and R. Bell. New York: Dorothy and Julius Koppelman Institute on American Jewish-Israeli Relations, American Jewish Committee.

Yoffie, E. 2001. Sermon by Rabbi Eric Yoffie at the Boston Biennial. Speech presented at the Union of American Hebrew Congregations Biennial Conference. Boston, Massachusetts.

Zerubavel, Y. 1995. *Recovered roots: Collective memory and the making of Israeli national tradition.* Chicago: University of Chicago Press.

Zvi, Y. I. B. 2004. *A nation's memories and hopes: Mount Herzl and the military cemetery.* Taglit–Birthright Israel.

Acknowledgements

Who is wise? One who learns from all people.
—*Pirke Avot* (Ethics of our Fathers)

Our goals in writing this book were to describe an extraordinary educational initiative and draw meaning from the effort that would illuminate its role in young adult identity development. Readers can judge for themselves whether we have succeeded in telling a compelling story and whether we have been able to illuminate lessons from Birthright Israel that can be applied elsewhere. It should be clear, however, that our understanding of Birthright Israel has been dependent on the help and cooperation of many other individuals. We are thankful to those who made it possible for us to be a part of the Birthright Israel endeavor and to those who helped us study and understand the program.

Our greatest appreciation goes to the thousands of Birthright Israel participants who allowed us to learn from them. Both metaphorically and otherwise, we joined participants on their physical and spiritual journeys, and they became our teachers. Their voices were with us as we wrote the manuscript, and we wanted readers to be able to walk in their footsteps and follow their paths of discovery and development. Parts of the book are based on findings of a series of Birthright Israel evaluation studies. Literally, tens of thousands of participants (along with others who did not participate in the program) completed lengthy evaluation surveys, some multiple times. We are extremely grateful for the willingness of our informants to share their experience and lives with us. The Birthright Israel generation whom we studied are an extraordinary group: well educated, highly motivated, and aware of their responsibilities to others. Almost without exception, they welcomed our questions and were eager to share their stories. We hope that we have listened well.

Along with the participants, our profound appreciation goes to Charles Bronfman and Michael Steinhardt who were responsible for founding Birthright Israel. They are extraordinary individuals, not only because of their generosity, but also because they are committed visionaries. We admire them for wanting to do something "big" and for their persistence in implementing their ideas. They have supported our work in a myriad of ways, and we are very appreciative. Their support, and our admiration notwithstanding, we have tried to describe and assess their role as accurately as possible. In doing so, we have not sought their review or approval, and the perspective offered about the program is ours alone.

Our work and the story of Birthright Israel would have taken a different course were it not for the presence of Andy Bronfman (*z"l*), wife of Charles Bronfman. Her steadfast and longstanding passion for the State of Israel, for young people, and for the role of travel to Israel and encounters with Israelis, made her one of the *halutzic* (pioneering) figures behind Birthright Israel. From the program's infancy through its early development, she was a strong voice. We are honored to have worked with her and to have been pushed, driven, and enlightened by her uncanny, nonconventional insights about the program's strategy. Her premature passing was an indescribable loss to her family, but also for us and all those connected with Birthright Israel.

Along with the founders, Birthright Israel was made possible by a unique group of philanthropists, by professionals and lay leaders at Jewish communal organizations worldwide, as well as ministers and professional staff of the government of Israel. We have learned invaluable lessons from our interactions and observations of these and others who are partners with Birthright Israel. Two individuals deserve special note: Marlene Post, past president of Hadassah, the Zionist Women's Organization of America, and philanthropist Lynn Schusterman. Both women were particularly passionate sources of insight for us. We are indebted to them in multiple ways and grateful that we have had a chance to get to know them.

The staff of Birthright Israel opened doors, their experience and understanding, enabling us to examine the innermost workings of the project. Shimshon Shoshani, *Taglit*–Birthright Israel's CEO, is a distinguished educator and educational leader. It is a privilege to work with him and be able to learn from a master teacher. Among the many staff who we have also been privileged to work with and learn from, we thank the senior leadership team, Ehud Afek, Zeev Boneh, Meir Kraus, Gidi Mark, and Elizabeth Sokolsky. We are also appreciative to other staffers who make the day-to-day work of the program possible; in particular, we thank Barbara Aronson, Ofira Bino, Mooli Brog, Hanna Chaddad, Deborah Goldberg, Hagit Polatov, and Sam Tuchman. We also thank Rabbi Sheldon Zimmerman (former North American Director) and Jay Golan of the Birthright Israel Foundation. Each of these individuals has taught us a great deal about how to nurture and shape ideas into programmatic reality.

Staff of the foundations connected with the founding philanthropists and their philanthropic partners are also key to the program and have been invaluable sources of insight and perspective. In particular, we thank Jeffrey Solomon and Janet Aviad of the Andrea and Charles Bronfman Philanthropies, two extraordinary thinkers and leaders. In addition, it is with profound respect and appreciation that we acknowledge Rabbi Yitz Greenberg, formerly of the Steinhardt Foundation/Jewish Life Network (JLN). He never failed to make each of our interactions a profound teaching moment. We also want to acknowledge the assistance of Rabbi David Gedzelman and Shula Navon (z"l) of JLN, and Sandy Cardin of the Schusterman Foundation. They, and many other foundation staff involved in Birthright Israel, have made innumerable contributions to our understanding and analysis of the program.

The directors and staff of the trip organizations that implement Birthright Israel trips were invaluable sources for this book, and without them the "thick description" to which we aspired would not have been possible. They are a dynamic and dedicated group of educators. We are, in particular, grateful to directors Rabbi Shlomo Gestetner, Avraham Infeld, Shlomo Lifshitz, and Joe Perlov, along with trip leaders "Francis" and "Udi" for agreeing to be interviewed. They taught us much, as have many of the other trip organizers and educational staff.

The evaluation study that played a key role in shaping our description of Birthright Israel was conducted at the Maurice and Marilyn Cohen Center for Modern Jewish Studies at Brandeis University. We are grateful for the support of the Cohen family, as well as other philanthropic supporters. From the inception of the Cohen Center's involvement with Birthright Israel, Brandeis' President, Professor Jehuda Reinharz, helped to make our work possible and was an invaluable advisor. To conduct the evaluation of Birthright Israel, the first author, Leonard Saxe, collaborated with a number of colleagues at the Cohen Center. Charles Kadushin, a distinguished sociologist, was co-principal investigator (with Saxe) of the evaluation for the first five years. Since 2005, another sociologist, Ted Sasson has taken over that responsibility. Shaul Kelner (now at Vanderbilt University) began as a junior colleague, but became a critical contributor. Mark Rosen conducted fieldwork at early stages of the program and did several observations that form a part of the book. Shahar Hecht, a research associate, has managed the datasets and conducted many of the analyses reported here. Ben Phillips, a research scientist at the Cohen Center, began with the project as a graduate student participant observer and become a key contributor to our increasingly sophisticated quantitative analyses of the program. We are thankful to our research colleagues for all that they have done to make our work possible.

A number of additional Brandeis staff worked on the evaluation studies and helped to shape our understandings of the program. In particular, we thank Graham Wright and MeLena Hessel who worked on surveys and survey analysis. Particular thanks go to the Cohen Center administrative team— Christie Cohen and Gloria Tessler—who have provided structure and support for the project. A number of staff, graduate students, and research assistants worked on the book itself. Deborah Grant and Katie Light provided invaluable editing assistance. And a set of research assistants, including Ari Abel, Miki Bard, and Rachel Maimin, tracked nearly impossible-to-find references, fact-checked, and helped to create a consistent format for footnotes.

We are also appreciative to a host of colleagues who read and commented on drafts of the book manuscript. Particular thanks go to Professors Sylvia Fishman, David Mittelberg, Jonathan Sarna, Ellen Winner, and a number of anonymous reviewers. As well, we thank Michael Bohnen and Rabbi Hershey Novack. The enthusiasm of our first readers has been incredibly rewarding, but also extremely helpful in shaping our arguments. In all cases, we learned from our readers' reactions and tried to take account of their suggestions. We have likely done so imperfectly, however, but that does not diminish our gratitude for their assistance.

We also express our appreciation to all those at the University Press of New England (UPNE) who helped us bring this book to life. Phyllis Deutsch, Editor-in-Chief, saw the potential of this project and both pushed us and supported our efforts. Sylvia Fuks-Fried, Brandeis University representative to the UPNE editorial committee, is a wonderful colleague and was tremendously helping in making our use of Hebrew consistent and understandable. Elizabeth Rawitsch, Assistant Production Editor, shepherded the volume through editing and design. We are very grateful for her care, thoughtfulness, and patience.

Our work on this project, and the book itself, would not have been possible without the support of our families. In literal and figurative ways, our families have accompanied us on this journey. They have contributed to this effort in ways that neither we nor they appreciate fully. We express our love for each of them: Marion Gardner-Saxe, Daniel Saxe, Ted Saxe; Anne Lanski, Shai, Tali, Idan, Adi, and Lia Chazan.

Our sense of gratitude is captured by another question posed and answered by the rabbis whose voices are recorded in Pirke Avot (*Ethics of the Fathers*): "Who is rich? One who has joy with his lot." We have been privileged to be part of a unique chapter in Jewish life called Birthright Israel. For that, we feel profound joy and deep gratitude.

INDEX

Israel trips, 9; and preconceptions about Israel, 24; psychological component, 106–107; revival in North America, 30; and social interaction, 108–109; and soldier's role, 82; strengthening of, 31; tourism as exercise in formation of, 39; trip providers' focus on, 128; and value of Birthright Israel, 184. *See also* Evaluation of program

IDF (Israel Defense Forces), 75, 90, 172. *See also* Soldiers

Immigrants: to Palestine in early 20th century, 19; participant perspective of, 168; from Soviet Union/former Soviet Union, 20, 52–53, 168; and State of Israel establishment, 25. *See also* Aliyah

Individualism vs. communalism, 16, 182, 184–185

Individual Jewish journey, participants' focus on, 141–142

Indoctrination, avoidance of, 40, 50, 64, 98–99

Infeld, Avraham, 35, 55–57, 134, 135

Information sharing, limitations of, 100–101. *See also* Cognitive learning approach

Innocents Abroad, The (Twain), 23

Institutional status for Birthright Israel, 182–185

Intellectual learning. *See* Cognitive learning approach

Intermarriage, 26, 29, 133, 143, 167–168

Internet and young adult mindset, 101

Intifada: beginnings of, 14–15; and challenges of starting Birthright Israel, 124; evidence at Gilo, 79; safety of German Colony, 46; soldiers as advocates for dealing with, 92; and tour guide availability, 64; violence levels vs. daily life, 191n33

Israel, State of: Arab population in, 19; Birthright Israel organizational role, 118–119, 121–123, 124; conclusions of

mifgashim, 89–90; as context for Birthright Israel, 169–170; Diaspora Jews' negative views of, 145, 146; diversity in politics and religion, 59–60, 62, 92, 145; immigrants and establishment of, 25; importance to Jewish identity, 7, 8, 26, 28, 49–50; relationship to Diaspora Jewry, 19–32; stereotypes about, 24; as Western society, 47, 49, 52, 58, 145; and Zionism, 22–24. *See also* Connection to Israel; Heritage; Modern state, Israel as

Israel Defense Forces (IDF), 75, 90, 172. *See also* Soldiers

Israel Experience, Inc., 9, 28

Israel experience field: anti-assimilation goals for, 6, 28; and Birthright Israel development, 5–10; Birthright Israel's impact on, 148; and group experience, 66–67; historical overview, 7–8; lack of oversight and evaluation, 106; and people-centered experience, 71

Israel Experts, Inc., 129–131

"Israel Express," 132

Israel-Hezbollah War (2006), 155–160, 169–170

Israeli-Palestinian conflict: diversity of opinion on, 81–82; Dolphinarium bombing, 20–22, 30; Israeli defensive position in, 58; and mifgash experience, 79–81; reporting on, 189nn50–51; War of Independence (1948), 25, 80–81, 171. *See also* Intifada

Israelis: and Diaspora Jews changing views of each other, 85–91; peer connections, 12, 70–71, 179–180; resolve in face of terrorism, 22; staff, 64–65, 119–120. *See also* Madrichim (tour educators/guides); Mifgashim (shared encounters)

Jaffa, 19

JAFI (Jewish Agency for Israel), 7, 99, 124, 194n8

Mifgashim (shared encounters): analysis of experience, 81–84; cemetery experience, 84–85; development of, 74–75; evaluation of role, 150; experience in northern Israel, 75–81; impact on soldiers, 90–91; introduction, 72–73; and Israeli society, 89–90; levelers and dividers, 87–89; and people-centered experience, 71; purpose of, 73–74; results of, 92–93; social interaction and identity, 108–109; and stereotyping, 85–87

Militaristic society, Israel as, 145, 146

Military, Israeli, 75, 90, 172. *See also* Israel Defense Forces (IDF); Soldiers

Mi-Shoah L'Tkuma, 49

Moach Eser, 105, 195n21

Modern state, Israel as: Birthright Israel's goal to present, 49; economic development heritage, 32; as Israel Experts focus, 129–130; and middle-class ambience of Emek Refai'im, 46–47; participant's perceptions, 145, 146; and peace goal, 58

Mount Herzl, cemetery at, 47–48, 84–85

Mount Moriah, 23

Mount Scopus, 79, 80–81

Multiple intelligences, theory of, 100–101

Narratives of Israel, variety of, 32

National anthem, 174

National Jewish Population Study, 27

National Military Cemetery, 47, 84–85

Nesiya program, 73

Netanyahu, Benjamin (Bibi), 104

North American Jews: dual loyalty question for, 25–26; fears of violence, 30–31; and Israel, 25, 26–30; Israeli perceptions of, 84, 85–87; on Israelis, 75–81, 85–89, 91, 180; lack of attention to Israel trip idea, 29; and organizational development, 123; overseas staff, 65–66, 110, 121; popularity of Birthright Israel for, 13. *See also* Federations, Jewish

Olmert, Ehud, 2, 95, 172

Operational targets vs. grand vision, educational, 104–105

Oranim Educational Initiatives, 126, 127–128, 177

Organizational culture: conclusion, 135–136; foundations of, 115–121; steering committee, 121–124; trip providers, 125–135

Orthodox community: dominance in religious life of Israel, 29, 83–84; encounter in Jerusalem, 80; and Kotel, 96; Lubavitcher-Chabad movement, 103, 131, 196–197n12; Mayanot trip provider, 103, 131–134, 177; participation levels, 8, 188n30; and stereotypes about Israelis, 47, 86

Outcome measurement, 111–112. *See also* Evaluation of program

Outsourcing of trip itinerary planning, 125–127. *See also* Trip providers

Overseas staff, 65–66, 110, 121

Palestinian Authority, 21

Palestinians, 12, 80. *See also* Israeli-Palestinian conflict

Paritsky, Dovi, 132

Participants: on behavioral outcomes, 165–169; on connection to Israel, 161, 165–167; criteria for trip eligibility, 13; denominational affiliations, 189n48; fun as primary motivation to apply, 106; on group experience, 163–164; immigrant perspective, 168; individual journey focus of, 141–142; on Jewish identity, 161–162, 166, 170; looking glass self through peers, 70–71; on *mifgash* experience, 75–81, 85–89, 91; on military culture in Israel, 48; and person-centered education, 109–110; on political diversity in Israel, 60; positive feedback from, 38; on sense of community, 162, 166; social life experience, 38–39; on soldiers, 180; voices